Media Politics

Media Politics

**The News Strategies of
Presidential Campaigns**

F. Christopher Arterton
Yale University

LexingtonBooks
D.C. Heath and Company
Lexington, Massachusetts
Toronto

Library of Congress Cataloging in Publication Data

Arterton, F. Christopher.
  Media politics.

  Includes index.
    1. Presidents—United States—Election. 2. Mass media.—Political
aspects—United States. I. Title.
JK528.A77   1984   324.7′0973   83–48735
ISBN 0–669–07504–3

Published simultaneously in Canada

Printed in the United States of America on acid-free paper

International Standard Book Number: 0–669–07504–3

Library of Congress Catalog Card Number: 83–48735

To Jeffrey Leonard Pressman
from whom I learned a great deal about
politics, political science, and life

Contents

Figures and Tables

Preface

The First Amendment may well be the most important part of the U.S. Constitution. The political rights provided there—"freedom of speech, or of the press; or the right of the people peaceably to assemble, and to petition the Government for a redress of grievances"—underwrite the other provisions for a democratic government and an open society. In two hundred years the norms of the American people and the behavior of their political leaders have envigorated these words on paper, building them into a first principle of popular government through the power of custom and legal precedent.

The rights of a free press have been integral to these political protections. They remain so even though the role of the press in politics has evolved considerably. In the early years, journalists were the handmaidens of politicians, subsidized by them, and kept in business by subscription lists of party adherents. Gradually over the nineteenth century, newspapers became financially independent and the concepts of factual news and objective news reporting emerged.

During the same period, the technology of news reporting and distribution changed markedly. Sole editor–printers were replaced by large corporations.

Today, most working journalists see themselves and their news organizations as being above politics, providing news and opinion about politics and public affairs without becoming part of the political processes that make events occur.

Their primary duty lies in providing readers and audiences with objective news reports about the activities of politicians. To preserve the credibility of this enterprise, they must not themselves become involved in the political debate. They must not become advocates.

While these changes have been taking place in the news industry, the communications needs and capacities of politicians have not grown commensurably. In fact, the principal link between candidates and voters, the party structure, has been deteriorating badly over the last eighty years, while the needs of politicians to reach voters with persuasive messages and of citizens to hear their arguments have not diminished. Political speech requires the transmission of both advocacy and objective information.

Given that communication is so central to their tasks, it is not surprising that campaigners should turn to the news-reporting industry as a means of reaching voters. In so doing, however, politicians place journalists into an awkward, undesirable position. Even while needing their services, some politicians are quick to criticize journalists for their presumed influence upon political processes.

These concerns have led me to present inquiry. I began with two questions: What are the influences of news reporting on the conduct of election campaigns? and, What are the consequences of this influence? The first question requires a detailed exploration of the perspective of those who run campaign organizations. I conducted an extensive series of long interviews with national campaign managers, press secretaries, and, where relevant, pollsters and advertising managers of presidential campaigns in 1976 and 1980. Rather than selecting a sample of these, I tried to interview them all. The initial model of interaction between campaigners and journalists was built upon my interviews in 1976 where my interviewing was more complete. This analysis was updated and revised by similar observation in 1980, though by and large I feel my arguments were sustained by a second look.

The research for this book was initially a team effort to assemble evidence. The interviews with politicians were supplemented by similar conversations with journalists and by a systematic effort to collect and analyze the news product, including the national and regional press, local newspapers in given primary states, and the network evening newscasts. These data are brought into the analysis where germane.

Assessing the consequences of exchanges between journalists and politicians is analytical endeavor. While the perspectives of both reporters and campaigners can be helpful in understanding these effects, essentially the analysis must rest on the cogency of my arguments. The very nature of the problem makes proof elusive.

The role of journalism in contemporary politics has indeed become controversial. This book will add to the controversy, but I should state emphatically at the outset that I do not feel the problems discussed in the chapters that follow should lead to any systematic attempts at remedies. Rather I hope by stating and analyzing the perspectives of those who conduct election campaigns, I will contribute to the public knowledge of how campaigns are currently conducted. Such information may help journalists understand their own impact from a more distant perspective, and may lead them to modify their relations with politicians.

Acknowledgments

In the course of three years of research and two more in writing, I have incurred debts far too numerous to be acknowledged individually. With few exceptions, categorical thanks will have to suffice.

The largest debt is owed to the many campaigners and politicians who consented to lengthy interviews in the midst of frantic efforts to capture the presidency. That they bothered at all to meet with an itinerant political scientist was surprising; that they gave their time so fully is deeply appreciated. This book would not have been possible without this cooperation.

Because I refused, on principle, to believe everything the politicians told me, I dispatched a large number of students to work as spies in state-level press offices of these campaigns. In New Hampshire, Massachusetts, Connecticut, Pennsylvania, North Carolina, and California, more than fifty students volunteered to work for the presidential candidate of their choice. With the knowledge and consent of the state press secretary, they reported to me the activities of their offices. Their observations provided a valuable inside view of the actual implementation of campaign press strategies, and generated examples and insights of how campaigns function as organizations.

I am extremely grateful for the financial support which this study has received. The initial research was funded by the John and Mary Markle Foundation and the Ford Foundation. In addition, a year's leave for writing was supported jointly by the Ford Foundation and the Russell Sage Foundation.

The original research conducted in 1976 was part of a joint effort with Donald Matthews, William Bicker, and Lawrence Goodwin and headed by James David Barber. I profited enormously from the interviews, which we all conducted, and the transcripts we all shared. In a few cases, I quoted directly from their interviews. A special debt is owed to Jonathan Moore and the Institute of Politics at Harvard for arranging (and allowing me to attend) postelection conferences of campaign managers. At many points, I have relied on the discussion at these conferences to supplement my interviews.

Friends and colleagues read and commented upon parts of the manuscript as it matured from 1978 to 1982. From a large list, I wish to thank Nelson Polsby and David Mayhew for their encouragement and help. John Griffen's editorial comments were invaluable in sharpening the final draft. Rob Fein, a student, research assistant, and friend, provided extensive help in analyzing press coverage of presidential campaigns. He is the coauthor of chapter 3.

In the course of this research, I lost my friend and colleague, Jeff Pressman. A gifted political scientist, Jeff taught me how to combine scholarship and a love of politics. He persuaded me that analysis that may improve political processes by illuminating "real-world" problems holds more merit than abstract theory building undertaken for its own sake. I hope I have fulfilled that teaching here.

Finally, friends, family—and especially Janet Bond Arterton—provided much-needed support throughout this endeavor.

I thank them all.

Media Politics

1

Presidential Selection and the News Media

The television news organizations in this country are an extraordinarily dominant force in primary elections. They're every Tuesday night! Not only counting the votes, but in some cases setting the tone and, in almost all cases, reinforcing the tone of what the issues are that week.[1]

The influence of the mass media in U.S. electoral processes has expanded dramatically over the past two decades. Newspapers, radio, newsweeklies, and television have become the major sources of information about election campaigns for most U.S. citizens.[2] Because presidential elections are newsworthy, the mass media devote substantial resources to reporting the actions of candidates, campaigners, other politicians, party activists, and voters. At the same time these news-reporting corporations sell or donate space to campaign organizations for political advertisements, public service broadcasts, or editorial statements. Thus, viewers, listeners, and readers receive the bulk of their information about elective politics through the media in two forms: advertisements and overtly partisan messages, as well as news stories generated by journalists who subscribe to a creed of partisan neutrality.[3] In either case, political information from the mass media has taken primacy to information from friends, family members, or work associates, or the direct efforts of political parties or candidate organizations.

Political campaigns are, in essence, efforts to direct persuasive messages toward a vast electorate; these messages are intended to maximize the number of supporters on election day. Presidential campaign managers believe, almost uniformly, that their most efficient means of persuasive communication is these preestablished communications media.[4] Rather than constructing direct organizational links to voters, campaigners rely on corporate media channels to give their candidates raw exposure and to cast them in a favorable light. This belief shapes their larger view of the campaign process and many of their activities to influence the voters. Indirectly, the process through which presidents are nominated and elected is thus heavily influenced by the way in which news is reported.

The literature devoted to the relationship between print and broadcast media and American politics is still in its infancy. Surprisingly, in view of the frequently expressed concerns about potential media manipulation of an unwitting citizenry, few careful studies have been made of the media's role in either the electoral or the governing process.[5] However, several approaches

1

have been attempted, all of which implicitly assume that reading, listening, or watching the media does affect individual attitudes and behavior.

In one approach, the political news produced by these corporations is analyzed to assess the biases—often political—in what is printed or broadcast. These works criticize the news media as, variously, a capitalist plot, a conservative cabal of small-town editors, or a liberal conspiracy against Republican politicians.[6] That is, all too frequently, our news is castigated as biased by a political philosophy. Second, other researchers have tried for over thirty years to measure the effects of the media on voters. Third, the values and norms of journalists' work have been examined. Even though journalism schools teach values governing news reporting, only a few empirical studies have been conducted on the values that are implicit in the actual production of news, especially political reporting.[7] Finally, because reporters and correspondents work as members of a large organization, there have been some detailed examinations of the effects of organizationally determined imperatives on the news.[8] In studying recent presidential campaigns, I adopt the last perspective. The way in which news-reporting corporations deploy their resources to cover the presidential race affects the product disseminated to the U.S. public as the events of the day.

To be relevant to politics, however, this inquiry must extend beyond the reporting process in one of two directions. First, by dissecting the relationship between the news product and citizen attitudes, we might be led to conclusions concerning the direct impact of the news on the election outcome. However, I have chosen a second direction that focuses on the effect of the news-reporting process on the behavior of those campaigning for electoral office. News reporting may have indirect effects shaping the process by which we select presidents and influencing the strategies of elites who seek political support. These indirect effects may be as profound as the direct effects: narrowing the candidate skills and characteristics that are offered through the electoral machinery, altering the uses to which a candidate's time is put by the campaign's strategists, and limiting the range of issues that can be discussed during the election campaign. The discussion will be from the perspective of political elites and will not illuminate the extent to which news reporting affects citizen attitudes during election campaigns.[9]

Inquiring into the dynamics of both presidential campaign organizations and news-reporting organizations, I will discuss how news organizations deploy their resources in covering a presidential campaign; what incentives govern the behavior of correspondents, reporters, editors, and news producers; how campaigners attempt to shape the news-reporting process; and what factors determine the adoption of a particular news strategy by a given campaign?

These questions cannot be answered in isolation. The behavior of campaigners is directly affected by the behavior of journalists. Because each depends on the other to accomplish its objectives, interactions between both organizations merit detailed attention. Accordingly, I will consider how news reporters react to the efforts of campaigners to obtain favorable coverage for their candidate, and, conversely, how campaigners react to what reporters write and broadcast.

The Importance of the Media: The Voters' Perspective

Before turning to the interaction of campaign and news organizations, however, I need to consider briefly the direct effects of the print and broadcast media on the behavior of voters. In fact, there is a host of reasons why voters might rely on the media for information and interpretation during contemporary presidential races. During recent nomination contests, several factors have obscured the progress of the race and the nature of options available to voters. As a result, voters may have relied on the simplification and interpretation inherent in news presentations to clarify candidates' characteristics, issue positions, and prospects.

For example, studies of U.S. voting behavior have repeatedly found that a substantial percentage of voters base their voting decisions primarily upon party identification.[10] Yet partisan labels are not relevant as a voting cue during intraparty nominations. The lack of party cohesion at the national level, evident in recent nominations struggles of both parties, implies that not all Democrats or Republicans are alike. Consequently, to affect public policy during the nomination process, citizens must rely upon other cues than party labels. The news media may supply these cues.

A second factor derives from the sheer number of candidates contesting contemporary presidential nominations. Both the growth in the number of primaries and changes in party rules since 1968 have opened up the selection process to a large number of unknown candidates without strong initial party backing. On the face of it, this proliferation could confuse voters, sending them to the mass media for information about candidates.

The expanded number of primaries itself provides a third source of confusion that could be alleviated by news commentary. For example, voters look to the media to identify which primaries were crucial and which could be ignored. Similarly, the rules under which delegates are selected in the various states add a degree of complexity that defies understanding by all but the most sophisticated observers. In this context, interpretation of winning and losing becomes a matter of judgment that news organizations seek to provide.

Finally, the absence of a single overriding issue (such as the war in Vietnam) or even a finite list of issues as in the last two campaigns, means that voters might find it difficult to differentiate among candidates. Reported news may simplify these necessary interpretations.

In the 1976 and 1980 general elections, the influence of reported news could, hypothetically, have been pivotal. Both races remained uncertain into the final week because a decisive proportion of the electorate were undecided until the end. In 1976, each candidate experienced a series of press crises when their campaigns were reported as in trouble and on the defensive. The televised debates drew substantial audiences as well as considerable news coverage and speculation about which candidate had won.

Given these arguments, it is surprising that social scientists have been unable to document these effects, even under carefully controlled conditions. In fact, the persistent finding of almost three decades of research has been that the mass media have minimal effects in changing voters' attitudes.[11] Repetition of studies first conducted in the 1940s by Paul Lazarsfeld and his associates have supported their conclusion that the influence of the media is limited to reinforcing the decisions of already committed voters and activating latent support.[12]

> Despite the flood of propaganda and counterpropaganda available to the prospective voter, he is reached by very little of it . . . all that is read and heard becomes helpful and effective insofar as it guides the voter toward his already "chosen" destination. The clinching argument thus does not have the function of *persuading* the voter to act. He furnishes the motive power himself.[13]

Although elective politics have changed markedly since 1940, social scientists studying media effects still reach roughly the same conclusions. The 1960 debates between Kennedy and Nixon were widely believed to have aided Kennedy; however, survey research was unable to document a substantial number of conversions.[14] At most, the debates reinforced the voting intentions of those who watched. Partisans tended to conclude that their preferred candidate performed better than his opponent. Similarly, research indicated that exposure to different mass media during the 1972 campaign was not systematically related to behavior or attitudes:

> Very little relationship between kinds of favorable and unfavorable perceptions of the major party candidates and exposure to any of the types of television-programming was present during the 1972 campaign.[15]

Finally, the long-run effects of the four debates held in Fall 1976 on voter choice were quite minimal.[16] Noting that "the goal of image improvement, which, in part, served to motivate debate participation for the candidates, was unattained," one study concluded, "the debates reinforced existing predispositions considerably but actually changed them very little."[17]

As is frequently the case, the research that supports the minimal-effects conclusion may be suspect. Most of these studies rely on measurements of the amount of exposure to different media as the cause of attitude change. That is, these studies compare the attitudes of heavy television viewers with those of nonviewers or newspaper readers. Meanwhile, the substantive messages have generally been neglected. Given crude survey questions and rather simple research designs, recording the effects of substance will take an entire new generation of research, especially considering the complexity of messages carried by the media and the very extensiveness of media-generated stimuli.

Research monitoring the content carried by the media has, in fact, demonstrated some tentative relationships. For example, Doris Graber found that voting in the 1968 presidential elections could be related to newspaper endorsements.[18] Michael Robinson, one of the most vocal critics of the law of minimal consequences, argued that overcoverage of the 1976 New Hampshire primary resulted in public misperceptions of the event's importance in the nomination process; those surveyed wildly overestimated the number of delegates chosen in New Hampshire.[19] Thomas Patterson suggested that undue attention to early primary winners can be systematically related to rapid jumps in name recognition and favorability ratings.[20] Finally, an effort to relate the content of the 1976 debates to changes in voters' understanding of candidates and their policy positions concluded that "those issues covered in the first debate were the ones on which there was an increase in knowledge."[21]

The law of minimal effects is also qualified by the timing of attitude measurement. Most such research is conducted during the general election phase of the presidential contest when many voters have already selected a candidate. The quadrennial surveys conducted by the University of Michigan indicate that elections do vary in the percentage of voters who delay making their choice until the fall campaign (table 1-1). As a result, the media may affect a larger number of voters in such elections.

Table 1-1
Timing of Voters' Decisions in Presidential Elections (1952-1976)
(Percentage)

	1952	1956	1960	1964	1968	1972	1976	1980
Before the nominating conventions	36	60	30	41	35	45	32	41
During the conventions	32	18	31	25	24	19	21	18
During the campaign	32	21	38	34	40	36	45	41

Source: Center for Political Research, University of Michigan, *American National Election Studies, 1952-1976.*

The media may also exercise greater effects during different phases of the campaign. Patterson reports marked changes in voter information about candidates and their policy proposals during the early nomination period when party identification does not serve as a vote cue.[22] The percentage of voters who decide late in the fall campaign has been rising in recent elections (figure 1-1). This trend is undoubtedly related to the declining influence of partisan identification on voting behavior and may portend an increasing reliance on alternative cues in selecting their candidates.

Reported news may also narrow the range of policy issues actively discussed by the public. This third qualification of the law of minimal effects has been called the "agenda-setting" function of the mass media. Researchers have long realized that even if a relationship between media messages and attitude change cannot be demonstrated, reported news still imparts information.[23] By deciding what to cover, the media may directly control what people believe to be the important questions of the day. As Bernard Cohen has argued, the press "may not be successful much of the time in telling people what to think, but it is stunningly successful in telling its readers what to think *about*."[24]

In covering presidential campaign politics, journalists are confronted with an enormous array of questions, issues, events, and statements that

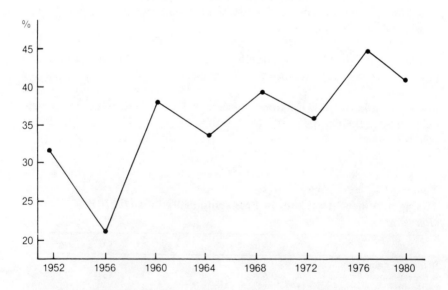

Source: Center for Political Research, University of Michigan, *American National Election Studies, 1952-1980.*

Figure 1-1. Percentage of Voters Deciding during the Fall Campaign

may be considered newsworthy. Reporting is only possible through selective judgments that may not only shape public perceptions of which issues or questions are seen as important, but may also benefit certain candidates. If, for example, the abortion question is perceived as a major element of the campaign, news coverage will highlight the candidates' positions on that question. The agenda-setting potential of the news media may be realized in yet another way. Journalists must decide which candidates have serious prospects for political success. These guesses will be reflected both in the content of their reports and in the amount of news devoted to the contenders. In the process, the media may indirectly suggest to voters which candidates they should consider supporting.[25]

The Importance of the Media: The Campaign Perspective

In contrast, presidential campaign managers have few doubts about the media's role in elections. The media are central to their efforts. Political organization for electoral competition is a communications process; much of the business of election campaigns involves contacting individuals, reaching them with persuasive messages. Although the task has remained constant, the techniques have changed markedly in the last 100 years.

U.S. political parties were established to facilitate this communications process. Constructed along geographical lines, parties served as vertical, interpersonal links, passing requests for support downward and demands and information upward. Initially, political parties resembled candidate organizations in that they were established as election committees for individual legislators. However, election committees and cliques within legislative bodies rapidly coalesced into multipurpose election organizations cutting across both geographical boundaries and political levels.

During the nineteenth century, political communications depended primarily on face-to-face contact. The wardheeler's job was to be personally acquainted with as many voters as possible within his territory. Regular contact was maintained and favors were distributed to ensure election victory. Few people moved, which stabilized the organization from election to election.

Contemporary candidate organizations, in contrast, are temporary, built anew for each election. They must overcome modern barriers to interpersonal contact: mobility of residence, suburban housing patterns, commuting distances to employment, and the atomization that has accompanied these changes. Communication techniques have also changed. Precinct captains and wardheelers have been supplanted by telephones, mass media, computer-assisted direct mail and targeting, and polling. The

traditional role of political parties—to provide a relatively permanent structure to communicate between candidates and voters—has been made super-
fluous by techological change.

Why should candidates and their close advisers prefer to construct a
new and temporary organization and use the apersonal communications
technology rather than an established vertical chain of personal contacts? One
reason is the reciprocal nature of the traditional structure. Wardheelers demand a price for the services they provide, replacing them takes time, and
their control of votes always gives them a certain power and independence
to make deals with other candidates. Rather than take on these problems,
candidates naturally prefer to reserve independence for themselves. The
mass media provides one mechanism by which they can maintain that independence and still communicate with the voters.

Many campaigners believe that modern presidential campaigns could
not be conducted without the corporately owned means of communication.
At the presidential level, relations with the press are inextricable from other
aspects of the campaign process. When campaigners are asked about the
importance of the media, most respond with disbelief that the question need
be asked and an inability to convey adequately the perceived importance.
That perception can be tangibly observed in major decisions concerning the
allocation of the two scarcest resources in campaigning: money and the candidate's time. Pointing to the amounts spent on advertising and candidate
travel by the 1976 President Ford Committee, for example, Comptroller
Thomas Moran explained them as "Here's our paid media, and here's our
free media.[26] Morris Udall's campaign manager noted:

> Everywhere we go, we're on a media trip, I mean we're attempting to
> generate as much free television and print, as much free radio, as we can
> get. Any angle we can play, whether it's his Congressional business or his
> campaign itself or the announcement of a state committee, anything that
> we can do that will generate a story everywhere we go. That's integral to the
> plans.[27]

Jody Powell, Carter's press secretary, summarized the process of campaigning for the presidency as a media event:

> You're really . . . running for President of the United States the way you
> would run for county school superintendent or state senator or governor or
> whatever, because . . . you're essentially going into a media market and
> trying to get all the good coverage you can there. And then you go to the
> next one and what happens in A has very little influence on what happens
> in B. . . . It's a very new audience, a new game, a new town, every
> day. . . .[28]

Many other managers emphasize the pivotal role assigned to the news media
by campaigners.[29]

The Media in the Campaign

The level of media emphasis can vary dramatically from campaign to campaign and across different levels of the political system. Reliance on the news-reporting process is most likely greater for presidential campaigns than for other elective offices.

The extent to which campaigners seek to use the news media depends on the amount of coverage that journalists will devote to a given election. The "news hole" on the total volume of daily news that can be carried by each news outlet is more or less finite.[30] Presidential campaigns, understandably, are deemed more newsworthy than other elections; as a result, presidential campaign managers can realistically aspire to making news, whereas campaigns for lower offices may not be able to count on communicating with voters through news coverage. Presidential campaigns are not only more likely to rely on media politics, but their reliance appears to have increased during the 1970s for several reasons.

The Decline of Parties

Party decline has forced politicians to rely more heavily on news coverage for three reasons. Although many voters once relied on party labels to aid their voting choices, they now use other information. Politicians must communicate such information to a larger segment of voters. The media are useful to this task. Second, as parties' abilities to communicate with voters have deteriorated, campaign organizations are unable to develop the needed financial and volunteer resources without relying on the media. In yet a third sense, party decline has contributed to the growth of media politics. Delegations to national conventions were once tightly controlled by strong state party leaders,[31] but changes in delegate selection rules enacted by the Democratic party in the early seventies reduced their powers.[32]

Gone are the days when a Mark Hanna or a Jim Farley could put together a convention majority by talking quietly to a few people who would deliver their delegations.[33] To contact or stimulate political activists, campaigns now need to reach beyond a tight circle of identifiable party leaders. The news media are potentially helpful in accomplishing this communication.

The Growth of Primaries

Many more state parties now hold presidential primaries than caucuses or conventions. The increased number of primaries has complicated the task of securing a presidential nomination if for no other reason than the number of voters involved. With the expanded number of primaries, the percentage of convention delegates now selected or apportioned by primary votes has increased (table 1-2), forcing candidates to enter numerous primaries to elect a substantial block of convention delegates. Caucus and convention states no longer can deliver significant delegate strength.[34]

The candidate organizations examined in this research were unable to reach directly a large number of voters in enough states to construct a convention majority. Initially, of course, many presidential campaigns begin in small states (such as Iowa and New Hampshire) where contacting high percentages of voters is more feasible than in larger states or in successive primaries. Limited resources inevitably force candidates to rely on the media for reaching voters. Reflecting on Carter's strategy in 1976, Joel Mc-Cleary, Carter's national finance director, commented: "We had no structure after Florida; we had planned only for the short haul. After Florida, it was all NBC, CBS and *The New York Times.*"[35]

The Campaign Finance Law

The laws regulating the finances of campaign organizations also accentuate the value of news reporting to presidential candidates.[36] The 1974 Federal

Table 1-2

Increases in States Holding Presidential Primaries and Convention Delegates from Primary States (1912–1980)

	Democratic		Republican	
	Primaries	*Delegates (%)*	*Primaries*	*Delegates (%)*
1912	12	32.9	13	41.7
1916	20	53.5	20	58.9
1920	16	44.6	20	57.8
1924	14	35.5	17	45.3
1928	17	42.2	16	44.9
1932	16	40.0	14	37.7
1936	14	36.5	12	37.5
1940	13	35.8	13	38.8
1944	14	36.7	13	38.7
1948	14	36.3	12	36.0
1952	15	38.7	13	39.0
1956	19	42.7	19	44.8
1960	16	38.3	15	38.6
1964	17	45.7	17	45.6
1968	15	40.2	15	38.1
1972	22	65.3	21	56.8
1976	30	76.0	30	71.0
1980	33	71.0	35	75.8

Source: *Congressional Quarterly Guide to U.S. Elections* (Washington: Congressional Quarterly, 1975); 1976 and 1980 documents supplied by the Democratic National Committee's Compliance Review Commission.

Election Campaign Act, which was designed to democratize the impact of money in elections, restricts individual contributions to any one campaign to $1,000. As a result, fundraising is much more time-consuming and expensive. The necessity of reaching a large number of smaller contributors has bound fundraising and electoral support tightly together as elements of the same strategic problem. Politicians now see a direct relationship between their success at fundraising and their treatment by the national media, especially in media assessments of their electoral prospects. As Fred Harris's press secretary noted:

> You're caught in a kind of vicious circle. In order to raise money, especially money from more than twenty states, then you have to have national media attention, not just good local media that Fred has been able to generate. . . . But in order to raise that kind of money dispersed among twenty states then you need national media exposure. You need it because people do judge by national media exposure as to whether the campaign is serious or not and, believe me, they hesitate before they give money. . . . They're going to wait until they see Fred's smiling face on national television.[37]

Campaigns rely on the media to reach a large pool of smaller contributors because the news is cheaper than advertisements or letters. For example, during the last two months of Ted Kennedy's primary campaign, he had "little more than free media" scheduled in his campaign stops. In each city he would spend 15 minutes with every political reporter of any standing in the area in an effort to substitute campaigning through the news for other types of contacts.[38]

The finance law also puts stringent limits on the amounts presidential candidates who accept public funding can spend. The act specifies the level of total spending for each candidate during both the prenomination and general election phases and, during the former, limits expenditures in individual state contests.[39] Almost uniformly, the campaigners interviewed complained that the legally permissible expenditure levels are inadequate to the tasks of reaching such a vast electorate. Spending restrictions have compelled campaigners to turn to the free media (news reporting and public affairs programming) as a means of reaching supporters.

Further, during the general election phase of the 1980 campaign, both the Carter and the Reagan staffs complained about the level of expenditures available under the finance act, echoing the complaints in 1976. In each instance, candidates have put about half their available capital into advertising; a significant proportion of the remainder goes to travel that reaps news coverage.[40] The televised debates in 1976 and 1980, of course, compensated significantly for tight campaign budgets by bringing the principals directly to very large audiences.[41]

The combination of expenditure limits and public funding have been widely assumed to encourage political competition during the primaries.

According to this argument, the spending limits provide a measure of equality among candidates, whereas subsidies offer weaker candidates the opportunity to survive the start-up period. At the same time, the act removed a financial screen that limited the number of contestants. Without that screen, other filters, such as the news-reporting process, have become more important in narrowing the competitive field.

Although many competitors, particularly from the "out" parties, entered the 1976 and 1980 campaigns, the finance rules were not the only factor enticing more politicians into the fray. The general opening of the nomination system is also the result of changes in party rules and the increased number of primaries.

In summary, specific institutional changes which have occurred over the last two decades have enhanced the importance of the news media in campaigning. As parties have declined as determinant of vote choice, more voters can be influenced by campaigning. As control over nominations has passed out of the hands of party leaders, candidate organizations are compelled to contact and stimulate a larger pool of political activists. The expansion of presidential primaries has involved a larger electorate in allocating delegates among the competing candidates. And, finally, reforms in campaign finance have curtailed the ability of politicians to raise and spend money, forcing them into greater reliance upon the media.

Media Politics: Do They Make a Difference?

If the importance of campaigning through the news process has increased over the last decade, what have been the consequences of this change? Interactions with journalists take up a major part of campaigners' time. Not only does media campaigning provide them with the best channel for reaching the voters, but journalists also become the prime conduit for exchanges with competitors. Charges and countercharges are made to the press corps as each candidate seeks to dominate the headlines to his or her advantage. The consequences of devoting so much time to the generation of news can be seen in organizational, substantive, and strategic campaign behavior.

Campaign Organization Effects

Relations with journalists have a major role in how campaigners allocate the organizational resources. The press office of a major presidential campaign organization takes up only a small proportion of the financial and staff resources available. Time is a more important drain. Campaign managers frequently report spending much of each day responding to journalists' inquiries. Candidates also have intensive daily contacts with newsmen in press conferences and exclusive interviews.

The campaign's daily schedule is also organized by the quest for news coverage. If a candidate spends one hour in a city, he is likely to receive the same amount of news coverage of that visit as he would during a four-hour or eight-hour campaign stop in the same location. Thus, modern presidential candidates are kept continually on the move by their desire for local news coverage. The scheduler's goal is to set up appearances in three or four major news markets each day.

Campaign Content Effects

All campaigns develop themes that they would like communicated to the electorate through the news-reporting process, persuasive messages that the campaigners hope will energize political support and differentiate their candidate from his competitors. Accordingly, media politics have implications for the substantive content of modern election campaigns.

Journalists, of course, retain ultimate control over what is disseminated as the news of the day. In making this determination, they respond to more than simply the desires of one campaign. As campaign-generated events are transformed into news, furthermore, they undergo a journalistic process that incorporates other information, points of view, and, perhaps unintentionally, the reporter's implicit values. Political journalists face an inevitable dilemma: by reporting events as they occur—and thus not intruding into the electoral process—they may be surrendering the content of their stories to politicians (who would like nothing better than to dictate the news).

To project appealing messages to the voters, campaigners must anticipate the transformation that their words and actions will undergo as they become reported news. A news strategy is, therefore, quite different from an advertising campaign in which the politician can control the content. Media politics demand that candidates and their operatives accommodate the values of journalists who will transmit their messages. Such accommodations distort—in some ways beneficially, in some ways adversely—the content of the campaign.

Journalists argue that campaign appeals are entirely the result of interactions between voters or party activists, on the one hand, and campaigners, on the other. Campaigners, however, react to news reports, regardless of what their polls tell them about voters' intentions. Candidates believe, for example, that if negative press commentary is not an electoral problem today, news reporting will make it a problem for them tomorrow. They expend a great deal of effort, therefore, to head off negative news before it creates a major political problem. In the process, the news-reporting industry can intrude into the content of the campaign, an indirect form of agenda-setting.

Media politics can influence the content of campaign in other subtle ways. Reporters often indicate that campaign speeches are appeals for votes, attempts to belittle the opposition, tries at putting the best face on a bad situation, or rebuttals to criticisms of public positions or candidacies. Such commentary alerts the audience that the speaker is trying to influence its thinking, in turn diminishing the impact of the campaigner's persuasive message.[42] The message is implicit: Politicians are manipulative, journalists objective.

In the following chapters, I distinguish between a candidate's image among the public at large and the labels that are consistently used to describe the candidate in news reporting. The two are obviously related. However, one difference flows from journalists' understandable reluctance to make positive statements about politicians. Although laudatory comments in campaign reporting can be found—mostly in discussions of the political acumen of winners—they are less frequent than critical comments and images. Journalists' reputation for objectivity may be easier to maintain if affirmative evaluations are kept to a minimum. Negative statements are less likely to be construed as partisan, particularly when all politicians are criticized equally. To the extent that the public holds positive images of candidates, however, there may be a disjunction with information carried by the news media.

Some authors have viewed this critical function of news reporting as a needed corrective to the efforts of politicians and their public relations advisers to manipulate public sentiment.[43] However, if carried too far, persistently negative commentary may have an adverse impact on the electoral process. As previously noted, political scientists have not been able to establish a definitive link between media content and citizen attitudes. If there are such effects, however, the content of the news is creating a greater cynicism about politics and politicians.[44]

Political Strategy Effects

Strategic planning is a third area in which media politics influence modern presidential campaigns. In practice, editors and producers must make certain decisions that significantly shape the political race. For example, since serious candidates are newsworthy, those without prospects for winning are given less of the limited news space available to electoral politics. Criteria must be established that distinguish candidates with serious electoral prospects to communicate as much information about them as possible to voters.

Editors and producers also have to decide on an approximate start-ing point for the campaign. The assumption is that voters are less atten-tive to campaign news during the preliminary stages of the campaign. Once the race is in full swing, journalists must give greater space to those events which they perceive as pivotally important to the outcome. Such advanced planning greatly facilitates the commitment of media resources, particularly for the networks who must deploy cumbersome equipment and numerous people.

In each case, news industry decisions affect the volume of coverage available to the contenders. As a result, campaigners conform to these deci-sions in their strategic planning. Once journalists decide on a given criterion for discriminating serious campaigns from those without real prospects for victory (say, for example, the ability to qualify for federal matching funds), campaigners compete along those dimensions. The timing of major cam-paign events also mirrors the decisions of journalists about when the cam-paign will begin to receive voluminous news coverage. Campaigners know, for example, that a policy speech will more likely be reported if scheduled during the so-called campaign season established by the media. These deci-sions create a cycle: as political events such as primary contests merit heavier news coverage, more competitors are drawn to them.

Media and campaign decisions are often intertwined. This cyclical pro-cess escalates the importance of some factors out of proportion to their political significance. In other words, the weighting given to certain achievements by the competitors or to certain events may be substantially different from pure political considerations once the news-reporting process is factored into the equation.

Does altering strategies potentially affect the election outcome? To answer this question, review any of the recent presidential races, eliminating sustained news coverage. Could Reagan have won the 1980 nomination without reports of his New Hampshire victory? Could Jimmy Carter have won in 1976 without the news coverage that accompanied his victories in Iowa, New Hampshire, or Florida? Probably not. But, without the pros-pects of this news coverage, in each case, the winners' strategies would have been quite different.

Thus, news coverage clearly creates a chicken-and-egg problem. Report-ing reflects the strategic calculations of campaigners, while campaigners take into account projected news coverage. When campaigners argue that the whole race hinges on media interpretations of events given by journal-ists, they are clearly wrong. However imperfect, news reporting is describ-ing a process of changing political support. The ambiguity of that process, however, means that media judgments can affect the decisionmaking of the participants. Journalists are, for this reason, equally wrong when they argue that they merely reflect events without contributing to them. The imprint of news reporting on what campaigners actually do, the media's influence on candidates' public messages, and the effects of media decisions on political strategies are all significant phenomena. Nor are they temporary or necessarily adverse. But, in order to comprehend the contemporary system of selecting U.S. presidents, the consequences of media politics must be understood and included in the analysis.

Notes

1. Personal interview with Barry Jagoda, Carter's television adviser, January 6, 1977.

2. Data on media-attending behavior during campaigns has been gathered regularly by the Inter-University Consortium for Political and Social Research since 1952. For the latest data see *The 1980 Center for Political Research American National Election Study* (Ann Arbor, Mich.: ICPSR, 1981). See also Robert T. Bower, *Television and the Public* (New York: Holt, Rinehart & Winston, 1973).

3. Information imparted by news organizations is rated as more credible by citizens. See, for example, The Roper Organization, Inc., *Trends in Public Attitudes Toward Television and Other News Media* (New York: Television Information Office, 1975), p. 3.

4. This book is based upon an extensive set of interviews with campaigners. See appendix I for a list of those contacted and chapter 2 for a discussion of how the research proceeded.

5. Studies of the supposed ability of media to manipulate the public are quite common; see Robert MacNeil, *The People Machine* (New York: Harper, 1968), and Frank Mankiewicz and Joel Swerdlow, *Remove Control* (New York: Times Books, 1978).

6. See, for example, Richard Bunce, *Television and the Corporate Interest* (New York: Praeger, 1976); Edith Efron, *The News Twisters* (Los Angeles: Nash, 1971); and Joseph Keeley, *Left Leaning Antenna* (New Rochelle, N.Y.: Arlington House, 1971).

7. See James David Barber (ed.), *Race for the Presidency* (Englewood Cliffs, N.J.: Prentice-Hall, 1978), and *The Pulse of Politics* (New York: W.W. Norton, 1978), esp. chaps. 1 and 15; and Herbert Gans, *Deciding What's News* (New York: Pantheon, 1979).

8. Paul Weaver, "Is Television News Biased," *The Public Interest* (Winter 1972), pp. 57-74; Edward Jay Epstein, *News from Nowhere* (New York: Vintage, 1974); Leon V. Sigal, *Reporters and Officials* (Lexington, Mass.: D.C. Heath, 1973); and Bernard C. Cohen, *The Press and Foreign Policy* (Princeton, N.J.: Princeton University Press, 1963).

9. See, especially, Thomas Patterson, *The Mass Media Election* (New York: Praeger, 1980), and Patterson and Robert McClure, *The Unseeing Eye* (New York: Putnam, 1976).

10. The voting studies include Paul F. Lazarsfeld, Bernard Berelson, and Hazel Gaudet, *The People's Choice* (New York: Duell, Sloan and Pearce; 1944): Angus Campbell and others, *The Voter Decides* (Evanston, Ill.: Row, Peterson, 1954); Angus Campbell and others, *The American Voter* (New York: Wiley, 1964); Warren Miller and others, "Majority Party in Disarray," *American Political Science Review* (September 1976). For evidence that partisan identification is decreasing see Norman H. Nie and others, *The Changing American Voter* (Cambridge, Mass.: Harvard University Press, 1976).

11. For a review of the law of minimal consequences, see Sidney Kraus and Dennis Davis, *The Effects of Mass Communication of Political Behavior* (University Park, Pa.: Pennsylvania State University Press, 1976); Donald R. Kinder, William M. Denney, and Randolph G. Wagner, "Media Impact on Candidate Image: Exploring the Generality of the Law of Minimal Consequences," Paper presented at the 32nd annual meeting of the American Association for Public Opinion Research, Buck Hill Falls, Pa., May 19–22, 1977.

12. Paul F. Lazarsfeld et al., *The People's Choice* (New York: Columbia University Press, 1944).

13. Ibid., p. 83. 3rd ed.

14. Elihu Katz and J.J. Feldman, "The Debates in Light of Research: A Survey of Surveys," in *The Great Debates*, ed. Sidney Kraus (Bloomington, Ind.: University of Indiana Press, 1962).

15. C. Richard Hofstetter, C. Zubin, and T.F. Buss, "Political Imagery in an Age of Television: The 1972 Campaign," Paper presented at the 1976 annual meeting of the American Political Science Association, Chicago, Ill., September 2–5, 1976; p. 25: see also Patterson and McClure, *The Unseeing Eye.*

16. Doris A. Graber, "Problems in Measuring Audience Effects of the 1976 Debates," in *The Presidential Debates,* Ed. G.F. Bishop, R.C. Meadow, and M. Jackson-Beeck (New York: Praeger, 1978). Some contradictory evidence for short-term effects of the second debate in which Ford discussed Poland and Eastern Europe is presented by Frederick T. Steeper, "Public Response to Gerald Ford's statements on Eastern Europe in the Second Debate," in *The Presidential Debates*, ed. Bishop and others.

17. Paul R. Hagnes and Leroy N. Riselback, "The Impact of the 1976 Presidential Debates: Conversion or Reinforcement?" in *The Presidential Debates,* ed. Bishop and others, pp. 172 and 178.

18. Doris Graber, "The Press as Opinion Resource During the 1968 Presidential Campaign," *Public Opinion Quarterly* (Summer 1971), pp. 168–182.

19. Michael Robinson and Karen McPherson, "Television News Coverage Before the 1976 New Hampshire Primary: The Focus of Network Journalism," *Journal of Broadcasting,* 21 (Spring 1977), pp. 177–186.

20. Thomas E. Patterson, "Press Coverage and Candidate Success in Presidential Primaries: The 1976 Democratic Race," Paper presented at the 1977 annual meetings of the American Political Science Association, Washington, D.C., September 1–4, 1977; and *Mass Media Election* (New York: Praeger: 1980), chaps. 10 and 11.

21. L.B. Becker, I.A. Sobowale, R.E. Cobbey, and C.H. Eyal, "Debate Effects on Voters' Understanding of Candidates and Issues," in *The Presidential Debates,* ed. Bishop and others, p. 138.

22. Patterson, *The Mass Media Election,* part 4.

23. See, for example, Lazarsfeld and others, *The People's Choice.* More recently, Becker and others made the same argument in *The Presidential Debates.*

24. Bernard Cohen, *The Press and Foreign Policy* (Princeton, N.J.: Princeton University Press, 1963), p. 13. See also J.M. McLeod, J.E. Byrnes and L.B. Becker, "Another Look at the Agenda Setting Function of the Press," *Communication Research* 1 (1974), pp. 131–166; D.L. Shaw and M.E. McCombs, *The Emergence of American Political Issues* (St. Paul, Minn.: West, 1977); and Philip Palmgreen and Peter Clarke, "Agenda-Setting with Local and National Issues," *Communications Research* 4 (1977), pp. 435–452.

25. Patterson, *Mass Media Election*, chap. 11, and "Press Coverage," 1977.

26. Personal interview with Thomas Moran, comptroller of the President Ford Committee, July 1977.

27. Personal interview with John Gabusi, campaign manager for Morris Udall, August 8, 1975.

28. Personal interview with Jody Powell, press secretary to Jimmy Carter, July 22, 1975.

29. A few respondents differed with the general conclusion of most campaigners that the media was all important to their efforts. For example, the Wallace campaigners felt strongly that they could not receive unbiased news reporting from the national media. Other instances in which campaigners broke with the consensus on the importance of the media resembled cautionary notes more than direct refutations. For example, John Sears, Reagan's campaign manager, told us (August 7, 1975):

> Television has probably oversold itself in the minds of politicians as a cure-all to the politician's drudgery in the past. Too many politicians have just assumed that you have this tube and you can just put someone on it and that's a hell of a lot easier than everybody knocking on doors and handing out literature and doing all the drudgery of campaigns. It's no substitute.

30. See Sigal, *Reporters and Officials*, for an explanation of this term.

31. See Denis G. Sullivan and others, *The Politics of Representation* (New York: St. Martin's, 1974); and Denis G. Sullivan and others, *Explorations in Convention Decision-Making* (San Francisco: W.H. Freeman, 1976).

32. F.C. Arterton, "The Changing Fulcrum," Paper presented at the 1979 meetings of the Social Science-History Association, Columbus, Ohio, March 1979.

33. On Hannah's activities, see Stanley Jones, *The Election of 1896* (Madison: University of Wisconsin, 1964); on Farley, see James A. Farley, *Behind the Ballets* (New York: Harcourt, Brace, 1938), and John T. Casey and James Bowles, *Farley and Tomorrow* (Chicago: Reilly and Lee, 1939). For an analysis of the way "bosses" operated, see Terry Sanford, *A Danger of Democracy: The Presidential Nominating Process* (Boulder, Col.: Westview, 1981).

34. I have elaborated on these points elsewhere. See "The Strategic Environment of Primaries for Presidential Campaign Organizations, 1976," Paper presented at the 1976 annual meetings of the New England Political Science Association Durham, N.H., April 9 and 10, 1976.

35. Joel McCleary, interviewed at a conference sponsored by Harvard's Institute of Politics on presidential campaign finance, Osgood House, North Andover, Mass., June 14–16, 1977.

36. For the provisions of the act as amended in 1974, see the Federal Election Commission, *Federal Election Campaign Law* (Washington, D.C.: Government Printing Office, January 1980).

37. Personal interview with Frank Greer, press secretary to Fred Harris, July 8, 1975. Greer refers to the number of states in which a candidate must raise $2,000 or more in contributions of less than $250 before qualifying for federal matching money.

38. Personal interview with Gary Orren, Kennedy's pollster, May 29, 1981.

39. Harvard's Campaign Finance Study Group, *Expenditure Limits in the Presidential Prenomination Campaign: The 1980 Experience* (Cambridge, Mass.: Institute of Politics, Harvard University, 1980); Kimball W. Brace, *The 1976 Presidential Primaries: An Analysis of How Many People Participated and How Much Money Was Spent* (Washington, D.C.: Democratic National Committee, 1977).

40. For a description of how campaigns used their money, see ibid., and Herbert Alexander, *Financing the 1976 Elections* (Washington, D.C.: Congressional Quarterly Inc., 1979).

41. Herbert Alexander and Joel Margolis, "The Making of the Debates," in *The Presidential Debates,* pp. 18–32. See also Edwin Diamond, *Good News, Bad News* (Cambridge, Mass.: MIT Press, 1978) for figures on the audience for the televised debates.

42. For the effects of innoculation in reducing persuasiveness, see William J. McGuire, "Inducing Resistance to Persuasion: Some Contemporary Approaches," in *Advances in Experimental Social Psychology,* ed. Leonard Berkowitz, vol. 1 (New York: Academic Press, 1963).

43. See, for example, Stanley Kelley, Jr., *Professional Public Relations and Political Power* (Baltimore, Md.: Johns Hopkins University Press, 1956); Melvyn Bloom, *Public Relations and Presidential Campaigns: A Crisis in Democracy* (New York: Crowell, 1973); and James Perry, *Us and Them* (New York: Potter, 1973).

44. Michael Robinson has attempted to draw a direct relationship between exposure to television broadcasting and the growth of cynicism in "Public Affairs Television and the Growth of Political Malaise," *American Political Science Review* 71:2 (June 1976), pp. 409–432; see also the subsequent exchange over this article in the *American Political Science Review*, 73:1 (March 1977), pp. 246–250.

2 The Campaign in the News

Politicians and journalists hold very different conceptions of the campaign process; each side ascribes a different role to campaign journalism. Reporters see electoral politics as a grand competition between contending candidates, each seeking support from a limited pool of party activists and voters. In fact, much campaign activity does involve exchanges between competitors: charges, criticisms, replies, competing suggestions for public policy, tactical moves and countermoves, and discussion of strategies. Journalists perceive their role in this process as observing these exchanges and transmitting them to the public.[1] As self-proclaimed observers, they are disturbed by the proposition that news reporting itself contributes to the growth or decline of political support. Most journalists hold firmly to the belief that campaign reporting merely conveys information among participants in a political process. Being factual, the content of news reporting has, they assert, a negligible independent influence upon the political process (figure 2-1).

At the same time, reporters view their relationship with politicians as inherently adversarial and therefore not entirely passive. Yet even while pressing candidates or their advisers on matters which they know are damaging to the campaign, journalists do not see their activities as intruding into the political process. Rather their efforts are necessary to ferret out the truth that politicians would prefer to obscure. Bringing that truth to light is seen as objective, neutral, and nonparticipatory, even if the exposure directly affects the electoral process.

This rationale hinges, of course, on the assumption that an objectifiable truth exists to be reported. Frequently, that assumption is tenuous at best. The belief in a nonparticipant status of news reporters is, furthermore, rooted in the assertion that journalists do not intend to influence events. The news, they argue, is neither selected nor distorted in such a way that will shape the behavior of either voters or politicians. I do not intend to challenge this latter belief—the news is not biased politically. But just because no influence is intended does not mean that no influence is exerted. Working journalists will, most likely, find this assertion disturbing.

Campaigners see things differently. For them, the news reporting process is central to their efforts. They conceive of electoral politics according to the relationships diagrammed in figure 2-2. Elements of the reporter's model coexist with, and in some cases are secondary to, linkages through

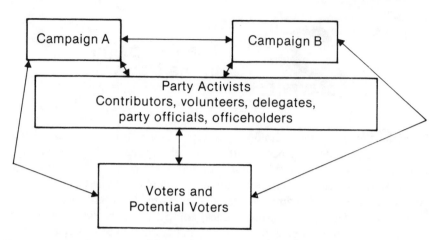

Figure 2-1. The Journalist's View of the Electoral Process

the news-reporting process. For example, the content of a campaign can be viewed as a competing struggle of ideas between two campaigns for news reporting. Sharp limits on news space force contending politicians to compete in "making the news", that is in dominating the headlines and controlling the context of news reporting.

Naturally, they also clash in their attempts to influence the content of what is reported. Journalists are viewed in this model not as objective conduits to the electorate, but as arbitrators over a very significant—the most significant by some tellings—area of campaign conflict. Most of the conflict between candidates takes place indirectly through the news-reporting process; situations in which competing candidates come face-to-face with each other during a campaign are exceedingly rare. In addition, campaigners acquire a large amount of their information about the activities of their opponents and about support groups within the electorate or politically active communities from news reports. Because producers and editors often ask their reporters to obtain the candidates' reaction to statements of their opponents, reporters frequently—if unwittingly—carry information between contestants. The candidates, for their part, reply to their competition most frequently through statements released to the media, rather than in private messages. For all these reasons, as well as those discussed in chapter 1, the content of the nightly news or morning headlines has become a tactical battleground over which presidential aspirants struggle for control.

The logic of the campaigner's position (figure 2-2) goes beyond the simple assertion that what is reported as news is integral to modern campaign discourse. News-making provides campaigners with access to large audiences as well as the credibility that comes with information provided

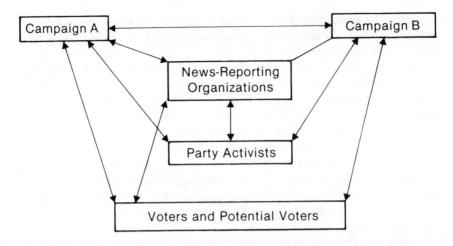

Figure 2-2. The Campaigner's View of the Electoral Process

through a conduit perceived as nonpartisan.[2] Both access and credibility are managed by the journalists who sit astride this channel. Because the attitudes of reporters affect both the amount of coverage available to a given candidate and the content of that coverage, political strategists make extensive efforts to influence the thoughts and behavior of journalists.

The Politics of Campaign–Media Interaction

The importance of media politics for contemporary campaigns arises out of the ambiguities inherent in electoral politics. Politicians are engaged in generating and organizing political support and manifesting it on election day. Meanwhile journalists are attempting to observe and chronicle this process. The ability to predict is essential to both tasks. Yet, for neither is prediction a simple endeavor.

Ambiguity and Complexity

The process by which candidates acquire political support is poorly understood, despite the professionalization of campaign techniques and the concentrated attention of a generation of political scientists. The effectiveness of different means for obtaining votes—the ultimate form of political support—is quite uncertain.[3] Politicians cannot be sure which appeals will prove successful nor how they should allocate the available resources to reach potential supporters. Instead, campaigners cope with their uncertainty by employing conventional wisdom, replicating strategies that proved successful in the past, using trial-and-error, and adopting the newest technology available.[4] Ultimately, however, campaign strategic decisions rest a good deal more firmly on the persuasive abilities or salesmanship of the participants than on any sure knowledge of what will produce votes.

The difficulties plaguing campaigners trying to assemble a plurality of voters, however, make forecasting results tenuous at best. Neither journalists nor campaigners can be certain which political resources will lead to eventual electoral success. Not only are the available indicators likely to contradict each other because different candidates have different strengths, but, taken alone, each indicator is also likely to be a poor predictor of ultimate success.

Consider, first, the early stages of an election contest. Poll standings, which are frequently cited as the most reliable indicator, changed dramatically over both the nomination and general phases of the two most recent races. Other possible indicators, such as organizational strength or support of the party activists, can be extremely difficult to observe or test. As the Connally campaign in 1980 amply demonstrated, still other indicators—the size of campaign treasuries or the number of important endorsements—may be easier to measure, but have questionable value in generating electoral support. Predicting the nomination outcome based on the results of early primaries involves the assumption that early states are representative of national trends. However, as the number of candidates increase in early primaries and because of the political nature of the early-primary states, this assumption can be quite dubious. Because nomination politics are ultimately competitions for delegate votes, the contours of the delegate race do not become clear until a number of states have held primaries. In the general election, of course, the electoral college provides a wealth of possible winning combinations.

No wonder that journalists are hesitant during the early campaign stages about whether to concentrate on issue positions, the charismatic appeal of the candidates, their conduct in office, their performance in face-to-face encounters with their opposition, their developing organizational strength, their cash balances, their performance in early primaries or caucuses, public opinion polls, reports of party dissension, the distribution of delegate votes, or all of these. As election campaigns unfold, this uncertainty is reduced but rarely eliminated. Delegate totals may not provide a definitive indicator of nomination success. In the 1976 Republican contest and, to a lesser degree, in the Carter-Kennedy clash of 1980, despite the best efforts of news-reporting organization to predict delegate intentions, the outcomes were uncertain until the votes were counted on the convention floor. Although Carter piled up a heavy lead in delegate votes in 1980, reporters still could not tell whether his losses in key primaries signaled the collapse of his support or whether Kennedy might be able to pull away enough delegates to break the convention open.

The general election is marked by similar confusion. Although great attention is focused upon the televised debates and most casual observers assume that these events are very significant, their effects upon the final outcome are highly ambiguous. Explaining their impact can be quite subjective. As demonstrated in both 1976 and 1980, moreover, the electoral college arithmetic provides a confusing array of contingencies that could tip the election one way or another right up to election day.

Campaign results are also difficult to forecast because political resources are obviously interrelated. Volunteers, endorsements, money, news space, votes, delegates, and poll standings—to name only a few indicators—can, in some circumstances, be causes and effects of each other. Television advertising evidently makes a campaign appear more newsworthy, thereby expanding the amount of news coverage.[5] Ample and favorable news coverage may stimulate campaign contributions.[6] Campaigners believe that success in generating primary votes has a snowball effect on attracting volunteers, endorsements, and votes in subsequent primary states. While campaign expenditures may be related to better performance on election day, the ability to raise money is itself an indicator of electoral support.[7]

The model of campaign success (or failure) emerging from these interrelationships evidently contains a multiplier effect. Improvement on one dimension is likely to be related to improvement in other aspects of support building. Journalists and campaigners call this dynamic momentum, although they rarely define the term precisely.[8] The converse, a pronounced deceleration in political support, is frequently described as the process by which candidates are "winnowed" from the field.[9] In either case, very little is known about the interrelationships among the various facets of political support.

Predicting success or failure in presidential nomination politics can be an especially hazardous undertaking for other reasons as well. The complexity of our electoral machinery reaches its zenith in the patchwork construction of institutions through which presidential candidates are nominated.[10] Although presidential candidates are formally nominated by delegate votes, these votes are accumulated during numerous discrete events stretched out over the six months before the convention. Winning a presidential primary is not like winning any other kind of election. Presidential primaries do not have the same degree of finality that we experience in other electoral processes where winning and losing are sharply distinguishable.[11] With each primary victory, the winning presidential candidate acquires only a percentage of the required delegates.

Essentially, the sequential nature of the nomination process means that changes in the measures of political support are more important than absolute amounts. Even if reporters could be sure what indicators provide reliable cues to success, they would still have to decide whether ambiguous measurements indicate growing, declining, or stagnating support. Success in a presidential primary must be judged within the context of how that event contributes to the overall contest. Even a majority of the votes for a given candidate could signal a weakness that might become consequential in succeeding primaries. A narrow loss may demonstrate growing strength.

Establishing that context is a matter of interpretation, and, needless to say, the evidence to support these interpretations is difficult to obtain. For example, there is no guarantee that a sequence of events will form a pattern similar to prior election cycles. Unknown candidates emerged from a crowded field in 1972 and 1976, but not in 1980. A stalemated primary process could result in a multiballot convention. Yet, reporters' assumptions about the likelihood of a given scenario occurring can significantly affect their interpretations of individual events.

The journalists' task of predicting outcomes is even more complicated by the candidates themselves. Reporters hear abundant and conflicting advice about how to interpret various factors by contenders and their supporters. Campaign politics—like many other forms of the art—places a premium upon persuasive abilities. Each campaign develops, refines, and advocates a plausible political strategy for achieving the nomination. To be sure, many claims can be dismissed as self-serving. However, the hazards of completely ignoring these conflicting arguments were demonstrated in 1972, when an unknown candidate emerged from obscurity to capture his party's nomination. George McGovern followed precisely the course predicted earlier by his campaign operatives to the overwhelming disbelief of most journalists. By 1976, newsmen, once burned, were less willing to dismiss the claims of any combatant.[12] During the preprimary period, one campaign manager, for example, described how her candidate profited from reporters' search for a dark horse candidate:

> The press this year is . . . so afraid that what happened to them in 1972 is going to happen again—that they're going to grasp the wrong candidate and run with the candidate and make a frontrunner of him and then have him fall while something is happening under their nose that they don't know about. And, they pay a lot of attention to me because I was part of that "under their nose."[13]

Carter's success in replicating McGovern's rise from obscurity only lent greater credence to the arguments of Republican contenders challenging the dominance of Reagan's lead in early 1980. The "last war" syndrome led to overenthusiastic interpretations of George Bush's victory in the Iowa caucuses. As the campaign evolved, however, that scenario did not lead to inevitable success.

Perceptions or Political Realities?

Neither journalists nor politicians, however, can afford to be hamstrung by patterns and problems of the past. But, if they cannot operate on realities, what do they substitute as a basis for action? Through their interaction, reporters and campaigners continually mold a shared consensus about the political processes at work, a system of beliefs or assumptions on which both can act. To the extent that these assumptions become widely shared, campaigners believe that they are more important than the concrete realities of political support, success or failure, strategies or tactics. Combined, these consensus beliefs form a perceptual environment within which campaigns must plan their strategies.

Sometimes, individual campaigns are able to influence these perceptions, but more frequently they have to accommodate their strategies to them. For example, campaign managers repeatedly voice the opinion that the perception of winning the New Hampshire primary is far more than the actual fact of winning or the margin of victory. George Bush's pollster, Robert Teeter, summarizes some of these consensus beliefs:

> We simply followed the rules that everyone has come to know: that primaries and early caucuses are far and away the most important—they're everything now; that what it takes in those early ones is a number of dedicated people within those states; that you've got to campaign full-time; and that you have to establish, in order to become that alternative, probably some uniqueness.[14]

Because a great many of the interpretations of political events are produced by journalists, campaigners believe that reporters are primarily responsible for establishing the perceptional environment to which they must respond. To the extent that journalists are able to achieve among themselves consensus that a given set of statements is descriptive of reality, they become reality itself for campaigners. Ultimately, politicians base their logic on their belief that news reporting does affect the behavior and attitudes of voters and political activists. If a candidacy is repeatedly described as "not living up to expectations" or "considered by many to be too old," these comments can take on a self-fulfilling quality, making support-building much more difficult.

Journalism exercises its greatest influence over the conduct of campaigns where ambiguity is highest. As documented in chapter 4, campaigners feel most vulnerable to the news process during the preprimary period. As the political process evolves, uncertainty is reduced, predictability improves, and the campaigns that survive become increasingly able to influence the content of news reporting. Success increases campaigners' ability to affect the consensus perceptions within which their activities will be interpreted.

The Alternative Electorate

Acting under these assumptions, presidential campaigns managers come to view the corps of journalists as an alternative electorate; they respond directly to the concerns and values of journalists in addition to, and sometimes in place of, forces in the electorate or the political system.

No doubt journalists would feel more comfortable with this notion if it were phrased as a "surrogate" electorate; "surrogate" denotes someone who serves in the place of another, a substitute. "Alternate," on the other hand, expresses a choice between incompatible directions. The concept of an alternative electorate is a more appropriate model of campaign-media interaction to the extent that one believes that campaigners seek to optimize the different values held by the voters and the media or that campaigners are forced to adopt different behaviors with regard to each. The politicians interviewed did believe they had to campaign separately on these two levels: the electorate and the media corps. In both arenas they respond to expectations while conducting a persuasive effort to shape attitudes and behavior.

During my research for this book, I found numerous examples of campaigners acting specifically to influence the thinking of journalists, on the one hand, and reacting to journalists' expectations on the other. One central conclusion of this research, therefore, is that newsmen occupy a separate sphere of persuasive activity for campaigners. Their messages to voters differ substantively from their messages to the media. Although reporters may have opinions about desired policy positions or candidate characteristics, a direct appeal to journalists on these grounds contradicts sensitive professional norms. Objectivity and neutrality keep reporters from publically endorsing a candidacy or proclaiming certain policy views as correct. Proselytizing journalists is rarely profitable.

Campaigners do try to persuade reporters that the campaign has serious prospects of attaining its objective—the nomination and election of its candidate. Voters and party activists are, to be certain, interested in horserace questions, and, as campaigners believe, many voters are influenced by their perceptions of which candidates seem realistic. But the intricacies of predicting future success on the basis of current events are a special concern of journalists. In dealing with reporters, campaigners attempt to persuade them to adopt the campaign's view of the horserace. In doing so, they are concerned with the application of images such as "winner" or "loser," and also with the decisions journalists make in allocating news coverage.

Intentionally or not, reporters shape the behavior of campaigners primarily through the questions they ask, the stories they file, and their demands for access to decisionmakers. Campaigners are hypersensitive to the beliefs and values of political journalists: media politics involves anticipating news reporting and accommodating campaign plans to those expectations. Without meaning to, journalists affect major campaign decisions.

A Political Relationship

Skilled campaign organizers offer journalists a reliable flow of reportable stories, especially those representing media with access to huge audiences. On the simplest level, the candidate's words, actions, and travels generate a steady stream of newsworthy stories. These are the heart of an election campaign's events planned with an eye toward how they will be reported. They are staged frequently enough to give the reporters something to do, partly to help them fulfill their jobs and partly to divert them from developing damaging stories.

Reporters and politicians engage in exchanges; each offers the other some valuable commodities. Only very rarely, however, does this relationship involve an explicit quid pro quo, which would compromise the independence of the reporter. Rather, their interactions form a relationship of reciprocal influence. Politicians are continually interested in shaping the timing, amount, and content of news stories. Journalists' influence is more subtle because it is not necessarily intended; few overtly or instrumentally seek to influence the course of events, the election outcome, or the behavior of politicians.[15]

The relationships we are discussing are, moreover, essentially political in a deeper sense. Their contacts involve more than mutual influence; both sides are actively seeking to alter their future terms of exchange.[16] Successful campaigners move from a position of supplicant—their need for coverage vastly exceeds the news space available—to that of regular dispenser of reportable news. Along the way, they are quick to exploit opportunities in which their own newsworthiness promotes competition among journalists and news media. By choosing among possible news outlets, campaigners can improve their terms of trade. Success, in turn, allows campaigners to take over much of the initiative in campaign reporting. Instead of responding to every individual request, they must deal with journalists in collectivities—the traveling press corps, the Washington media, or the local press.

Journalists, for their part, are equally concerned with these terms of exchange. Most wish to develop sources of reliable information within each candidate organization that will provide them with continuing access to campaign decisionmaking. Successful upper-level advisers become increasingly insulated over the course of the campaign, so journalists seek to establish contact, trust, and access early.[17] Such sources can be invaluable to reporters once the momentum builds and press officers stop responding to individual requests. At the same time, journalists often become restive about the efforts of the candidate and his organization to control the content of the daily news. When things are going most smoothly from the campaign's viewpoint, reporters feel that nothing is happening because the initiative is out of their hands.

The journalists interviewed for this book are highly sensitive to the political aspects of their relationship with campaigners. They worry continually about the possibilities of being manipulated by candidates. Upon occasion, they react collectively to the dominance of campaigners in initiating most news. A perceived error by the candidate can become a focal point, concentrating the vast majority of news about that contestant upon a single topic. In these episodes, perceived as "press crises" by campaigners, journalists reinforce each other, defining the news themselves through persistent questioning of the candidate's position, the answers to which serve to perpetuate reports on this topic.

Politicians perceive these crises as essentially political.[18] Rather than conceding that reporters are responding to an important, substantive issue, they view newsmen as out to test the mettle of the candidate under fire, or as seeking to compensate for earlier, more favorable writing.

The Campaign News Strategy

Campaigners use whatever means lies at their disposal to achieve beneficial news coverage. Their strategy is based on their desire to pass some major communication costs over to the media corporations, an understanding that news has more credibility than advertising, and a firm belief that reported news does shape their political support.

By making desired stories easy to report while attempting to obscure or detract news value from stories deemed harmful to the candidate, campaigners maneuver to limit the agenda of the daily news. Yet, even when they are successful in influencing the content of news reporting, politicians are never able to dictate a journalist's report. Reporters and correspondents retain final control over what they print and broadcast. Yet because politicians normally hold the initiative in generating events that can be reported, they can control—at least to some extent—the range of stories that are available. The predictability in the news process does permit campaigners to plan their political efforts with the headlines in mind.

To what ends do politicians pursue media politics? Campaigners report that several distinct goals shape the development of the campaign news strategy.

Name Recognition

The first concern of campaign operatives is to achieve access to voters through the news media. They are interested in sheer exposure. Whether accurately or not, politicians assume that name recognition is fundamental to the process of securing votes. If candidates are not covered, they will not become known. The era in which voters pull the lever for their party's candidate—whether or not they have ever heard of him—is over, if it ever existed. Name recognition has become a critical ingredient in the calculus of electability, particularly in primary elections where party identification has less influence and differences in recognition levels can be substantial.[19] But even in general elections, campaigners believe that voters will not support a candidate whose name they do not recognize.[20]

Promoting name recognition by maximizing news coverage is, therefore, the initial step of the campaign's news strategy. For example, during the 1976 presidential campaign, Senator Church and his advisers decided to start late in the primary season when, presumably, the other candidates would be nearing exhaustion. However, by mid-May, when Church began to recruit voters in the Nebraska primary, most reporters had already been assigned to other candidates. His political strategy, thus, ran counter to the practical need to provide visibility. Despite their best efforts, Church received very little coverage both before and after his win in Nebraska:

> In April, the networks waited until just before the Nebraska primary to assign crews to Church. They were traveling permanently from that point on. . . . They gave us a few bad shots, but they're not as damaging as just nonexposure. You can't overcome other candidates who are on the screen two or three nights per week.[21]

The goal of expanding name recognition is not, however, as straightforward as it first appears. We cannot predict that campaigners will seek to maximize their news coverage indiscriminantly under all circumstances. Some campaigners may target segments of the electorate and, consequently, focus on gaining exposure through specific news outlets. These segments can be based on policy interests, the probability of campaign involvement (for example, party activists versus mere voters), or geographic concerns. As the general election campaign nears a conclusion, for example, local media in pivotal states may become more important to the candidates than those which deliver a nationwide audience. On the other hand, little-known candidates may count upon the news exposure accompanying early primary victories to boost their national ratings:

> In the primaries, your basic thing is to get known, at least in the states where you're running early, and if you're successful then that takes care of your national recognition problem overnight.[22]

> The places that our name recognition had better be high are New Hampshire and Florida. We don't have to worry about the rest of the country. But if we do well in those states, particularly if we win New Hampshire where we're not expected to do well at all—a Southerner in a New England state, you know—we could get on the cover of *Time* and *Newsweek* and all of a sudden this guy nobody ever heard of before is, maybe, the probable nominee. . . .[23]

Finally, during the year preceding the primaries, most campaigners recognize the impossibility of attracting television coverage. Accordingly they devote their efforts to reaping newspaper coverage, knowing that clippings, particularly those from prestigious national papers, can be photocopied for mass mailings to party activists and local journalists. During these initial stages, campaigners seek to communicate with attentive publics through media like newspapers or magazines which may have lower salience to the mass electorate.[24]

In practice, the pursuit of name recognition can include efforts to associate a candidate's name with a particular office. Even well-known politicians will seek news coverage to link their candidacy to a position. The Reagan campaign in 1976 and the Kennedy campaign in 1980 experienced great difficulties in generating a continuous flow of news coverage between the end of the primary campaign and the opening of the August conventions.[25] Each sought to maintain public awareness that its man was a credible candidate for the nomination; both faced the obvious disadvantage of an incumbent candidate who could command legitimate news coverage.

Campaigners' attention to the quantity of news coverage, therefore, does not cease with the attainment of a given level of recognition. Campaign personnel attempt to pace the news flow so that the candidate's activities will be continually reported. These considerations can affect such critical decisions as which primaries to enter. Quite apart from the value of votes and delegates, a continuing calendar of state primaries could ensure that a candidate will not drop out of the national headlines.[26]

Patterson has provided empirical support for the relationship between news coverage and name recognition.[27] The number of respondents who felt they "knew something" about Jimmy Carter rose from only 20 percent in February before the New Hampshire primary to 77 percent just after the

Pennsylvania primary in late April. Patterson found that, after his New Hampshire victory, Carter received fully half of the news space devoted to the Democratic race, more than three times the volume allotted to any other candidate.

Occasionally, campaigners may seek to limit the quantity of news reported about their candidate. For example, in the latter stages of the 1976 primary campaign, Carter's strategists became convinced that voters were becoming annoyed at seeing Carter on the network news every night.[28] They limited press access to the candidate and his family and decreased the scheduling of reportable political events in the months before the convention.

Favorable Images

The quest for volume in news coverage is based on the campaigners' acceptance of the hypothesis asserting the media's agenda-setting capacities. Journalists are perceived as able to establish the range of candidates from which voters will choose. Campaigners also desire to use the media to project persuasive information about their candidates.

Substantively, the campaign news strategy consists of persuasive messages about the candidate's personal characteristics, policy stands, or prospects for achieving victory. From the politicians' viewpoint, much of the effort of their campaign consists of repeated attempts to cast essentially the same, simple message into seemingly new forms, such that it will continue to be newsworthy. Each campaign organization seeks to communicate a unique theme or message to the electorate. This message is simultaneously intended to attract political support and differentiate the candidate from his opposition. The appeal may emphasize either images or issues. By informal convention, the discussions between politicians and journalists over campaign themes are usually phrased in terms of their attractiveness to the electorate, rather than as a straightforward debate over the virtues of the candidate or his policy positions. In the process, politicians and journalists cooperate in emphasizing the manipulative aspects of the electoral system, rather than leadership. The ethos of the democratic system in their dialogue becomes primarily the mechanics of how a politician achieves electoral victory rather than a presentation by political elites of the policies they believe correct for the country.

The Prospects of Victory

Political reporters frequently comment upon the progress of the race itself, combining reports of the election strategies of the contenders with forecasts of probable outcomes. These stories are called "horserace reporting," referring to the interpretations and projections of the likely result of the nomination or election, the "thrill of victory and the agony of defeat" of those who would be president. Politicians perceive such stories as a critical element of their news strategies. Few voters, they assume, will support a politician who has no chance for victory. John Anderson's independent campaign in 1980 and numerous nomination candidacies have been caught in this bind. Many campaigners believe that these horserace stories provide voters with a chief source of information about which candidates have serious prospects.

Accordingly, campaigners make a considerable effort to mold the perceptions of journalists as about their candidate's electoral prospects—the likelihood of his eventual success, the standards according to which his progress should be measured, the levels at which his achievements ought to be labeled "expected" or "surprisingly strong" or "disappointing," and the implausibility of his opponents' strategies.

As perceived by these politicians, the media's role in establishing and applying these standards to each campaign is most significant during the preprimary period, when there is an absence of concrete events, and a multitude of possible predictors. Later, success is more and more measured by primary delegate counts, so that room for plausible criteria is narrowed sharply. Nevertheless, in framing political strategies for gaining the nomination, most campaigners assume that interpretations by journalists continue to be important throughout the election. As one press secretary remarked:

> the interpretation of the media will be that much more important . . . because, I think, that coming into the convention, if you're short of delegates, the real determining factor's going to be the psychological momentum the press creates. Is he the winner? Can he get the nomination? Is he acceptable? Given that it's not going to be a clear and away winner . . . that interpretation, that psychological momentum, is very important.[29]

Insulation

A fourth goal of the campaign news strategy is to handle the organizational problems that journalists create for politicians. Once journalists decide that a campaign is newsworthy, they can become quite intrusive into the campaign's activities. The press office not only secures news coverage, but fends off reporters to enable other campaign officials to do their jobs.

Most presidential campaigns adopt specific procedures for responding to reporters' inquiries. All contact with reporters, for example, is usually coordinated through the press office, both to achieve coordination in the flow of information from the campaign and to insulate campaigners from journalists. Of course, there are numerous instances in which these rules were violated by individual campaigners.

Intracampaign Communication

Campaigners might circumvent the centralized press office approach to advance their individual goals through news coverage. For example, campaigners often use the news media to communicate to other compaigners or the candidate himself, particularly when internal channels have proved fruitless. Such attempts need not be entirely self-serving, as, for example, when state-level coordinators are quoted by the press saying that the state will be lost unless the candidate appears there.[30]

The use of journalists for internal communication is not limited to attempts by subordinates to signal their superiors. In July 1975, Terry Sanford used a press conference to commit his campaign organization to qualifying for federal matching funds within one month. Internal memoranda would not have had the same compelling effect, since in his press conference Sanford invited journalists to enforce this policy upon his own campaign organization. Once the campaign was committed publicly to that goal—particularly one so easy to measure—subordinates knew that newsmen would continually measure their progress.

Technically, this use of the news reporting process falls outside our definition of a campaign news strategy. Rather than securing the goals of individual campaigners, a news strategy refers to the objectives of the organization. Nevertheless, these examples provide a reminder that campaigns are composed of individuals with diverse goals.

To what degree can campaigners rationally plan and implement their strategies? These organizations are composed of individuals operating to fulfill their own agendas.[31] They may produce either strategy by committee or an amalgam of the disjunctive action of campaigners striving to reach individual goals.[32] Yet upper-level campaign personnel do carefully plan the organization's political efforts.[33] Furthermore, at least some evidence indicates that campaigns behave rationally.[34]

For the purposes of this study, I assume that campaign organizations are able to develop strategic plans that include goals and actions necessary to achieve these goals. Whether or not the campaign management can ensure that subordinates actually do what they are supposed to is, for the purposes of this study, less important.[35] I do not intend to assert that they are successful in achieving all their goals. However, an understanding of the assumptions about news reporting that guide their actions will illuminate why they adopt given political strategies, what substantive messages they seek to communicate to the electorate, and how they organize and structure their activities.

The Nature of This Study

The relationships between presidential campaigns and news media organizations can take very diverse forms. Candidate organizations differ markedly in resources, structures, strategies, and themes. As a result, each deals differently with journalists. Even greater diversity exists among news-reporting organizations, which includes local dailies and weeklies, dailies with national visibility, wire services, radio and television, networks, and newsweeklies. For this book, the differences in interactions between the media and the campaign organization are simplified for clarity and succinctness.

Documenting the "influence relationships" shown in figure 2–3 is exceedingly difficult. In chapter 1, we examined the literature that discusses the media's impact on voters' ideas and behavior (arrow 4). Very little research has focused upon whether party activists differ from voters in their reliance upon the media (arrow 3). The influence of campaigners upon journalists' work (arrow 1) proves difficult to isolate, although numerous examples of such influence are brought to light in chapters 4, 5, and 6. Ultimately, however, journalists respond to manifold considerations as they turn out the reported news.

For these reasons, the interactions between candidate and news organizations will be examined here from the perspective of upper-level campaign management (arrow 3). Media politics have the most pronounced consequences for the political system through the belief structure of campaigners.

For example, during the 1976 primary campaign, Jimmy Carter's beliefs about public policy options were widely regarded as "fuzzy." While

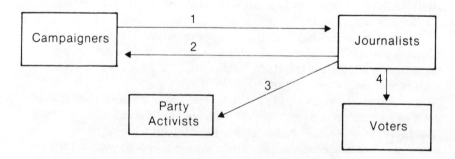

Figure 2–3.   Influence Relations in Media Politics

this label can certainly be found in much of the journalistic commentary about the candidate, other important pieces argued that he was no less precise than most other candidates. A detailed analysis of media content would be necessary to uncover whether either label became a consensus judgment among journalists. For this study, however, we are less concerned with press labels than with the perceptions of Carter's managers—how widespread did they perceive the use of that label; to what did they attribute its development; what kinds of problems did it become both in their press and in the minds of voters; and, especially, what steps did they take to counter its effects on both the media and the voters?

Although campaign managers' arguments should not be accepted without question, eventually political actors respond to their perceptions, rather than to the realities of the situations they confront. Those perceptions become politically significant, and it is that political significance which this study seeks to describe and analyze.

Chapter 3 describes the organizational dynamics and strategic problems of newsreporting corporations, paying particular attention to those forces which shape the dissemination of news about the presidential race. To a degree, the discernible continuities in how election campaigns are reported provide a level of predictability upon which campaigners can plan.

Campaigners and reporters interact on three conceptually distinct levels—personal, organizational, and substantive. They are thrown into close proximity for as long as a year of long campaign days. On a personal level, not only do they develop a camaraderie, but also their separate careers become intertwined. Organizationally, both the campaigns and the news corporations become symbiotic, interacting structures. Journalists seek to report the events of the day; campaigners wish to generate such stories. Finally, campaigners and journalists interact over the substance of what is reported as news. Chapters 4, 5, and 6 illustrate and elaborate these levels of interaction, particularly the organizational and substantive dimensions.

Obviously, the nature of competition for the presidency evolves markedly throughout the election year. Preprimary, early primary, late primary, nominating conventions, and the general election are distinguishable stages. Because the structure of the race and the candidate organizations themselves change over these stages, interactions between the politicians and journalists also undergo a metamorphosis throughout the campaign year.[36] Rather than discussing the campaign chronologically, the following chapters analyze the modes of interaction between campaigners and journalists, their organizational symbiosis, and their mutual influence over the substance of campaign news reporting.

Notes

1. The best evidence for the perspective journalists bring to reporting campaign politics often comes from the books they subsequently write about an election. I have found Jules Witcover's *Marathon* (New York: Viking, 1977) very helpful in presenting the reporters' answer to the media critics.

2. "Credibility" is a technical term borrowed from communication studies. For an early introduction to this abundant literature see C.I. Hovland and I.L. Janis (eds.), *Personality and Persuadability* (New Haven, Conn.: Yale University Press, 1959). Estimates of the added value to a campaign of having its message carried as news can be found in Arnold Steinberg, *Political Campaign Management* (Lexington, Mass.: D.C. Heath, 1976), chap. 7.

3. Marjorie R. Hershey, *The Making of Campaign Strategy* (Lexington, Mass.: Lexington Books, 1974).

4. These strategies are discussed by Hershey in *The Making of Campaign Strategy,* and in "A Social Learning Theory of Innovation and Change in Political Campaigning," Paper presented at the 1977 annual convention of the American Political Science Association, Washington, D.C., September 1-4, 1977. See also Xandra Kayden, *Campaign Organization* (Lexington, Mass.: D.C. Heath, 1978), chaps. 4, 5. These strategies are considered more formally in Larry Bartels, "Resource Allocation in the 1976 Presidential Campaign: Strategic Responses to the Campaign Environment," unpublished master's thesis, Yale University, 1978.

5. Mary Ellen Leary, *Phantom Politics: Campaigning in California* (Washington, D.C.: Public Affairs Press, 1977.)

6. Personal interview with David Keene, campaign manager for George Bush, February 2, 1980. This interview took place after the Iowa caucuses results, news coverage of which had resulted, in Keene's opinion, in a massive flood of contributions to the campaign.

7. Gary C. Jacobson, *Money in Congressional Elections* (New Haven, Conn: Yale University Press, 1980).

8. A discussion of momentum is contained in John Aldrich's *Before the Convention: Strategies and Choices in Presidential Nomination Campaigns* (Chicago: University of Chicago Press, 1980), and in F. Christopher Arterton, "The Concept of Momentum in Presidential Campaigns," a paper presented at a symposium on presidential nominations at Dartmouth College, January 14, 1980.

9. Donald R. Matthews, "Winnowing: The News Media and the 1976 Presidential Nominations" in *Race for the Presidency,* ed. James David Barber (Englewood Cliffs, N.J.: Prentice-Hall, 1978).

10. For a discussion of the workings of the nomination system, see John H. Aldrich, *Before the Convention* (Chicago: University of Chicago Press, 1980); John Kessel, *Presidential Campaign Politics* (Homewood, Ill.: Dorsey, 1980), pp. 3–23; Nelson Polsky and Aaron B. Wildavsky, *Presidential Elections,* 4th ed. (New York: Scribners, 1980); and Stephen J. Wayne, *The Road to the White House* (New York: St. Martins, 1980).

11. I am indebted to David R. Mayhew for his help in developing these thoughts about the nature of victory in presidential primaries.

12. For a discussion of the lessons learned by reporters following McGovern's victory, see Timothy Crouse, *Boys on the Bus* (New York: Ballantine, 1973); James Perry, *Us and Them* (New York: Clarkson Potter, 1973); and Witcover, *Marathon.*

13. Personal interview with Jean Westwood, campaign manager for Terry Sanford, July 9, 1975.

14. Robert Teeter, pollster for George Bush, in *Campaign for President: 1980 in Retrospect,* ed. Jonathan Moore (Cambridge, Mass: Ballinger, 1981), p. 3; emphasis added.

15. While anticipated reactions constitute a difficult research problem, they must be considered a major form of influence. See Jack Nagal, *The Descriptive Analysis of Power* (New Haven, Conn.: Yale University Press, 1974), chap. 2.

16. Central to a power relationship is what Frey refers to as the "power over power," structural relations through which the power to influence substantive outcomes is distributed. See Frederick W. Frey, "Comment: On Issues and Non-Issues in the Study of Power," *American Political Science Review* 65:4 (December 1971), pp. 1081–1101.

17. For a discussion of the use of "sources" and the imporance to newsgathering of this form of exchange, see Leon V. Sigal, *Reporters and Officials* (Lexington, Mass.: D.C. Heath, 1973), chap. 6.

18. By conceptual standards within the literature on the study of power, the relationship described here would be termed "political" or concerned with power and influence. See Frey, "Comment," or Nagal, *Descriptive Analysis of Power.*

19. See, for example, the role assigned to name recognition in a study of congressional races by Thomas E. Mann, *Unsafe at any Margin* (Washington, D.C.: American Enterprise Institute, 1978).

20. For example, Gerald Rafshoon, Carter's advertising manager, worried as late as mid-October that substantial segments of the electorate still knew very little about Carter (speech before the American Association of Advertising Agencies, New York, October 14, 1976).

21. Personal interview with Deborah Herbst, press aide to Senator Frank Church, October 7, 1976.

22. Personal interview with Richard Stout, press secretary to Morris Udall, January 12, 1976.

23. Personal interview with Hamilton Jordan, campaign manager for Jimmy Carter, July 22, 1975.

24. On the notion of "attentive publics," see Donald J. Devine, *The Attentive Public* (Chicago: Rand McNally, 1970); James N. Rosenau, *Citizenship Between Elections* (New York: The Free Press, 1974); Gabriel A. Almond, *The American People and Foreign Policy* (New York: Praeger, 1960), pp. 137ff; or V.O. Key, Jr., *Public Opinion and American Democracy* (New York: Knopf, 1961).

25. Personal interview with Lyn Nofziger, convention coordinator for Ronald Reagan, August 16, 1976.

26. Personal interviews with John Gabusi, campaign manager for Udall, December 10, 1976, and Bob Neumann, press secretary to Udall, July 6, 1976.

27. Thomas Patterson, *Mass Media Election* (New York: Praeger, 1980), p. 109, and "Press Coverage and Candidate Success at Presidential Primaries: The 1976 Democratic Race," Paper presented at the 1977 meetings of the APSA, Washington, D.C., September 1-4, 1977.

28. Personal interview with Hamilton Jordan, campaign manager for Carter, December 3, 1976.

29. Personal interview with Frank Greer, press secretary to Fred Harris, July 7, 1975.

30. See, for examples, the remarks by the Carter coordinators in California and New Jersey, the *New York Times,* October 29, 1976.

31. This is explicitly argued by Kayden, *Campaign Organization,* and implicitly by Hershey, *The Making of Campaign Strategy.*

32. For a discussion of how organizational outputs may be other than rationally calculated, see Graham T. Allison, *The Essence of Decision* (Boston: Little, Brown, 1971) or John Steinbruner, *The Cybernetic Theory of Decision* (Princeton, N.J.: Princeton University Press, 1974).

33. Rational theory's strongest advocate for campaign organizations can be found in Arnold Steinberg, *Political Campaign Management* (Lexington, Mass.: D.C. Heath, 1976).

34. See Aldrich, *Before the Convention,* and Hershey, "Social Learning Theory.

35. In the literature on governmental policymaking, this would be called an "implementation" problem; see Jeffrey L. Pressman and Aaron B. Wildavsky, *Implementation* (Berkeley: University of California Press, 1973).

36. For 1976, see Witcover, *Marathon,* or Martin Schram, *Running for President* (New York: Stein and Day, 1977). A very useful descriptive account of the 1980 campaign is contained in Elizabeth Drew, *Portrait of an Election* (New York: Simon and Schuster, 1981).

3 Reporting the Campaign: The Journalist's Perspective

F. Christopher Arterton with
Robert A. Fein

From right to left on the political spectrum, critics charge the news media with political bias and incompetence in their coverage of politics.[1] Those who make these charges, however, have failed to capture the subtle reality of media coverage of national politics. Most journalists working in major news organizations are intelligent and competent in what they do; more to the point, their work is not shaped by a systematic pattern of political bias. News organizations do not intentionally distort their interpretations of the events they cover. Nevertheless, a central thesis of this book is that the methods these organizations use to gather, select, and report can result in unintentional bias—in both campaign coverage as well as reporting the daily news.[2]

To understand the activities of campaigners in reaping news coverage for their candidates, we need to explore the predictable patterns in what reporters write or broadcast. Politicians anticipate these patterns in planning their news strategies, sometimes taking advantage of them, and, at other times, compensating for them. (One important caveat: Using the term "journalists" to embrace all those working in the production and dissemination of news necessarily blurs some important distinctions. Individual journalists differ radically in their abilities and in their approach to their work, as do the various news-gathering organizations. Daily newspapers, wire services, radio and television stations, broadcast networks, weekly publications, and monthly magazines all have different routines, different decisionmaking structures, and different metabolism rates. This discussion of broad similarities should not minimize the importance of these differences nor demean the individual skills of working journalists.)

What's Today's News?

Journalists write the news in an uncertain environment. Whether their topic is campaigns, presidential trips abroad, or embassy attacks, uncertainty affects their decision-making. In part, the ambiguity of their work derives

41

from the absence of a universally shared conception of what constitutes news. Many studies of journalists at work have concluded that the selection of what to report is not rooted in a unitary principle or principles that objectively define the concept of news. For example, Bernard Roshco, in a study of U.S. journalism, found that journalists were unable to advance a general definition that determined what they should report as the news of the day.[3] Both Leon Sigal and Paul Weaver came to similar conclusions.[4]

Instead of being determined by an objective criterion, news reporting is invariably judgmental and selective. Journalists rely on their professional training and experience to isolate each day's reportable news from the continual flow of events.[5] They adopt the view, "I may not be able to define what news is, but I know it when I see it." The number of events that should be covered and the amount that could be said about each are far greater than the limited space available in any newspaper or broadcast. David Broder of the *Washington Post* argues that the selectivity demanded by the space limitations on reporting produces circumstances in which objectivity is impossible:

> It is a journalistic myth . . . that argues that something we can honestly call objective news coverage can be obtained through a sort of universality of reporting. . . . The problem that all of us live with constantly in journalism is what to leave out—what can be safely left out with minimum distorting effects. . . . Selectivity, which is the essence of the procedure, involves criteria. Criteria mean value judgments.[6]

William Grieder reaches a similar conclusion:

> The fact is we reduce news every day drastically. That's part of what our thing is about—singling out incidents, events, information, and deciding, by our secret, hierarchical scale of values, which of them is entitled to space in the newspaper. We do it all the time. That is our job.[7]

Not only must individual reporters ferret out a single story from a mass of events, the news organizations themselves must select the stories they use. Selectivity begins with the decision of which stories to cover.

Economic considerations underlie all these organizational constraints. Operationally for campaign reportage, limited funds translate into limited space, manpower, and time. These constraints increase the arbitrary nature of making, reporting, and using the news. Without a conceptual definition of what constitutes news, the journalist has no general principle to guide the selection of news; organizational constraints curtail the process of gathering the news. Moreover, such uncertainties are magnified by the high degree of ambiguity in reporting election politics. As a result, reporters find it extremely difficult to cover election campaigns fairly. Both participants and

observers have significant stakes in the outcome; deeply held and contradictory values are involved. The careers of politicians are directly pitted against
each other. In this charged atmosphere, complaints of political bias flow
quickly from compaigners who see themselves as under attack in the media.
Without an ironclad definition of news and forced to select some stories and
details while ignoring others, how can a reporter defend himself or herself
against charges of political bias?

Under these conditions, journalists tenaciously cling to the principle of
objectivity. They resist suggestions that what they report as news is anything
but a reflection of actual campaign events. Their assertion of objectivity
defends them against charges by politicians and political scientists that the
newsmaking process is uncertain, ambiguous, and indefinite.

These points are not made to criticize journalists, but rather to express
my sympathy about the demands of their profession. Reporting is a hard
job, especially when it comes to covering events as complex and as amor-
phous as a presidential campaign. How do journalists cope with these ambiguities?

The marked continuities in how elections are reported arise not so much
from objective aspects of the campaign process, but from standing
presumptions journalists bring to covering election politics. I believe these
continuities do not originate in political biases; rather, I suggest that they
can be traced back to the organizational constraints which structure the
news-gathering process.

To reduce the ambiguity involved in selecting the daily news, reporters
must adopt some decision rules. These rules are not necessarily neutral between candidates, yet they can be defended by journalists as objective indicators that help them to compare and allow them to measure the progress
of one candidate during the campaign process. Because these shared conceptions are so pervasive during a presidential campaign, journalists and
political activists alike have come to regard them political realities. In turn,
they can have pronouced, though unintended, effects on the news-reporting
process and on the behavior of candidates and campaigners.

Campaign Newsmaking by Rules of Thumb

Like most other corporate structures, news organizations choose to subor-
dinate other problems to the maintenance of the organization itself.[8] The
uncertainties in newsgathering threaten the attainment of such organizational
goals as the production of the daily broadcast or paper, the financial security of the enterprise, and even individual performance. Accordingly, news
organizations adopt routines that reduce ambiguity. To a certain extent,
every decisionmaker functions under some decision rules or rules of thumb.

No one can be expected to calculate all the options for each decision that must be made; standing policies provide a necessary shortcut. However, to analyze the effects of the media on the campaign process, we must examine how these organizations and individuals avoid uncertainty.

Horserace Coverage

Political reporters, perhaps to a greater extent than those in other news environments, believe that an overriding principle guides what they decide to report. Journalists must cover the horserace because they believe that is what elections are all about, that is what their audience wants to hear, and that is what they like to cover:

> We've got to concentrate on the horserace because that's where the news is. . . . If we were a monthly magazine and we were concerned with some of the esoterics of politics—yeah, we could sit back and do that kind of thing [cover issues in detail], and I think we should do some of it. But we're a newsmagazine and we've got to interpret for people what's happening this week, what does it mean. I think we've got to tell people this week that this race in the Republican side is so close that if Rockefeller doesn't deliver what's expected from New York, Ford's in trouble. If we don't do that, I think we're cheating our readers.[9]

> There is more results news in this campaign than ever before, and results news tends to dominate press coverage. . . . For all its good intentions and its extraordinary conscientiousness this time around about avoiding the excesses of the boys on the bus, we're dealing with a new terrain and it has resulted paradoxically in a less issue-oriented kind of coverage than you have seen before.[10]

> I think [horserace coverage] is inevitable, and it *is* a horserace. I mean it is an elimination contest, particularly so this time with the proliferation of candidates . . . [which] tends to make the campaign soupy in terms of issues as well as just fogging it up in the sheer numbers of candidates. And so, I think, it is unavoidable that the early reporting this year has been in terms of the whittling down—who is going to survive and who isn't going to survive—and how much money they have. . . .[11]

This horserace aspect becomes an operational definition of what constitutes news in presidential elections. "When in doubt," the rule counsels, "the horserace is always good news." If the presidential selection process is conceived of as a year-long national horserace, the task of selecting (or ignoring) news is greatly simplified. This proposition is, furthermore, reinforced by the intrinsic interest of the horserace to journalists themselves:

> It would be naive to suggest that this kind of who's ahead, instant analytical reporting can ever be stopped entirely. Our editors and even our

publishers want to know who's ahead and what's happening. We [reporters] are under great pressure to respond.[12]

We love suspense; we love horseraces; and we love good stories, good copy.[13]

Several social scientists have systematically attempted to measure the patterns of coverage found in campaign news reporting.[14] These studies mostly agree that a very high percentage of news coverage is normally devoted to stories about the horserace—that is, to the strategies of the contenders, their prospects for winning or losing, their gaffes and mistakes, and their appearances and scheduled campaign events. Examining the content of campaign coverage from 1968 to 1976, Doris Graber found that the proportion of campaign news dealing with the "hoopla and the horserace aspects of the contest" has been increasing in both television and newspapers (see table 3–1).

Graber used the same coding scheme to analyze the 1968, 1972, and 1976 coverage of elections. Even studies of a single campaign year support her findings, however. During the 1972 general election campaign, Patterson and McClure found that 72 percent of the network news coverage of the campaign dealt with the drama, excitement, and adventure of the race, almost four times the coverage given to the candidates' policy positions. During the 1976 campaign, Patterson later observed different news outlets with similar results. Networks covered the campaign game an average of 58 percent of the time, newspapers about 56 percent; and *Time* and *Newsweek*

Table 3–1
Television and Newspaper Coverage in Presidential Campaigns (1968–1972; percentage)

	1968	*1972*	*1976*
Television			
Campaign Events	26	60	63
Foreign Affairs	37	12	10
Domestic Politics	19	18	14
Social Problems	9	4	4
Economic Policy	9	5	9
Newspapers			
Campaign Events	14	42	51
Foreign Affairs	30	18	14
Domestic Politics	21	24	19
Social Problems	22	7	5
Economic Policy	13	10	11

Source: Doris Graber, *Mass Media and American Politics,* (Washington: CQ Press, 1980), p. 179.

an average of 54 percent. In each case, the horserace took up about three times the space or time given to policy issues.

At first, the 1980 campaign appeared to be following the same mold. From October through the first half of December 1979, fully 77 percent of the stories in the *New York Times, Time, Newsweek,* and three local papers dealt with campaign events.[15] Even the hostage crisis in Iran did not evoke an analysis of the advantages and disadvantages of various candidates' foreign policies; instead, the news articles examined the effects that the crisis was having on the horserace. Later in the primary campaign, Michael Robinson and Margaret Sheehan found that 67 percent of CBS's campaign coverage was devoted to the competition.

Measurements of the 1980 general election coverage indicate that these patterns may have shifted somewhat. Robinson and Sheehan report that during September and October 1980 the networks dramatically increased their reporting of the candidates' policy views. Citing the fact that much of the changed coverage pattern came about in special segments produced at the networks' initiative, they argue that criticism of horserace news was responsible for the change.

If these figures are confirmed by other measurements and analyses, this change could be taken as further confirmation of the role of selectivity taking precedence over objectivity (what actually happened) in campaign coverage. As Robinson and Sheehan note, Reagan and Carter were quite close at this point, whereas the gap between Nixon and McGovern was widening in 1972 when Patterson and McClure recorded the peak in horserace reporting. Robinson and Sheehan also ruled out another case for objectivity in 1980: neither Reagan nor Carter appeared to be any more interested in discussing policy views than they had been during the primary campaign.

To interpret such assertions fairly, we must also examine the coding schemes used by the authors. For example, during the preprimary period in 1979, 77 percent of the sampled news articles dealt primarily with campaign events; 52 percent of these same articles, however, contained at least some mention of the candidates' stands on policy disputes. Individual stories cannot always be classified as pure horserace examples. More frequently, they contain issue coverage mixed with horserace news. Yet it is also true that the treatment of issues in the media was extremely superficial. In most discussions of issue stands, the reporter did little more than mention the policy problem touched upon in a candidate's speech and seldom specifically analyzed the candidate's views. It is possible to blame the candidates for the absence of concrete proposals, but journalists rarely used their media to force candidates to be specific. Dan Dorfman's recognition that Kennedy avoided articulating his policy views is too rare a phenomenon in campaign reportage:

I turned to the growing housing crisis, pointing out that the prices of new homes were going through the roof. . . . And I asked Candidate Kennedy what President Kennedy would do to ease the situation.

He did it again; it was simply a replay of my question on inflation.

"Housing is getting out of reach," replied Kennedy, raising his voice and clenching his fist. "I don't believe we've made a serious effort."

His specific recommendations: You guessed it—none.[16]

Given the ambiguities implicit in electoral politics, particularly at the presidential level, horserace reporting poses the distinct danger of being proved wrong by subsequent events. Predictions, of course, can be hedged with all manner of caveats ("if these trends continue"); even so, no one likes to have his or her objective statements about reality turn out to be erronous. In light of these hazards, why should horserace reporting be such a major component of campaign coverage?

One answer can be found in the career incentives of the working journalist. Not only does the horserace rule of thumb provide an easy rule for selecting the daily news, it serves as a litmus test for professional prestige and career advancement. Ultimately, reporters compete with each other in calling the horserace. Each seeks to decipher the signs of growing political support and thereby to understand the meaning of current events in relation to final outcomes. Enormous respect and prestige among colleagues flow to the individual who, either through sagacity or serendipity, correctly diagnoses the flow of events.

Beyond the career incentive, their publishers or networks pressure reporters to predict the horserace. Each competes with similar and different media to provide their readers, viewers, or listeners with rapid yet accurate reporting. Early in the nomination races, these newer organizations may have another reason for predicting the outcome. A large field of presidential contenders presents most news corporations with a major problem of distributing their limited resources. Because they cannot cover all the candidates simultaneously, editors and producers must decide which candidates have serious prospects of capturing the nomination to give them the necessary coverage. Because of space and resource limitations, reports on contenders with slim chances of victory necessarily must be minimized. The earlier this decision can be reached, the better.

I am sure that there is a subconscious desire [among the press to reduce the size of the field to make things simpler to cover]. . . . The size of the field created all kinds of difficulties. Issue coverage, for example. . . . To give one paragraph to each of the candidates on a given issue, you used all your story up. There's no analysis. There's just one example. The manpower problem was extremely serious. This is the first campaign that I've been involved in in the *Times* where we didn't have a *Times* person on every candidate from the very start. We did pretty soon when they started thinning out, but we just didn't have enough people.[17]

By concentrating on the win/lose elements of the campaign, journalists limit their coverage of the issues raised during the election and the character of the candidates. If the political process is ambiguous, judgments on issues and character are even more uncertain. At least by reporting the horserace, the press can produce a number—how many votes each candidate received, the size of a campaign treasury, the number of prominent endorsements, or the results of an opinion poll.

The Search for Credibility

As it turns out, the standing decision to focus on the horserace is not, by itself, a sufficient guide for the selection of campaign news. Further rules of thumb are necessary to point journalists toward specific stories, allowing them to select which horserace stories will be more newsworthy.

In coping with the uncertainties of the horserace, reporters and correspondents advance statements about the progress of the candidates on three different levels. On the most general plane, they convey notions about the dynamics of the race as a whole. Elaborate scenarios are usually developed from the statements of campaigners as to how they plan to secure electoral victory. For example, most of the profiles published in the *New York Times* or broadcast by the television networks at the beginning of the election year discuss the candidate's strategy for gaining his party's nomination. Scenarios are general conceptions as to how the race will evolve over the long run. In any case, they are highly contingent propositions.

Where campaigners advance guarded statements about their long-run strategies, these scenarios, once accepted by news organizations, take on a life of their own. They provide a general theme that organizes news coverage and makes sense out of disparate events. The 1980 Republican campaign was broadly interpreted as the final refusal of the party's ideological wing to accept another centrist and the efforts of an extremist to moderate his stands for the general electorate. In 1976, Carter's race was described as a long march from obscurity, capitalizing on the new openness in party rules. Both the Democratic nomination struggle in 1980 and the Republican race of 1976 were summarized as a bitter struggle of each party's ideological core against the advantages of incumbency. And so on.

Second, on a less global level, scenarios point toward the selection of certain standards that provide a means to assess and compare the performance of contending candidates. For example, during the primary period, victory in close races and the results of early primaries become two accepted criteria by which candidates are rated, dwarfing other possible measures. Even earlier, before the actual selection of delegates begins, press commentary comparing the competing candidacies tends to focus heavily upon straw votes, polls, and endorsements, financial strength and organization building receive less attention.[18]

Finally, at the most specific level, newsmen develop benchmarks to rate the progress of individual candidates. Given the ambiguity of the selection process, agreement on appropriate standards will not suffice. Journalists must also judge what level of performance on those indicators constitutes adequate performance for each campaign. For example, the news reports in October 1979 discussed at length whether Kennedy had to win the straw vote held in Florida caucuses to demonstrate that his candidacy was making progress.[19] If fundraising success becomes an important standard, not only must the campaigns be compared against each other, but they must also be examined against expectations of what the campaign should have achieved.

These three levels of the horserace—scenarios, standards, and benchmarks—can become generally accepted in campaign reporting. Understandably, campaigners compete fiercely to have journalists accept their scenario rather than those of their opponents. Similarly, the application of different standards may generate alternative perceptions of which candidates have serious prospects for electoral success. Finally, benchmarking shapes the interpretation given to an objective performance. At each level, statements are advanced to assess the credibility of each candidacy. If these statements are repeated often and by enough journalists and politicians, the judgmental and ambiguous nature of these propositions becomes obscured by their seeming objectivity. Although consensus does not define reality, it can become a substitute framework by which politicians shape their actions and a background against which reporters describe campaign events.

I refer to this evolving consensus as the perceptual environment within which the campaign is conducted. Jules Witcover illustrates the firmness with which these judgments dominate the campaign's environment:

> The fact is that the reality in the early going of a presidential campaign is not the delegate count at all. The reality at the beginning stage is the psychological impact of the results—the perception by press, public, and contending politicians of what has happened.[20]

Not only are these statements advanced in the content of campaign news as the perceived status of the horserace, but they also help shape coverage decisions by media organizations. Serious candidates deserve coverage; those without reasonable prospects must, unfortunately, be neglected. But, as noted in chapter 1, without access to the news conduit, a campaign's internal resources are too meager to reach the vast electorate.

A vital part of the campaign is to convince these guys [the press] that you're serious and . . . [your're] going to be viable. Because of the limitations on spending, on contributions . . . I think it's going to be a lot more important how you're perceived by the national press immediately and . . . what kind of impression they create. . . .[21]

For example, during the earliest phases of prenomination campaigning, journalists rely on fundraising as a standard for ranking the progress of the competitors. During the 1976 campaign, candidates' abilities to qualify for matching public funds became almost a concrete marker separating serious candidates from the others (even though the subsidies are not actually turned over until after January 1 of the election year). One campaign manager lamented in July 1975:

The media start looking for the most simple benchmarks they can. For instance, they've all hopped on the idea that qualifying for matching funds means something more significant. . . . It really doesn't matter to our campaign . . . [if we] qualify on December 31st or July 1st because they still get the same amount of money on January 1. . . . But in the minds of the media, they have found a simple measuring tool that says, "Ah ha, that makes them more significant because they can do it earlier."[22]

The reporters' emphasis on matching funds was their way of saying: "We are not intruding into the electoral process; rather, we've chosen a criterion that objectively represents electoral success." While horserace coverage can, by this logic, be defended as objective, the standard would certainly not stand up to detailed scrutiny as a reliable indicator. Nor is it neutral between candidates; in fact, its utility derives from its ability to discriminate among the successes of the contenders.

Whether defensible as objective indicators or not, once such standards become widely accepted to the point of allocating news coverage, campaigners feel they have little choice but to compete in meeting the journalists' expectations. It is ironic that by trying to avoid intruding into the political process—to stand as neutral witnesses—journalists create political realities that directly affect the behavior of the candidates and their campaigns.

The Early Primary Emphasis

The early primary contests constitute such an important standard for horserace reporting that their role as a rule of thumb must be examined separately. The primary campaigns since 1964 indicate the decisive nature of the early primaries in the election process; however, the early primaries become even more significant because of the heavy emphasis of the press. Some have labeled the phenomenon the "New Hampshire syndrome", because of the disproportionate coverage received by such a tiny state with so few delegates. Robinson and McPherson, for example, analyzed the content of both television and print journalism coverage of the 1976 primaries.[23] They found that all media have marked affinity for New Hampshire stories. Television coverage was particularly intensive: 53.5 percent of all television stories and 60.1 percent of the time spent in television primary election coverage dealt with the New Hampshire primary. Print journalism was more equitable, but New Hampshire stories still took up 34.3 percent of all stories and 42 percent of all space. Overcoverage does not arise from a last-minute blitz in coverage by news organizations. Robinson and McPherson found the emphasis on New Hampshire just as strong in November, December, and January as in February just before the primary.

From the journalist's viewpoint, the decision to cover the early primaries extensively requires no elaborate justification. These events are viewed as the first real hard news.[24] Journalists, therefore, are able to transform a complex decision of what to cover into the application of an unexamined criterion.

The emphasis by the press on the early primaries is, of course, no secret. Campaign activists fully understand this tendency. "The New Hampshire primary . . . is, as you know, for a small number of delegates, but [mostly] for a lot of press attention—because it's first."[25] In 1976, the Carter campaigners knew that, if successful in New Hampshire, their early wins would be translated into cover stories on *Time* and *Newsweek*.[26] Both Carl Wagner, Kennedy's campaign coordinator, and David Keene, campaign manager for George Bush, predicted in advance how the media would cover the early primaries, geared their strategies to these press tendencies, and both knew they were in trouble when they failed to win.[27] They would certainly agree with the comments of John Gabusi, who piloted the 1976 Udall campaign:

> [The role of the press] . . . was no surprise to us . . . because we were working on the assumption that we might be the beneficiary of their method of reporting. . . . The easiest and clearest example was the magazine coverage after the New Hampshire primary. The fact of the matter was that Bonnie Angelo was writing the story on Mo Udall and somebody else was writing the story on Jimmy Carter. And we knew for a month that whoever was perceived as the winner was going to get the cover story of *Time* magazine.[28]

This overemphasis on early primaries also affects those candidates who remain until the late primaries. Once a candidate emerges as the clear frontrunner, the theme that dominates coverage thereafter casts the other candidates as spoilers. That is, they have little chance to win the nomination, but do possess the capacity to deny the nomination to the frontrunner. In the 1980 Republican race, George Bush assumed this role around the time of the Illinois primary. If he succeeded in stopping Reagan, the presumed beneficiary would have been Gerald Ford. In the 1976 Democratic race, the same situation arose well before half the delegates were selected.[29] After Pennsylvania, the press argued that only Carter would win the nomination among the candidates then entered in the primaries. For example, in reporting on Carter's victory in Pennsylvania, *Time* proclaimed:

> Suddenly only a third of the way through the obstacle course, the race was all but over. . . . Last week by triumphing decisively and against formidable odds in Pennsylvania's pivotal primary, [Carter] all but crushed his remaining opposition, including Democratic senior statesman, Hubert Humphrey. . . . Morris Udall, the primaries' perceptual runner-up, pushed on with characteristically good humor, but nobody took his candidacy seriously. Latecomers Frank Church and Jerry Brown were still running, but some political analysts thought that Brown at best was running for Vice President and Church perhaps for Secretary of State.[30]

The Use of Polling

One way to translate uncertainty and ambiguity into reportorial simplicity is to assign a number. The use of survey research provides the press with a fourth, quantitative rule of thumb. Kenneth Auchincloss, the managing editor of *Newsweek*, notes:

> I've been very bearish on polling, which I think has been very much overdone. It's a very handy journalistic device because it has a sort of scientific cast to it, and it reduces complicated questions to numerical quantities. These are things that journalists find easy, and are attracted to.[31]

The problem with polling, as Hadley Cantril explains, is that the world is not so simple, and the press fails to tell its audience that simplest fact of all:

> The percentages in poll reports have a way of acquiring a legitimacy and life of their own—particularly so when they are dramatic. Yet the mood of the people is elusive. It operates on many levels: from opinions on topical issues to basic hopes and fears. It is sometimes stable, other times volatile. It is often ignorant, but almost always able to respond to pollsters' queries. No matter how finely tuned the poll, there is always a question about what it is bringing in.[32]

Examples abound of the questionable use of polling in the coverage of campaigns. The most obvious example was the widely held belief that in 1976 Carter lost a 30-point lead in the polls over his opponent, Gerald Ford. *Newsweek's* preelection wrap-up illustrates the point: "[Carter] has, moreover, gone from new face to old in a single year; familiarity has bred, if not contempt, a 30-point slide in his standing against Ford in the polls."[33]

Of course, Carter never held such a wide lead, but there was a "halo" effect from all the favorable exposure received during the Democratic convention. A more equitable assessment of his lead could be based on the polling data after the Republican convention (when Ford gained favorable exposure) that showed Carter with a lead of 9 or 10 points. However, the press latched onto the 30-point lead as if it were a hard news event. Just as a primary result requires interpretation due to its ambiguous nature, so does poll data. Four years later, polls taken at a similar point in the campaign gave Reagan a 20-point lead. However, having learned from the last war, journalists treated this figure with some skepticism, in some cases even criticizing the Harris organization for releasing and promoting results measured between the two conventions.

Although news organizations conducted more polls in 1980, these polls frequently contradicted each other. Nevertheless, journalists were no more cautious in their use of figures. For example, on September 28, the *New York Times* and CBS released a poll that called a slippage in Anderson's support (from 14 percent to 9 percent) a "marked decline."[34] At first, these data were accompanied by statements about the possible margin of error (4 percent) and the required caution about putting too much emphasis on survey results. Although polling changes for Reagan and Carter were ambiguous enough to fade quickly from view, later stories emphasized Anderson's drop and ignored the tenuous nature of the data. The initial story in the *Times* commented that the debates with Reagan had failed to "reverse John Anderson's decline and revitalize his candidacy," citing a mid-June apex in Anderson's support measured by a Gallup poll (24 percent). However, the accompanying chart showed Anderson rising from 13 percent in early August to 14 percent in middle September and then down to 9 percent in late September.

On the same day that the CBS/*New York Times* poll was published, a *Newsweek* poll showed Anderson's support constant at 14 percent.[35] Two weeks later, on October 14, a Gallup poll also put Anderson at 14 percent. During this period, however, data from their September poll appeared in three subsequent stories in the *Times*.[36] In each case, selected data were used to discuss the Anderson decline; in no case was the margin of error in the poll results noted. On October 4, for example, the poll figures were mustered to reinforce a story by Steven Roberts based primarily upon "person-in-the-street" interviews in northern Illinois: "Mr. Anderson fell to a 9 percent rating in the latest national *New York Times*–CBS News Poll and the feelings expressed by Miss Pantsios and others here illustrate some of the reasons for his decline."

Anderson did decline in the polls, receiving about 7 percent of the final vote. However, that fact does not validate the substance of these treatments of poll data, for the media may have contributed to Anderson's slide. Robinson and Sheehan reported that during September, television news stopped covering Anderson as a horse in the race.[37] In campaign coverage, the agenda-setting capacity of the media works to establish some candidates as serious prospects, relegating the candidacy of others to a hopeless quest. The effect of Anderson's lack of coverage may have been to decrease the number of voters who were willing to consider his candidacy seriously. The process may create a vicious cycle: as Anderson was seen as dropping in the polls, journalists gave him less news coverage, and his standing dropped with voters.

Polls also allow the press to turn debates between candidates into pseudo-primaries. Again, quantifying an ambiguous situation imparts a greater sense of objectivity. For each of the debates held in 1976 and 1980, journalists used poll data to determine the winner. They also established benchmarks before the debates to assess the candidates' performance. This use of victory-related concepts implied a direct relation between performance in the debates and electoral fortune, where no such relation necessarily exists.[38] A supporter of one candidate could easily think that the other candidate won the debate.[39]

"Victory" in debates can have many meanings. A campaign may gear its efforts to a specific group of voters in the electorate, while pollsters measure the perceptions of the entire electorate. A candidate could achieve his goal of reaching a certain audience in the debate and still "lose" the debate. The Reagan campaign, for example, sought to avoid mistakes and the appearance of being an unacceptable extremist to independent and wavering Democrats.

In each case, there was no need to publish poll results—except the media's need to reduce uncertainty by using numbers. The goal of debates, after all, is to present a discussion of the issues and the men themselves, not to provoke a discussion of how to win a debate. By applying these four decision rules, the press reduces uncertainty to facilitate journalistic decision-making. Intentional partisanship does not appear to exist, although the organizational imperatives of newsmaking can produce systematic biases.

Inertia, Change, and Consensus in News Reporting

News is trendy. Stories that appear in today's coverage provide a simple, empirical definition of what the news of the day is. Therefore, in searching for tomorrow's story, the journalist is likely to start with those which seemed to be developing the day before. These stories have been legitimated by editors and producers as newsworthy. As long as a new detail or angle can be found—repetition is an anathema—further developments on yesterday's news provide the easiest means of reducing uncertainty in selecting today's story. The effects of this "inertial" nature of news production are described in the following sections.

Inertia

Stories can develop a life of their own as journalists collectively prod politicians for details or new statements. Ultimately, this inertial quality depends on the development of consensus among journalists that a given story is worth pursuing. The process by which this consensus is established is little understood, though amenable to empirical research. Two standards appear to determine whether a story will be continued: first, if a large number of news organizations are devoting substantial amounts of news space to a particular story, or second, if a prestige news organization or individual journalist legitimates an item by presenting it as news.[40] The journalist gains confidence by following the judgments of his or her peers. Cohen demonstrates how the prior definition of news leads to the development of the news consensus:

> What is reported, then, becomes news; it takes on a new quality, like a successful candidate who is suddenly vested with the mystique of his freshly won office. It exists, almost independently of the myriad of choices that made it exist. In this sense, news takes on a kind of objective reality: what was reported is news; what was not reported—for whatever reasons—is not news. And once it is news it exercises a powerful claim on the attention of reporters.[41]

For example, in September 1980, Reagan was put on the defensive for several days by his remarks suggesting a return to the two-China policy.[42] Later, in September and early October, reporters began to discuss the "gutter politics" that both major party nominees were pursuing. The story was published as an underlying theme of the campaign until President Carter finally apologized for his remarks charging that Reagan's election would divide the country.[43]

About a year earlier, the Kennedy campaign was both the beneficiary and the victim of similar inertia. According to Carl Wagner, the campaign's national coordinator, Kennedy was on evening network broadcasts twelve times from June through October of 1979. Almost anything he did was deemed newsworthy. Yet, when he announced his candidacy (November 8), that story was seventh or eight in line after coverage of the events in Iran. For the next month, Kennedy was only able to get network coverage five times—and then for such items as Jane Byrne's indecision as to who to endorse or the fees being charged news organizations for air travel with the campaign. On December 6, when Kennedy expressed some opinions critical

of the Shah of Iran, his remarks became the lead story on the three networks for three nights running.[44] During that period, Iran, the campaign,
and Kennedy-in-trouble became wrapped together by the inertial nature of
news coverage.

The importance of consensus became evident in the *New York Times*'s
editorial decisions on Warren Weaver's 1975 articles on the Federal Election
Commission (FEC). William Kovach, the national news editor of the Washington bureau, feared that Weaver's articles would eventually be killed by
his superiors in New York because no other papers were covering the FEC.
At the same time, Kovach felt that the new campaign finance law would be
an important factor in the 1976 primaries. To encourage other papers to
carry the story, he asked R.W. Apple, Jr. to write a lead front-page article
on the FEC. The news consensus, not the reporter's perception of reality,
became the crucial factor in the decisionmaking process.[45]

These maneuvers also demonstrate how journalists rely upon the output
of prestigious reporters and newspapers to shape the news consensus. In our
interviews, a number of journalists spoke frankly about following the leads
taken by such well-respected journalists as David Broder, Hedrick Smith,
Jack Germond, and Johnny Apple. As John Chancellor says:

> I look to Dave Broder, for example, as a leader in this. His columns are
> very valuable and, I think, they are very important in terms of what other
> political reporters think and do. I think Broder is probably the most impor-
> tant single one that we have. I wouldn't miss a Broder column.[46]

Change

The inertia built around a particular story cannot last forever. Sooner or
later the dominant story loses its newsworthiness—its freshness, novelty, or
surprise value—and reporters begin to search for other stories. What is in
the headlines or newscasts one week cannot, almost by definition, appear
there the following week; to remain in the news, a story must continue to
evolve.

The same proposition applies, albeit less dramatically, to the shared
conceptions journalists develop about the dynamics of the race or its participants. Once a consensus is established on the basic scenario, the boldest
journalists are sure to search for evidence to demonstrate its frailty. Again,
respect and prestige can be important incentives to journalists who are pre-
scient enough to identify a new trend that reassembles consensus around a
slightly different understanding.

A minor though persistent theme of campaign reporting, therefore,
consists of confronting the old consensus with new interpretations. Such
stories may counsel that candidate X should not be counted out yet, that

although no one has ever heard of the former Southern governor he seems to be making progress, that a former Governor commonly considered too conservative to win the presidency is making inroads in the other party's traditional coalition, and so forth. Nevertheless, because these assertions run counter to the perceived certainty, the old consensus dies hard. Many of these divergent themes never strike a responsive chord and are quickly forgotten.

Consensus

What effects do inertial tendencies have on the campaign? The development of a consensus among journalists and the subsequent inertia that maintains it can have pronounced consequences in both major aspects of campaign reporting. First, at all levels of horserace journalism, the development of a perceptual environment will affect the subsequent activity of campaigners. For example, a primary competition may become cast as a hopeless quest by an ideological wing of the party against a centrist incumbent. Once established, such a conception can be almost impervious to change; needless to say, it benefits one candidate to the disadvantage of the other. Similarly, standards and benchmarks can become matters of consensus behind which inertia develops.

Second, journalists describe candidates or their campaigns with images and labels—catchphrases that, to be sure, capture some of reality, but not all of it. These partial truths spread to other news reports and become accepted truths about the race and its participants.

If journalists are quick to criticize politicians for image-making, why do they resort to shorthand labels themselves? Lester Crystal, a producer for NBC News, argued that the need for images and labels derives from the short-term focus of coverage.[47] Reporters save both time and space by characterizing a politician's appeal or liabilities with the consensus label. One of the campaign managers interviewed agreed:

> I think the media looks for a handle on a guy because it's a shorthand method of . . . cutting their space and description. . . . [T]he handles vary from trying to label a person philosophically to the label Senator Jackson has on him . . . if he gave a fireside chat the fire would fall asleep . . . that kind of labeling. . . . Bentsen's sometimes identified as a "slick Texas oil millionaire. . . ." If you have a *Washington Post* deadline to make your first edition at 10 P.M. and your story's at 9:30 you have a half hour, you have twenty minutes to write and five minutes to file. Are you going to sit and explain the fact that Lloyd Bentsen has never made any money in oil—that his money came from insurance? No . . . you fast-label him or . . . you condition yourself to look for a lot of things.[48]

In its last issue before the 1976 election, *Time* provided a striking example of the imagery developed by journalists during the campaign. After claiming that "there has been too much attention paid by the press to relatively minor flaps: Carter's Playboy interview, Ford's tangled tongue, what to do about Earl Butz," the article characterized each of the candidates:

> Carter's is by far the *quicker* mind. He is both bolder and capable of more brilliance than Ford. His compassion for the underdog in U.S. society seems sincere. But he is also *shifty*. He showed that in Georgia by campaigning as a *conservative* and governing as a liberal. His religiosity is genuine, yet there is a *mean streak* in him. The blue eyes can turn *cold*, and his *ready tongue* can lacerate a foe. When he cools off, he often apologizes. Whether it is out of Christian charity or practical considerations is unclear. Carter is supremely *ambitious, self-confident* and *stubborn*—qualities that are both helpful and potentially divisive in a President. Going with Carter is clearly a greater gamble. His supporters would claim that to risk nothing is to gain nothing.

> Ford is *likable, unpretentious, undevious.* He looks uncomfortable when stridently attacking his opponent. He appears similarly forced and *unconvincing* when he makes a blatant specific pitch for votes, as he did in the South with his contrived emphasis against gun controls. While he is certainly a bright man, his image as a *verbal bumbler* nevertheless is not totally unfair; he is also a man who can forget three times in a day which town he is in, as he did recently in Illinois. Far from an inspirational leader, Ford has a limited let's-not-rock-the-boat perspective on the presidency. He offers a prospect of predictability that may reassure many—assuming no *imaginative initiatives* may be needed over the next four years.[49]

These images may have simplified *Time*'s decisionmaking process, but they grossly oversimplified the characters of the two men running for the presidency.

Campaigns must deal with these tendencies. Attempts to counteract unfavorable images generally fail; some campaigns survive the unfavorable coverage by hiding from the press until the wave of inertia dies down. Others live with the image until events prove it wrong. Some even try to accommodate their political and substantive strategies around them.

Campaign Reporting

The presidential race begins long before most news reporting organizations are willing to devote substantial resources to covering its events and personalities.[50] After an initial decision to run, each politician gradually hires staff, raises money, builds a campaign organization, and recruits support. Planners in the news media are not idle either. Long before the primaries begin, they are scheduling public opinion polls, establishing facilities in key primary states, switching reporters or correspondents away from other assignments, and reserving space at convention sites. Such arrangements provide an implicit answer to the question: What is news in an election campaign?

The Press Corps Structure

Unlike campaigns, news reporting corporations do not come into existence solely for presidential elections. Detailed coverage begins with the decision of the editors and producers that the time for campaign news has arrived. Only the networks and a few of the major newspapers can afford to assign a star reporter or correspondent and film crew to cover national politics on a continuing basis. In recent cycles, increased coverage began around September in the year before the general election and expanded gradually through early December. In-depth reporting, a product of rather arbitrary decisions to assign reporters to cover the race and to print or broadcast their work, did not begin until late December or early January when many major news outlets produce a series of background reports on each candidate—including his positions, support, electoral prospects, strategy, and character.[51] These reports marked the end of the preprimary phase and the real beginning of the primary season. The public campaign begins in earnest, mainly set off by the decisions of news reporting organizations.

Before detailed coverage begins, reporting on candidates and their activities is heavily influenced by the way media resources are generally distributed. A political base in Washington is useful because many major news reporting organizations concentrate their reporters and correspondents there. Epstein, for example, reports that NBC maintains five network crews in Washington and three full-time crews in Los Angeles, Chicago, and New York.[52] Sigal finds 60 percent of the *New York Times* staff is located in Washington as are 75 percent of *Washington Post* reporters.[53] This concentration not only reflects expectations of where the news will occur, but also determines which events will be reported. For example, after observing how the networks cover the news, Epstein is convinced that:

> In choosing among equivalent stories in different cities, assignment editors therefore tend to select the ones that can most easily be reached by crews—or at least the ones that require no additional resources being expended.[54]

Most candidates respond to this concentration by establishing headquarters in Washington.[55] In turn, this facilitates such campaign tasks as distributing press releases or holding well-attended press conferences.

There is further concentration in Washington itself, reflecting news hot spots. Obviously, the White House is a major focal point for the press corps, providing an incumbent candidate with built-in access. Capitol Hill, particularly the U.S. Senate, is another center of press activity. During the preprimary period, presidential candidates from the Senate enjoy an organizational (though not always a politically decisive) advantage in access to media. In explaining why Howard Baker delayed so long in initiating his campaign, his advertising adviser, Doug Bailey, noted this advantage:

> While his position on the SALT Treaty was determined by personal belief, politically he was aware that it was important for him in the campaign. . . . A debate on the SALT Treaty is news night, after night, after night, after night. And, while not dominating the news every day, that issue—while it was on the floor of the Senate—would be the major event in the news for as long as it lasted.[56]

Four years earlier, Jackson's news strategy was based on the same assumption:

> The Senate is where the action is, not touring around the country. . . . If we have something to say we can go to the Senate [press] gallery.[57]

Simon Fentiss of *Time* magazine and Daniel Schorr, then of CBS, make the same point. First, Fentiss:

> The media are concentrated, is concentrated, here in Washington, in the Capitol. That's where the reporters are by the thousands almost and the TV cameras and the networks. And they tend to focus too much, I think, on the candidates who are here, and that's why in recent years the U.S. Senate has become the pit from which candidates come.[38]

Then Schorr:

> The agenda is set more by network national television than it is set by local television. That brings in a certain imbalance in . . . things that are considered to be of national significance. . . . The effect these have with regard to candidates, then, is you get an awful lot of Senators and very few governors appearing on television nationally. . . . Therefore, there you have an obvious bias when the political campaign comes along in that your Senators, good or bad, are recognizable persons which offers enormous advantages in getting yourself into the stream of an election campaign.[59]

This national orientation of major news organizations goes beyond unequal access; it can create a propensity to view candidates with a Washington base as more credible, as a *Time* representative notes:

So it's very difficult for a governor in any one state to say anything that is
necessarily newsworthy in some other state; whereas in the Senate . . . and
in the House, they are dealing with national issues. And it just seems to me
to be perfectly reasonable that they would be better known and have a better shot at the Presidency than some guy who was in the statehouse in Min-
nesota.[60]

Although poll results that demonstrate the frontrunner status of—for
example—a former California governor can override this propensity, current national officeholders have the newsmaking edge.[61] Kennedy and
Baker in 1979, like Jackson in 1975, built their news strategies on their
Senate responsibilities, thus ensuring legitimate claim to coverage. Even
though journalists are aware that a desire for exposure may be motivated by
campaign aspirations, their assumption is that the holding of public office
constitutes a more justifiable "news peg" than mere candidacy.

The results of Carter's 1976 efforts, and Reagan and Bush's 1980,
however, may have destroyed this presumption. In fact, the heavy travel
demands imposed by the increase in state primaries may tip the balance
toward the candidate who is essentially unemployed. Even though the organizational edge held by senators is mitigated once full primary coverage
begins in January, the perception of enhanced credibility may carry over
into the assignments of journalists and the allocation of news space in the
pre-New Hampshire period.

Coverage Patterns during the Early Primaries

The exceptionally large candidate fields impose a difficult organizational
problem upon news corporations. On January 1, 1980, nine major candidates were reaching for their party's nomination; a slight drop from the
13 entrants in the 1976 race. None of the news outlets could afford to assign
a reporter to every presidential aspirant. Instead, they practice so-called
zone coverage. A reporter or correspondent is assigned to cover a state
primary, reporting on the activities of all candidates entered in that race.
As candidates travel in that state, reporters join up with them for a day or
two, dropping off to cover the other competitors. This technique allows
reporters to develop a comparative understanding of the competitors.

The larger outlets may assign one reporter, correspondent, or film crew
to the major candidates; darker horses might be covered by a journalist
assigned to a given primary. Because each organization usually assigns a
reporter to the White House press corps, fairness dictates assigning someone to cover his opponents when one candidate is the president. In covering
the "out party" competition, many news organizations use a mixture of
zone and candidate coverage as editors and producers attempted to place

their resources where they believe news will occur. Thus, George Bush picked up a sizable traveling press corps after his victory in the Iowa caucuses, while his opponents' press aides (other than Reagan's) were still trying to convince journalists to spend a day with their candidates in New Hampshire. During this phase of the campaign, Bush held a considerable advantage in making the news over candidates Crane, Dole, and Baker.[62]

Zone and partial-zone coverage patterns are, however, inevitably unstable. Candidate coverage—assigning a journalist to cover one candidate all the time—remains the preferred and most used pattern of presenting the news.

Candidate Coverage

Many editors and producers find numerous advantages in so-called candidate coverage. Reporters develop much of their information through establishing regular contact with a finite number of individuals occupying key campaign roles.[63] Because those at the top become increasingly insulated as their organizations increase in size, journalists wish to develop strategic sources within the campaign early. Personal acquaintance with the candidate and his top staff yield valuable insights into the campaign's activities. In addition, reporters covering the same candidate become as familiar with his public policy stands as the candidate himself; in theory, at least, they are sensitive to shifts of position.

Administratively, candidate coverage is more convenient for journalists and their organizations than any other assignment pattern. Once the reporter joins the campaign, most arrangements for transportation, meals, accommodations, and communication are taken care of by the campaign staff. Zone coverage, in contrast, creates substantive and administrative problems. For one thing, the work of a reporter assigned to a primary may not be used if the election is several weeks off, particularly if other events crowd the headlines. Then too, reassigning reporters after the primary has been passed can become a problem, since primaries vary enormously in their perceived importance and, hence, newsworthiness. Candidate coverage reduces these problems. Each journalist will have the opportunity to have his or her work carried daily, depending, of course, on the newsworthiness of that competitor. Reassignment is not a problem, as long as the candidate is perceived as a serious competitor.

Candidate coverage also tends to separate the journalist's career advancement within the news organization from internal politics. Assignment to a successful candidate increases a reporter's access to front page or prime time space. If the candidate happens to be elected president, an assignment to the White House press corps is usually in store for the reporter. In other words, decisions about individual advancement of political reporters are deferred to an external process.

Understandably, then, zone coverage has not proved to be a long-term solution to assignment decisions for most news organizations. Internally, pressure develops to eliminate the less serious candidates at an early point so that the organization can revert to candidate coverage.[64] (This point is fully discussed in chapter 5 in the context of the organizational pressures that shape the substance of campaign reporting.)

On the other hand, the disadvantages of permanently assigning one journalist to each campaign are less immediately obvious. Candidate coverage constitutes an organizational commitment that each candidate will receive some coverage. The traveling journalist is continually filing stories, at least some of which must be broadcast or put in print. According to Irv Horowitz, deputy national news editor for the *New York Times:*

> A reporter gets more and more nervous when a story he has written has not been printed. After about three days they get pretty paranoid—we don't like him, we want to deprive him of his means of livelihood, etc. You can be sure of one thing. After not printing one or two stories written by a reporter, you just *have* to print the third![65]

Describing one day's efforts to present the news, Henry Rosenthal of the *Washington Post* notes that including separate stories on each candidate is a natural outgrowth of the assignment process:

> I question whether we really serve the reader by . . . a separate story on the day's doings of four different candidates. I question the efficacy of that approach. It's inevitable because we have four different staff reporters, each one anxious, after a very important [group of] primaries, to want to write something.[66]

Bill Chesleigh, political editor of NBC News, discusses the pressure that can build up within an organization once assignments have been handed out:

> You do get a correspondent who will occasionally call and say, "Why hasn't my candidate been on this week? You've had three Carter spots and you've had none of my candidate." But he would say the same thing if he were not doing politics and doing general news, wondering why he's not getting on the air.[67]

Ultimately, candidates who win primaries deserve and receive abundant coverage. Between primaries, however, a large volume of campaign news is heavily influenced by these organizational commitments.

Second, candidate coverage is grounded in the assumption that the essence of presidential nominations and elections is found in the behavior of the individual candidates. However, this is only one aspect of the selection of a president. The slow construction of political organizations, the advertising campaign, and the raising and spending of campaign dollars are but a few others. More to the point, systemic trends, such as the strength of the traditional party coalitions, the growth or decline of support in pivotal states or among key population groups, the development of stands on policy questions, and the changing acceptance by local and national party leaders are important election events not readily observable by reporters traveling with candidates.

Furthermore, candidate coverage seldom allows reporters to compare the various contenders. Although comparisons can be achieved through the editorial or production process, most news organizations accept, modify slightly, or reject the work of reporters in the field. Synthesis is difficult to achieve organizationally.

Finally, the institutional problems of candidate coverage are magnified by the personal difficulties of journalists assigned to cover a single candidate during the entire nomination–general election cycle. Perpetually on the move, surrounded primarily by the candidate's staff and other journalists with the same assignment, reporters perceive all of their political information as polarized by the filtering question: "What does this mean for the electoral prospects of this candidate?" This is not to contend that they develop a bias in favor of that candidate.[68] Rather, the demands of the assigned job—to report upon the activities of a candidate and how they affect his prospects for election—may reduce the reporter's comparative or systemic perspective.

The problem of perspective is not new; it was touched upon by Crouse's critique of the campaign media in 1972.[69] In fact, many of our respondents in major news organizations echo the concerns of David Jones, national news editor for the *New York Times:*

> The experience of our political reporters is that when they get on that campaign plane, they get trapped; they're in a cocoon and it distorts their perception of everything that's happening in the campaign because they don't see the broader dimension. . . .[70]

A mixed assignment pattern employing some "zone" coverage, therefore, is not simply a response to the large number of candidates or the need for administrative simplicity, but a decision designed to enhance—not eliminate—perspective. Many of the larger media, like the *New York Times* and CBS, now keep their top-ranked reporters free to consider systemic or comparative trends, while the more junior reporters travel regularly with the candidate. Inevitably, however, the vast bulk of campaign coverage is still organized around the activities of the individual candidates.

Career Success and Campaign Reporting

The politicians are not the only ones whose careers are on the line in presidential campaigns. Covering election campaigns has become an established route to success for journalists. Often, after the prominence obtained by covering a campaign, reporters move on to reporting politics in Washington and then on to editorial or columnist status:

> If he is writing about the frontrunner, he is guaranteed front-page play for his articles. . . . A campaign reporter who covers one of the two major candidates is usually headed for bigger things. "The presidential politics beat is one or two steps down from being a junior or senior executive on the paper," David Broder said after the election.[71]

Whether their career goals become entangled with the content of their reports is, of course, the critical question. In the previous section, we surmised that career incentives influence the content of campaign reporting. Journalists who first predict the outcome of an election contest gain enormous prestige among their colleagues, which then can also spill over into the political community to promote better access to news sources. Just as momentum may be a key concept in the gathering of political support by politicians, so too success in predicting the horserace can accelerate the careers of journalists. This snowball effect may cause reporters and correspondents to predict the outcomes prematurely:

> They're all giant egos—just like the politicians—reporters are. They like to have been there first, by God. Carl Leubsdorf's got one of the biggest egos there is. He always likes to be first and he likes to let people know about it. . . . He's very good, and I'm taking nothing away from him. They like to be first, you know, and there's a little pressure, maybe, sometimes, to shave it close, in order to be first.[72]

Once out on a limb, campaigners argue, the journalist is naturally reluctant to see his or her prophecies turn sour. An interpretation is likely to be reinforced in subsequent reports via inertia. During the early stages of the 1976 primary campaign, while her candidate was falling further behind each day, one strategist complained:

> Nobody's going to write a story that says, "I was wrong." I think that Johnny Apple has created—to a large extent—Jimmy Carter. He went out and wrote the first stories out of Iowa and said that Jimmy Carter's a candidate. He got a vested interest. I don't really mean "a vested interest"—that's too strong. But it would be contrary to the laws of God and human nature for him not to feel some sort of satisfaction that what he said is coming true. I am no more likely to talk him out of that, than I am to convince my mother that I'm not one of the best people you ever met. . . .[73]

The argument can be extended to describe the interests of different generations of journalists. Perceptive reporters worry that, given the essential ambiguities of presidential campaigns, their predictions can become self-fulfilling and that there is every incentive to make them stick. For example, writing after the 1976 campaign, Richard Reeves contrasted the interests of younger journalists assigned to the legwork of the campaign with those of their older colleagues. The latter had come to prominence earlier, their careers entwined with the success of politicians who were thoroughly part of the Washington establishment. The younger group was seeking to gain admission to the pinnacle of their profession; to some extent, Carter was a vehicle for their own success:

> Then *we* found someone *they* didn't know—an outsider. We began touting Jimmy Carter in early 1976; they began mocking him. . . . We were already committed to Carter. We knew him, we had forecast his triumph, we had checked out our new desks at the White House and we had begun our Carter books—the books we expected to take us into the first rank of our business. . . . I'm not saying that we liked Carter. Liking was never part of it. Our lives and ambitions happened to come together—to mutual benefits.[74]

Reeves quotes Curtis Wilkie, who covered Carter for the *Boston Globe:*

> I'm going to be in a position to actually know a President and Vice President of the United States and be able to say to my kids—if Carter wins—that I covered probably the most remarkable political story of the century. The political thing to do is to say it doesn't matter to me. Shit, it does . . . if Carter ever sees me, he'll know who Curtis Wilkie was.[75]

Ultimately, we can never demonstrate conclusively that career considerations influence the interpretations the working journalist brings to campaign events. The argument that these incentives reinforce other propensities to concentrate on the horserace aspects of a campaign does appear plausible. Given the uncertainties in measuring political support, we can justifiably criticize journalists' rush to judgment, even while recognizing their reasons for reaching for early predictions. These ambiguities make it difficult to prove any self-fulfilling prophecy at work in their projections. It must stand as a necessary caution for campaign reporters; the most perceptive are already mindful of this danger.

Despite the unsatisfying nature of this conclusion, essentially the same point needs to be made when we consider whether the personal likes and dislikes of reporters can sway their judgments. Nevertheless, the possibility needs to be examined.

The Campaign Journalist's World

In its very early stages, presidential campaigning involves very few people. Later—some time about a year and a half before the general election—candidates and their senior political aides put aside their personal lives, climb on an airplane, and enter a small but rarified community for over a year and a half. This community includes political reporters from news organizations that can afford to devote resources to a presidential election in the distant future. As the campaign year progresses, more of their colleagues are pulled from other beats to cover the campaign.

This small world fosters a certain camaraderie among its inhabitants, even though both sides are certainly involved in a struggle to determine the substance of news coverage and candidates themselves may remain somewhat aloof from the press corps. Hours of riding in airplanes or buses and relaxing in bars facilitates friendship among reporters and staff aides. As well, each profession provides reasons for wishing to cement personal ties. Reporters are anxious to develop sources that may provide reportable information in the future; politicians seek public outlets for their views. Both meet in the context of their shared interest in politics and a small reference group of colleagues. A campaigner and a journalist agree:

> I really like reporters. . . . 95% of the population just doesn't give a damn about politics, and the only people who care are people that are in the same business I am and reporters. . . . we know all the same people, and it's a great source to sort of exchange information and to tell stories and to tell jokes. . . .[76]

> It's a little in-world that we have. You see it—when I was up at that thing in Boston in a modern hotel with all those people, and you could have picked that hotel up and put it in Kansas City in December and it would have been the same people there. Some of them anyway. You know, the reporters, the political hangers-on, and operatives and staff people. And every time you go to one of these places, it's a reunion in another bar or hotel in another city. In fact, you wouldn't even know where you are.[77]

Both the journalist and the politician attempt to enter into these personal relationships without losing sight of their professional objectives. The reporter seeks to develop information, a good deal of it antagonistic to the campaign's news strategies. Casual conversations may provide a lead; personal acquaintances can be called on to answer specific questions:

> I guess there's a certain amount of human nature involved. You get a call from some person [reporter] you know, and you get one from some person that you don't know. And [if] you've only got time to talk to one of them,

you're probably going to talk to the one you know and then do your best to get back to the other one.[78]

Many campaigners also believe that such personal friendships aid them in achieving desired news coverage for their candidate:

> I think it [personal friendship] can and does have a major impact—I really do. I think that good reporters will always say, "Well, hell, even if my deskmate became this guy's press secretary, it wouldn't matter."
>
> [But] . . . I tell you how it can make a difference: maybe he'll change his adjective in the description of the campaign; maybe he'll make a little bit of difference in his lead; maybe he'll put a comma where a period ought to be; you see, maybe he'll soften the story a little bit. Maybe he'll do it unconsciously, or she'll do it unconsciously. . . . Those are the kinds of very imperceptible things you see that, I think, do make a difference. . . .[79]

The impact of friendship—as asserted by campaigners—arises not in direct influence, but in the opportunity to be heard and believed by the other side:

> I think it helps to know people in the media. There's no point in getting to have some hotshot PR guy to come in and run the media, if he doesn't know his way around a newspaper office, or doesn't know some people specifically, 'cause I think it takes a while to build up your own credibility with the media.[80]
>
> They [friendships] help, because people—not that people do me favors, but they believe me. That's the only thing I can sell, is credibility and some experience.[81]
>
> Carl Leubsdorf, for example, he's a particularly close friend . . .I could talk to Carl; it's easier because I know him. "Of course, you'll write what you want, but I think that observation's pretty god-damned flimsy, Carl!"[82]

Of course, asking journalists to confirm that their friendships ever affects their reporting constitutes a direct challenge to their professional standards. Campaigners, for their part, are aware of these canons of journalism. Perhaps for this reason, some denied that reporters would allow personal friendships with campaign staff to affect their work. Even those agreeing that friendships could be useful refused to cite specific instances.

In the final analysis, the personal dynamics between reporters and politicians remain idiosyncratic. Although both groups feel that there may well be instances in which personal relationships can be consequential for campaign reporting, generalizing beyond this statement can be hazardous.

However, these personal relationships can become important to the implementation of the campaign news strategy simply because of the ambiguities in the presidential selection system (see chapter 2). In circumstances in which judgments and interpretations are as important as concrete evidence of political support, other factors—in this case, personal dynamics—may intervene. Credibility and personal trust are more likely to affect interpretative journalism than on the reporting of strictly factual matters.

In fact, the ambiguities imbedded in these personal relationships are a microcosm of the ambiguities imbedded in the news-gathering process. Combined with a subject matter of considerable uncertainty, they make reporting extremely difficult. Where journalists see their profession as objective and concrete—"that's the way it was," their task is much more judgmental. To reiterate, the procedures by which the ambiguities are surmounted—the routines, the decision rules, the organizational array of resources, the continuities of coverage, and the personal dynamics—neither arise from nor produce any systematic political bias in campaign reporting. The influences that exist derive from the organizational necessities of conducting the news business. Some can become quite consequential for campaigners, as the next three chapters document.

Notes

1. Edith Efron, *The News Twisters* (Los Angeles: Nash, 1971); Joseph Keeley, *Left Leaning Antenna* (New Rochelle, N.Y.: Arlington House, 1971); Frank Mankiewicz and Joel Swerdlow, *Remote Control* (New York: Times Books, 1978); Richard Bunce, *Television and the Corporate Interest* (New York: Praeger, 1976).

2. See Paul Weaver, "Is Television News Biased," *The Public Interest* (Winter 1972), pp. 57–74; Edward Jay Epstein, *News from Nowhere* (New York: Vintage, 1974), pp. 231–236; Leon V. Sigal, *Reporters and Officials* (Lexington, Mass.: D.C. Heath, 1973), pp. 1–2; and Herbert Gans, *Deciding What's News* (New York: Pantheon, 1979).

3. Bernard Roscho, *Newsmaking* (Chicago: University of Chicago Press, 1975), chaps. 1–6. For studies of the reporter's craft, see Mitchell V. Charnley, *Reporting* (New York: Holt, Reinhart & Winston, 1966) and Nicholas Tomalin, *Reporting* (London: Andre Deutsch, 1975).

4. Sigal, *Reporters and Officials,* pp. 1–2; and Weaver, "Is Television News Biased."

5. Bernard C. Cohen, *The Press and Foreign Policy* (Princeton: Princeton University Press, 1963), pp. 22–53.

6. David S. Broder, "Politicians and Biased Political Information," in *Politics and the Press* ed. Richard W. Lee, (Washington, D.C.: Acropolis, 1970), pp. 61–62.

7. William Grieder, interview with James David Barber, June 13, 1975.

8. Sigal, *Reporters and Officials,* p. 9.

9. Interview with Hal Bruno conducted by James David Barber, May 21, 1976.

10. Interview with Ed Kosner conducted by J.D. Barber, June 8, 1976.

11. Interview with Jules Witcover conducted by J.D. Barber, March 26, 1976.

12. James Perry, *Us and Them* (New York: Clarkson Potter, 1972), p. 257.

13. Interview with Peter Goldman by J.D. Barber, June 4, 1976.

14. Thomas Patterson, *Mass Media Election* (New York: Praeger, 1980) and "The 1976 Horserace," *Wilson Quarterly* 1:3 (Spring 1977), pp. 73–79; Patterson and Robert McClure, *The Unseeing Eye* (New York: Putnam, 1976); Doris Graber, *Mass Media and American Politics* (Washington, D.C.: Congressional Quarterly, 1980) and "Press and TV as Opinion Resources in Presidential Campaigns," *Public Opinion Quarterly,* 40 (Fall 1976), pp. 285–303; Michael Robinson and Margaret Sheehan, "The Eleventh Hour Conversion of CBS," *Washington Journalism Review* (December 1980), pp. 15–17; and Michael Robinson, *Over the Wire and on T.V.* (New York: Russell Sage, 1983).

15. I am indebted to Ms. Nancy Marder for her research analyzing coverage patterns during the preprimary season.

16. Dan Dorfman, "Sound, Fury, But Short on Significance," *Boston Globe,* November 9, 1979.

17. Personal interview with R.W. Apple, Jr., national political reporter for the *New York Times,* September 9, 1975.

18. Marder's research revealed that 36 percent of the horserace stories in the 1979 preprimary period dealt with polls, 33 percent with endorsements, 15 percent with finances and 13 percent with organization building.

19. See Adam Clymer, "Florida to Provide Early Test for '80" *New York Times,* September 18, 1979; *New York Times,* September 21, 1979; Hedrick Smith, "President, in Rebuttal to Kennedy, Calls Florida First 'Significant' Test," *New York Times,* October 10, 1979; H. Smith, "Carter and Kennedy Camps Mount Strong Last-Minute Efforts For Florida Caucuses Today," *New York Times* October 13, 1983; and "Carter's Delegates Take Lead as Party Caucuses in Florida," *New York Times* October 14, 1979. *Washington Post* stories on September 24, 1979, October 13, 1979, and October 14, 1979.

20. Jules Witcover, *Marathon* (New York: Viking, 1977), p. 208.

21. Personal interview with Don Pride, press secretary to Sargent Shriver, August 6, 1975.

22. Personal interview with John Gabusi, campaign manager for Morris Udall, August 8, 1975.

23. Michael J. Robinson and Karen A. McPherson, "Television News Coverage before the 1976 New Hampshire Primary: The Focus of Network Journalism," *Journal of Broadcasting,* 21 (Spring 1977), pp. 177–186.

24. Interview with R.W. Apple, Jr., by Donald R. Matthews, September 4, 1975.

25. Interview with Peter Kaye, campaign press secretary for Gerald Ford, by Arterton and Pressman, January 13, 1977.

26. Personal interview with Hamilton Jordan, campaign manager for Jimmy Carter, July 22, 1975.

27. Personal interviews with Carl Wagner, campaign coordinator for Ted Kennedy, February 2, 1980, and with David Keene, campaign manager for George Bush, December 5, 1980.

28. Interview with John Gabusi, August 8, 1975.

29. See the analysis by Perry in *Us and Them,* p. 150.

30. "Jimmy Carter's Big Breakthrough," *Time,* May 10, 1976, pp. 11 and 12.

31. Interview with Kenneth Auchincloss by J.D. Barber, June 4, 1976.

32. Albert H. Cantril, "The Press and the Pollster," *Annals of the American Academy of Political and Social Science* (September 1976), p. 49.

33. *Newsweek,* November 1, 1976, p. 29.

34. *New York Times,* September 28, 1980.

35. *Newsweek,* October, 1980.

36. *New York Times,* September 30, 1980, October 1, 1980, and October 4, 1980.

37. Robinson and Sheehan, "The Eleventh Hour Conversion of CBS."

38. That perceptions of who won or lost had little effect on voting is supported by data published by Paul R. Hagner and Leroy N. Rieselbach, "The Impact of the 1976 Presidential Debate: Conversion or Reinforcement," and by Frederick T. Sleeper, "Public Response to Gerald Ford's Statements on Eastern Europe in the Second Debate." Both are found in *The Presidential Debates* ed. George F. Bishop and others (New York: Praeger, 1978).

39. Ford's pollster Robert Teeter observed massive changes in the percentage of voters who thought Ford had lost the second debate. He argued that news reporting was the only possible reason for this shift, which had little to do with voting intentions. Jonathan Moore and Janet Fraser, *Campaign for President* (Cambridge, Mass.: Ballinger, 1978), p. 142.

40. Sigal, *Reporters and Officials,* pp. 37–42.

41. Cohen, *The Press and Foreign Policy,* p. 59.

42. See the initial article by Stephen Rosenfeld "Reagan's Ifs . . ." *Washington Post,* July 11, 1980; and Kathy Sawyer, "Reagan Sticks to Stand on Taiwan Ties," *Washington Post,* August 23, 1980; Philip Geyelin, "Reagan's China Syndrome, *Washington Post,* August 25, 1980; and the

text of Reagan's statement, *Washington Post,* August 26, 1980. Other articles appear in *Washington Post* on August 20, 1980, August 26, 1980, and September 1, 1980, and in the *New York Times,* August 23, 1980 and August 25, 1980.

43. See "Two Candidates for Reform" *Newsweek,* October 20, 1980, pp. 26-28.

44. Remarks by Carl Wagner before symposium organized by Americans for Democratic Action, Washington, D.C., January 16, 1981.

45. Interview with William Kovach by D.R. Matthews, October 28, 1975.

46. Interview with John Chancellor, Anchor, NBC News, by J.D. Barber and Lawrence Goodwin, May 15, 1975.

47. Interview with Lester Crystal by J.D. Barber, May 15, 1975.

48. Personal interview with Robert Healy, campaign manager for Lloyd Bentsen, January 2, 1976.

49. "D-Day, and Only One Poll Matters," *Time,* November 8, 1976, p. 14 (emphasis added). To be fair, *Time*'s summary article in 1980 made similar comparisons but was not nearly as loaded with shorthand labels: November 3, 1980, pp. 22-25.

50. Arthur Hadley, *The Invisible Primary* (Englewood Cliffs, N.J.: Prentice-Hall, 1976); Witcover, *Marathon,* pp. 1-184.

51. In 1979 and 1980 these series were run by the *Associated Press,* the *Boston Globe, CBS, NBC,* the *New York Times,* the *Washington Post,* and possibly others.

52. Epstein, *News from Nowhere,* p. 147-148.

53. Sigal, *Reporters and Officials,* p. 38.

54. Epstein, *News from Nowhere,* p. 148.

55. The Wallace and 1976 Carter campaigns were exceptions to this observation.

56. Personal interview with Doug Bailey, advertising manager for Howard Baker, December 7, 1980.

57. Personal interview with Brian Corcoran, press secretary to Henry Jackson, June 12, 1975.

58. Interview with Simon Fentriss, *Time,* by J.D. Barber, May 8, 1975.

59. Interview with Daniel Schorr, correspondent for CBS News, by J.D. Barber, April 5, 1975.

60. Interview with Stan Cloud, *Time,* by J.D. Barber, March 21, 1975.

61. For a comparable observation see Mary Ellen Leary, *Phantom Politics* (Washington, D.C.: Public Affairs Press, 1978), p. 25.

62. Keene interview, February 1980; Bailey interview, December 7, 1980.

63. On the use of sources see Dan Nimmo, *News Gathering in Washington* (New York: Athenton, 1964); or Sigal, *Reporters and Officials.*

64. Donald Matthews, "Winnowing," in *Race for the Presidency* ed. James David Barber (Englewood Cliffs, N.J.: Prentice-Hall, 1978), pp. 55–78.

65. Interview with Irving Horowitz, *New York Times,* by Matthews, November 13, 1975.

66. Interview with Harry Rosenfeld, editor, *Washington Post,* by J.D. Barber, May 26, 1976.

67. Interview with William Chesleigh, political editor of NBC news, by William Bicker, June 1976.

68. This argument was also made by William Grieder, *Washington Post,* in an interview with J.D. Barber June 13, 1975, and by Gerald Rafshoon, Carter's advertising adviser, personal interview, December 12, 1976.

69. Timothy Crouse, *Boys on the Bus* (New York: Ballantine, 1973).

70. Interview with David Jones, national news editor, *New York Times,* by D.R. Matthews, November 13, 1975.

71. Crouse, *Boys on the Bus,* p. 55.

72. Interview with Richard Stout, January 21, 1976.

73. Personal interview with Ann Lewis, national political coordinator for Birch Bayh, January 22, 1976.

74. Richard Reeves "On Political Books," *The Washington Monthly* (December 1977), p. 58.

75. Remarks of Curtis Wilkie, quoted by Reeves ("On Political Books"), is originally from a story by Ken Auletta in *MORE* Magazine.

76. Interview with Ann Lewis, January 22, 1976.

77. Interview with John Margolis, *Chicago Tribune,* by D.R. Matthews, July 8, 1975.

78. Personal interview with Billy Joe Camp, press secretary to Governor Wallace, July 24, 1975.

79. Personal interview with Robert Healy, campaign manager for Lloyd Bentsen, January 22, 1976.

80. Personal interview with Paul Clancey, press secretary to Terry Sanford, July 7, 1975.

81. Personal interview with Peter Kaye, press secretary for the President Ford Committee, January 13, 1976.

82. Richard Stout, January 21, 1976.

4 Organizational Interaction

Relations between politicians and the press have a necessary adversarial element. Campaign operatives seek to reach the voters by shaping the work of reporters and correspondents, while journalists ferret out details of the strategy, organization, and issue positions that campaigns would rather keep hidden.[1]

> The result is a highly charged adversary relationship—often tempered by personal cordiality, good will, and good sense on both sides, but always there. Since a political candidate is in the business of putting his best foot forward to get elected, and the press is in the business of holding that foot to the fire, the adversary relationship is inevitable.[2]

An inherent clash of interests, a built-in antagonism, sooner or later pits the judgment of newsmen against the designs of the candidate.

From an organizational perspective, however, the goals of candidate organizations and media corporations are, to a large extent, harmonious; the interactions between these organizations are symbiotic rather than antagonistic. News-reporting organizations view the presidential race as a series of events that must be covered.[3] To meet this goal, they are willing to expend significant resources in news gathering and to devote substantial space to campaign events and commentary.[4] Campaigns seek to use the news-reporting process as a relatively inexpensive means of communicating with voters and political activists.

The news media begin the reporting of presidential elections by building on resources already arrayed in an organizational pattern. Coverage decisions, particularly in the early months, reflect these existing arrangements. As noted in the previous chapter, media corporations develop special yet fairly standard plans for shifting resources to cover the serious presidential candidates.

Unlike media organizations, campaigns are not permanent; they are built solely for contesting the nomination and election. They begin without an established organizational pattern or a baseline. The organizational structures designed to implement different candidates' news strategies vary in important ways, reflecting the political circumstances of the candidate.

The initial structures of both news and candidate organizations evolve as the campaign progresses and the political competition changes. As the number of serious contenders narrows to two, the number of journalists traveling with the survivors increases. This numerical change qualitatively alters the relationship between candidates and newsmen.

The race begins long before most voters turn their attention to presidential politics and before most news-reporting organizations are willing to devote substantial resources to coverage.[5] Congressman Philip Crane was the first candidate to announce in August 1978; four years earlier Morris Udall had announced almost two years before the November general election (see table 4-1). Even before these early dates, the candidates were framing their plans and traveling in search of support. Many of the early tasks faced by their organizations precede the visible campaign when a candidate needs to reach for support among rank-and-file voters.

During the campaign season, the goals which politicians seek to achieve in their dealings with journalists change. For example, in the early months, candidates may be more concerned with reaching party activists and attentive publics. As the primary season develops, party voters in certain states become the primary target. As the field narrows, those who survive begin to reach out more broadly to a national electorate. Despite this evolution of goals, reporters and correspondents remain essential to campaigners, both as gatekeepers to news coverage and as an alternative electorate judging the candidacies.

Organizing the Campaign News Strategy

Despite differences in the messages they would like to convey to voters and political activists, all campaigns construct a remarkably similar organizational array for achieving news coverage. Any differences in candidate organizations are, moreover, largely attributable to specific political circumstances. Surprisingly, choice or skill in organizing the news strategy appears to be less important. Accumulated and shared experience, modified by the campaign's political position, seems to be much more determinative of campaign attempts to influence news coverage.

The deployment of campaign resources to affect news coverage reflects the goals of the politicians, the structure of the news organizations to be influenced, the expertise available for dealing with journalists, the campaign's resources, and the perceived seriousness journalists accord to the campaign. The first three factors produce broad similarities in how campaigners attempt to deal with the media, whereas the latter factors—that is, whether political support is growing at a rate that will produce victory—create variation in candidates' media strategies.

Competing campaigns confront the same news reporting corporations. Although the structure of the news industry remains constant, the media treat candidates differently. In both 1976 and 1980, some were assigned full-time reporters, photographers, correspondents, and film crews, depending on editors' and producers' assessments of the probability of a candidate's success. In chapter 2 and 3, however, I questioned the validity of these

Table 4–1
Announcement and Effective Withdrawal Dates for Major Presidential Contenders

Order of Statement of Candidacy	Announcement of Date of Candidacy	Effective Withdrawal Date	Rank of Withdrawal
	1980 Campaign		
1. Phillip Crane	Aug. 2, 1978	April 17, 1980	9
2. Benjamin Fernardez	Nov. 19, 1978	June 3, 1980	12
3. John Connally	Jan. 24, 1979	March 9, 1980	6
4. Lowell Weicker	March 12, 1979	May 16, 1979	1
5. George Bush	May 1, 1979	May 16, 1980	11
6. Robert Dole	May 14, 1979	March 15, 1980	7
7. John Anderson	June 8, 1979	April 24, 1980	10
8. Larry Pressler	Sept. 25, 1979	January 8, 1980	4
Gerald Ford	—	October 19, 1979	2
9. Howard Baker	November 1, 1979	March 5, 1980	5
10. Edward Kennedy	November 7, 1979	August 12, 1980	13
11. Edmund Brown	November 8, 1979	April 1, 1980	8
12. Ronald Reagan	November 13, 1979	—	—
13. Jimmy Carter	December 4, 1979	—	—
Alexander Haig	—	December 22, 1979	3
	1976 Campaign		
Edward Kennedy	—	September 23, 1974	1
Walter Mondale	—	November 21, 1974	2
1. Morris Udall	November 23, 1974	June 14, 1976	13
2. Jimmy Carter	December 12, 1974	—	—
3. Fred Harris	January 11, 1975	April 8, 1976	8
4. Eugene McCarthy	January 12, 1975	November 2, 1976	16
5. Henry Jackson	February 6, 1975	May 1, 1976	10
6. Lloyd Bentsen	February 17, 1975	February 10, 1976	4
7. Terry Sanford	May 29, 1975	January 23, 1976	3
8. Gerald Ford	July 8, 1975	—	—
9. Sargent Shriver	September 20, 1975	March 19, 1976	7
10. Milton Shapp	September 25, 1975	March 12, 1976	6
11. Birch Bayh	October 21, 1975	March 4, 1976	5
12. George Wallace	November 12, 1975	June 9, 1976	11
13. Ronald Reagan	November 20, 1975	August 18, 1976	15
14. Edmund G. Brown	March 12, 1976	July 14, 1976	14
15. Frank Church	March 18, 1976	June 14, 1976	12
Hubert Humphrey	—	April 28, 1976	9

Sources: ABC News Special Events, *The '80 Vote: Republican Convention Handbook,* Jeff Gralnick, exec. producer (New York: ABC, 1980); ABC News, *Factbook: The 1976 Democratic National Convention* (New York: ABC News, June 24, 1976) and Jules Witcover, *Marathon* (New York: Viking, 1977). Announcements of withdrawal were taken as statements that candidates were suspending their activities in pursuit of delegate votes. (Most maintained organizations to continue FEC reporting; as the convention approached, they released their delegates.)

estimates and proposed that consensus rather than objectifiable criteria forms the basis for suppositions of likely victory and therefore the relative amount of news space available to that candidate. In turn, access to news space (as well as campaign finances and staffing) governs how politicians mold their candidate organizations to implement their news strategies.

These campaign-media dynamics are analyzed at the end of this chapter. First, I discuss the techniques commonly used by campaigners to obtain news coverage and the environmental factors that produce variation in their behavior.

Techniques

In organizing their news strategy, campaigns can rely upon a substantial body of accumulated expertise. Numerous written manuals describe the demands of news reporting, the deadlines of different media, the need for communication facilities, the appropriate positioning of television cameras versus print reporters, the requirement for advance transcripts, and so on. The behavior of journalists, to the degree it can be predicted, imposes a known range of tasks upon the campaign.

One campaign manager described these tasks:

> Press includes everything from national press secretaries, traveling press secretaries—which are one kind of operation—to press coordination—which is the production end; the radio releases, TV film on the news, and photo distribution. . . . One [task] is deciding what should be in the press; the other one is the distribution of the press. They're separate operations and too often confused as all being press relations. The third area is the clippings and analysis, not only of yourself (and how your events—whether they've come across through the press as you perceived they would or whether they have not and you need to change it) but also of other candidates and how they're doing. Then a separate area is issues and research which feeds not only into press but into media production. . . .[6]

This campaign manager presided over a skeletal organization in the very early stages of development. Even though only two people were performing these press office tasks, she had a picture of a full-blown media operation and all the steps necessary for its development.

Arnold Steinberg has given us a more complete list of the media office tasks; this list reflects the fairly standard division of campaign duties:

1. Spokesperson: speak on behalf of candidate and campaign.
2. Liaison: contact with all media to handle queries, problems, requests for information and materials (candidate's biography, issue papers, photographs, etc.).
3. News releases: create ideas for news releases: write, edit releases; oversee their production (typing, duplication) and delivery (by hand, mail, etc.).
4. News conferences and visuals: create ideas for news conferences and visuals (i.e., television-oriented, action events); oversee writing, editing, production, and delivery of related news releases.

5. Scheduling: liaison with scheduling to advise regarding media implications of schedule, assess schedule in terms of publicity value, and help alter schedule to achieve maximum media attention; assure that press gets candidate's complete and accurate schedule promptly and that traveling press is properly serviced.
6. Traveling with candidate: provide assistance to candidate in dealing with media; provide drafts of statements and ideas for statements; serve as communications link with campaign headquarters regarding media matters.
7. Administering news operation: manage aides, secretaries, clerks; provide for orderly office operation; oversee local campaign committee media activity.
8. Evaluate and serve media: relate the campaign to appropriate media (e.g., print or electronic weekly or daily newspapers, radio or television) by making news for each type of media and providing relevant delivery mechanisms (e.g., telephone audiofeeds to radio stations).
9. Strategy and counsel: propose ideas and counsel candidate and campaign in formulation of strategy and plans to market candidate through media (i.e., issues selected, emphasis, positions taken, frequency and types of statements); handle overall public relations, including tactics (interviews, syndicated columnists, editorials and editorial board meetings, etc.) and guidelines for local campaign committees.
10. Special projects: draft and send telegrams to groups (especially when candidate has turned down invitation) and deal with ideas, drafting, writing, and editing of brochures, advertising materials; research for statements and issue papers; speechwriting, media liaison with ethnic radio and press; television debates.[7]

Despite this level of campaign planning, reporters and correspondents retain the ultimate determination of what will be reported as the daily news. As a result, they are able to hold their sources to subtle, ethical boundaries that campaigners must respect. Journalists, for example, highly resent being deceived; outright lying to reporters is strictly taboo. Blatant efforts to manipulate journalists can be detrimental to the long-run relationship between an individual politician and a journalist. Campaigners and their press secretaries, must, therefore, guard their reputations for credibility:

You cannot lie to the press; at least in a campaign you cannot. It doesn't work. A couple of press secretaries for a couple of the so-called major candidates have bad reputations with the national political reporters . . . as either liars or people who are going to distort things for their person's benefit. And, I don't intend to get that kind of reputation.[8]

There's no point in getting some hot shot PR guy to come in and run the media, if he doesn't know his way around a newspaper office, or doesn't know some people specifically, 'cause I think it takes a while to build up your own credibility with the media.[9]

[Reporters] believe me. That's the only thing I can sell, is credibility and some experience.[10]

Journalists know that their new sources are instrumental actors who bring a bias to the information they impart. They do not expect campaigners to be dispassionate and objective. Although there is nothing subtle about the campaigner's objective in having news reporting serve the interests of the candidate, the means to achieve that end must be subtle indeed. Yet the space between deception and objectivity leaves ample room for manipulation or, as campaigners prefer to think of it, "orchestration."

Even though they ultimately control the news-reporting process, reporters and correspondents depend on campaigners to maintain a daily flow of reportable news. Because of this initiative, campaigners are able to craft their words and actions to narrow the range of reportable stories. That is to say, campaign politicians seek to limit the latitude that reporters exercise in selecting the daily news to stories that favor their candidate.

In initiating news stories, campaigners rely on their understanding of the media rules of thumb (see chapter 3). (In many cases, press officers have worked as reporters themselves.) As a result, they recognize what events or statements will appear newsworthy to journalists; they attempt to giftwrap some stories and make others more difficult to report. As media critic Joel Swerdlow writes:

> From the candidate's perspective, a major element in planning the day became control over the all-important lead. Campaign strategists determined the day's principal story—a Reagan statement on the economy, a Carter attack on Reagan's judgment—and they constructed a vacuum around that story, forcing reporters to use it.[11]

By visiting one state rather than another, by giving speeches on one topic rather than another, by appearing with carefully selected audiences, campaign organizations make it easy for reporters to prepare the "right" kind of stories. For example, when polling data revealed that Carter was doing better than Reagan among women, they turned to the news process to attract more middle-income women, in particular, to his candidacy. The Carter campaign began to schedule meetings between the president and volunteer women's organizations, hoping they would be covered by local TV and press. News coverage of these events would convey to female viewers and readers the subrosa message that Carter was responsive to their views.[12]

Reporters, for their part, find it difficult to circumvent the campaign's objective. NBC's Heidi Shulman comments:

The Reagan staff knows that the picture carries an impact no matter what the correspondent says, so they give us a picture with a message, "Reagan likes blue-collar voters." And even if I say, "Reagan is out to get the blue-collar vote," people will remember the picture and not my words.[13]

Campaigns attempt to deny reporters information needed to write damaging stories, especially those stories not conforming to the campaign's objectives. Defensive techniques can be as simple as refusing to answer a reporter's questions; for example, in public forums, candidates may fend off difficult questions with their standard campaign messages instead of direct answers. The press office is the center of the campaign's effort to coordinate the release of information to the media, and to deny access to reporters working unfavorable stories. Campaigners can become quite skillful in manipulating journalistic values using five different sets of tactics.

Adapting to the Routines of Journalism. Campaigners adapt their behavior to the imperatives of news production. For example, campaign events are scheduled to meet the deadlines of the major news outlets. Morning speeches or statements can be easily reported by the wire services. Afternoon events have a decreasing likelihood of being carried by the networks as the main story of the day. These deadlines can be used to accent some stories and obscure others. For example, running as an outsider in 1976, Carter held his meetings with Democratic party leaders in the evening to minimize network news coverage.

Campaigners also arrange hotel and travel plans for reporters (leaving them free to file stories), provide them with the means to communicate with their organization's headquarters, write press releases that can be easily paraphrased into a story, phone local radio stations offering tapes of the candidate's remarks ("this is Jim Smith reporting from the Reagan campaign"), and so on.

Beyond these simple techniques campaigners also try to pace the flow of news about the campaign to ensure regular coverage over the long term. For example, important policy statements are spread out over the entire campaign. The Reagan organization set out in September 1980 to focus its campaigning on a different policy issue each week as a way of maintaining its control over news content. In 1976, feature stories on Carter's family and top-level staff were deliberately rationed so that each story would be given maximum exposure.[14]

The timing of campaign events such as conventions, primaries, or caucuses can be critical to the campaign's effort to pace the news. In 1976, for example, Udall's advisers made a major mistake by planning a month's hiatus in their major efforts in Massachusetts (March 8) and Wisconsin (April 6); without the news peg of an upcoming primary, the campaign became virtually invisible at a critical period. In early 1980, the Reagan campaign decided not to campaign heavily in Iowa, thereby passing up opportunities to create its own news. During this period, it lost control over press coverage; as a result, Reagan's ability to dominate the headlines during the month before the New Hampshire primary was sharply curtailed.[15]

Travel. Media considerations affect how modern presidential candidates spend their time. Campaigns realize diminishing returns in news coverage by investing the candidate's time in a single media market. A candidate's first stop in a given city receives the lion's share of local news coverage. To reach more people as rapidly as possible, candidates travel to as many media market areas as possible each day. In an extreme example, Ronald Reagan visited seven cities in North Carolina the day before its 1976 primary, and then flew off for an appearance in Wisconsin. At each stop, his sole event was to hold a news conference at the airport.

> You're really . . . running for President of the United States the way you would run for county school superintendent or state senator or governor or whatever, because . . . you're essentially going into a media market and trying to get all the good coverage you can there. And then you go to the next one and what happens in A has very little influence on what happens in B. . . . It's a very new audience, a new game, a new town, every day. . . .[16]

Such whistlestopping helps campaigns limit the journalists' access to sources outside the candidate's traveling party. This in turn reduces the number of "enterprise" stories, in which reporters piece together material supplied from several sources offering very different perspectives. Rapid travel probably reinforces the consensus nature of campaign journalism as individual reporters turn to the judgments of their colleagues as a means of preserving some independence from the campaign's perspective.

Accommodating to News Values. Campaign-media interactions provide a myriad of examples of how campaigners accommodate their activities to the values of news production. An exclusive story, for example, has heightened newsworthiness to the reporter and organization. Campaigners know that once this story appears in the news, other organizations are more likely to report it themselves. Thus, competition between journalists and between news organizations affords campaigns with many opportunities to play one off against the other.

Other things being equal, stories that have an unexpected, conflictual, or dramatic element or that illustrate a new trend or change are preferred. Reporters have a penchant for stories relating to the horserace aspects of electoral contests, perhaps because they usually contain many of these elements. Campaigners know they are more likely to make the news if they discuss the race's progress rather than trying to communicate the campaign theme. Because news reporting is a highly selective and simplifying endeavor, candidates quickly learn to summarize their thoughts into brief statements that can be sliced out for a television news segment or quoted in a written story. Even though they run the risk of being charged with sloganeering, they have a better chance of having their actual words transmitted to the voters rather than a synopsis or an extract.

A more detailed example further illustrates how campaign techniques conform to journalistic values. By using the quick-response tactic, campaigners seek to capitalize on the inertia of newsmaking and on reporters' preference for stories that involve conflict. In campaign politics, this tendency means that a candidates' statements in reaction to the actions and words of other political actors can be deemed as newsworthy, other things being equal. On-the-spot comments on a major breaking news story have a higher probability of being reported than, for example, a speech on some unrelated public policy proposal. Campaigns often establish informal groups to prepare their candidates' statements of his reactions to current events on very short notice.[17] Especially during the preprimary period—when political coverage is minimal—this tactic constitutes one of the most successful means of "breaking into the news" and thereby gaining national exposure. As one press secretary notes:

> One thing that you can do is play the "quick response game," which means that whatever is today's headlines in terms of policy matter that might come out of the White House or out of one of the federal agencies or departments, you immediately have a response available. If you do that . . . then you can get very good exposure. . . . Once you start engaging in that, then the media begin to think of you as a source, as someone who represents another point of view or as the loyal opposition to the administration, and so they have the tendency to call on you every time something breaks. . . .[18]

Most campaigners rely on this technique from time to time. For example, it was successfully used by the Jackson for President Committee in 1975.[19] Capitalizing on his Senate responsibilities, Jackson received news coverage for his statements on a wide range of public policy issues.[20] Between January and October, the Senator's activities were reported directly in thirty-four stories in the *Washington Post* and eighteen in the *New York Times*.[21] Of these, twenty-four *Post* stories and six *Times* stories (71 percent and 33 percent respectively) were related to his policy stands, the remainder being reports of his presidential campaign. During all of 1975, Jackson appeared on the evening network news shows a total of sixty-eight times. Of these, 93 percent of these telecasts dealt with policy questions, covering Jackson's reactions to current events.[22]

Although this Jackson example demonstrates that quick responses can secure news coverage, there are, however, several limitations upon the usefulness of this technique. The ability to command news coverage, particularly during the early phases of the campaign, requires a legitimate reason other than one's candidacy. A public office, particularly in the U.S. Senate, appears to have the greatest potential. Senators can hold forth on a wide array of committee responsibilities, and they have ready access to the broad number of Washington-based reporters.

Jackson's experience also implies that, as journalists come to expect reactions from a vocal source over a range of questions, the strategy can have a multiplier effect, spreading from policy issues to his candidacy itself. Quick responses can become a two-edged sword, as another campaign press secretary noted:

> If you're only available when you want to be, then the game doesn't work very well. You have to be available when they want, as well as when you want to make a particular point. It's a hard thing to do in a stop-go fashion. So that can be a problem if a guy is, you know, he's commenting on everything, and some of those things may be things that he'd prefer not to comment on.[23]

Reacting quickly on unfamiliar ground, a candidate can make mistakes that can potentially damage his press relations or his credibility.

Journalistic Competition. Both news organizations and individual reporters constantly compete to be first with an important story. Invariably, campaigners seek to turn these competitive urges to their own benefit. Leads to major stories can be surreptitiously channeled to one reporter and away from others. A reporter given an exclusive may be less willing to spend the time necessary to check all the details or to balance the campaign's interpretation with other views. As the demands for access to the candidate and upper-level staff increase, campaigners are able to escape somewhat from responding to requests of individual journalists. In the name of fairness to all, they deal collectively with the press corps in most interactions and single out journalists for special access when it suits the campaign purposes.

Feedback and Learning. Campaigns continually monitor news products to sharpen their media techniques. Each campaign studied maintained clipping files, either using contract services or relying on volunteers. In addition, many campaigns videotaped the network news to study and improve the candidate's televised appearances.

Occasionally, such evaluations can go beyond simply improving campaign news strategies. During the 1976 Massachusetts primary, for example, the Bayh campaign analyzed the space devoted to different candidates in the

Boston Globe and brought a complaint of unequal coverage to the *Globe's* editorial board.[24]

The news strategy is different in at least one essential way from other aspects of campaigning. The results are known on a continuing basis. The press office does not need to wait until election day to evaluate its performance. Thus, for campaigners, cause and effect appears to be easily observable. Perhaps this seeming clarity helps explain why they devote so much of their attention to their relations with reporters, settling for a tangible but less than final measure of success since no one can be certain how reported news will affect voting behavior. The number of favorable news stories may document the effectiveness of the press office; it does not indicate whether the news strategy is contributing to the overall success of the campaign.

Variations in Organizing the News Strategy

Although standardized techniques are generally used by all campaigners, news strategies vary considerably both across campaigns and within individual campaigns. How campaigns organize to conduct media politics is largely determined by environmental constraints—the subject of the next section—or to the skill of the campaigners in recognizing and making the best of forced choices.

Initiation versus Inertia. Campaigners sometimes can gain media exposure by capitalizing on stories already in the news agenda. Consider, for example, Ted Kennedy's dramatic statement about the Shah of Iran in the middle of the Iranian hostage crisis.[25] After November 4, 1979, the Iranian crisis consumed a large percentage of the front pages and evening network news. As a result, most campaign stories were blanked out. Kennedy's remarks did serve to thrust him back into the headlines. By jumping onto an existing story, campaigners can reap a large amount of coverage, but not always to their liking.[26]

Therefore, when few news-reporting resources are directed toward covering campaign politics, campaigns tend to rely on existing stories. Initiating stories is much more difficult, particularly during the preprimary period. Nevertheless, inasmuch as the campaign controls the subject matter of the stories it initiates, politicians are always staging events that they hope will be newsworthy.

Political success is the major factor in initiating stories. Weaker campaigns require a greater effort to generate coverage of their activities. The party's nominee is guaranteed news coverage. An incumbent president enjoys the luxury (and the hazard) of being constantly newsworthy. By legitimately upholding the country's interest, the president can attempt to

convert voters into supporters without giving the appearance of campaigning. Both Ford in 1976 and Carter in 1980 found that they were better able
to orchestrate their news coverage by remaining in the White House—the
so-called Rose Garden strategy.

Carter's decision to stay in the White House during the Iran crisis forced
him to cancel an Iowa debate with Kennedy. As the crisis lengthened, however, Carter was increasingly criticized for cynically exploiting the crisis and
the White House, particularly after he called a press conference on the
morning of the Wisconsin primary to announce progress in the hostages
negotiations.[27] Even then Carter's strategists recognized the advantages in
their ability to create and control news by remaining in the White House:

> If we just dropped him on the campaign trail at a point when things looked
> like they were going to hold up all right for a while, we would face the prob-
> lem that he might do something that would cause problems electorally, or
> in fact, refocus attention even more starkly on himself. And the truth of
> the matter is that the one campaign trip he took worked against us.[28]

Ford campaigners four years earlier made parallel statements:

> If Truman had to implement his 1948 campaign today, he would probably
> lose because of TV. Truman was not that good on the stump (his speeches
> were awful!) and, while his "Give 'Em Hell, Harry" style was pleasing to
> relatively small crowds—who would only see it once—it probably would
> have quickly worn thin if seen nightly by millions in living color.[29]

> So this was the basis for the campaign strategy in the general election, the
> Rose Garden Strategy. The president [Ford] simply did better in communi-
> cating with the voters when he was perceived as president, not as a candi-
> date for president.[30]

Like an incumbent president, candidates can choose whether to initiate
news stories or capitalize on stories already being reported. But they may
not be as successful in generating their own news. As Anderson's press
secretary notes, initiation can be more difficult for nonincumbents and less
successful candidates:

> When Anderson . . . was out front on the Cambodian famine issue in the
> fall of 1979 I'd call reporters by the dozens and invite them to press con-
> ferences. If they showed up they wouldn't necessarily write a story. . . .
> Anderson started talking about it several weeks before the more important
> politicians. We did everything we could, I must have called 40 or 50
> reporters. . . . And nobody covered it, I don't think there was a story
> about it. . . . Somehow two or three weeks after Anderson took the lead,
> Kennedy and Carter started talking about it. . . . [Then] it was front page.
> Nothing different was being said; it was just a matter of different actors
> saying it.[31]

Press-Directed Activity. Presidential campaigns are politics on a national scale. Usually, the candidate organizations are headquartered in Washington and oriented toward the national news media. When the candidate travels, local newspeople are contacted and urged to report his activities. All campaigns maintained press lists of journalists in their target primary states and mailed material to them frequently. Nevertheless, in most campaigns, the upper-level staff concentrated on national press attention:

> The place to get known is out of Washington. That's the media center of the United States. That's where any newspaper worth its salt has a bureau. They have a 1,000 press corps in Washington. We can get on CBS Morning News, A.M. America, and so forth.[32]

> The more column inches I saw in national publications, the better . . . We operate in the Washington milieu, and we tend to think of ourselves in terms of what we see in the big Washington papers. . . . The opinion-makers reside around here, in the Washington–New York axis; the stuff they read will trickle down. . . .[33]

> I think in the early days of the campaign, print media and the kind of established and more well-respected and more nationally focused papers are important, like the *New York Times* and the *Washington Post*. We recognize that there is a tendency . . . on the part of people like Broder and Jack Germond of the *Washington Star* to find out what's happening before it becomes really public knowledge, to find out how the campaign's going in New Hampshire and report that long before the television networks will catch up. . . .[34]

Another press secretary remarks on the attractiveness of the national news coverage:

> We had been invited to the California State Democratic Convention. . . . We had to get there, however, by Saturday night, because Sunday there's not much left of the convention. Saturday night, unfortunately, Jackson had a long-term commitment right here [in Washington]. . . .

> Well, when we arrived in Los Angeles on Sunday for our big fundraiser that night, on page 1 of the *Los Angeles Times* was a major Jackson story out of Washington, D.C. It was on foreign policy, a major Jackson story all over page 1 of the *L.A. Times*. The Sacramento convention was about on page 12. . . . Here we had gotten, with our essentially Washington-based campaign, better local press than you got by those who had been in the state. Which is often the case. We've seen that many times, we've been moving around the states, and our best press will come out of Washington. . . .[35]

Other campaigns are forced to organize their news strategy with little expectation of national press attention, at least until they demonstrate political progress. For example, during the 1976 campaign Jimmy Carter was neither based in Washington nor an established candidate. His early efforts were not directed toward national coverage; Carter was such a long shot that committing major resources to national press coverage would have been wasted. Instead, Carter and his staff sought to maximize their exposure in states where they planned an early political effort. That is, they decentralized their news strategy, putting their resources into the courting of local press and broadcast exposure: "the *Des Moines Register* became more important [to us] than the *Washington Post*," Jody Powell recalled to Jules Witcover.[36] In July 1975 alone, Carter spent a considerable proportion of his time seeking local media coverage, following this strategy:

> Jimmy's in Dallas tomorrow [July 23]. He's doing radio and TV news cuts in the morning, a half-hour segment for their morning show to be run the next day, editorial board [meeting] with the morning newspaper and the *Times Herald*, a luncheon speech, a speech to the AFL-CIO convention in the afternoon, a meeting with Democratic leaders after that, a half hour number on their statewide public television network show called "Newsroom," and then a short meeting with political and money folks after that.[37]

On a trip to the AFL-CIO convention, Carter spent at least half his time in interviews with *local* journalists, even though the Texas primary was over nine months away.

Carter's decentralized approach was not an effort to circumvent national political reporters. Rather, it grew out of a realistic appraisal of the campaign's potential for generating national news:

> I would suspect that we concentrate more heavily on the local media than anybody else does, if for no other reason than . . . the national media . . . is not there for us. We've got to do the best we can. . . . I have a feeling just from some of the candidates' schedules that I've seen, that even amongst folks like us who can't command the national media attention, that we're still placing more emphasis on the local media than they are.[38]

Making Carter more accessible to the Washington press corps would not have increased his national coverage:

> [Reporters] that cover Washington usually have covered the Congress or the White House. They generally have more knowledge of other presidential candidates that have Congressional backgrounds. . . . That is a built-in disadvantage. I'm sure you could make a list of the 50 top press people in the nation's capital, and I'm sure that most of them at some point in their career had interviewed Scoop Jackson or Mo Udall. . . . So there's that disadvantage that would not be overcome just by having our headquarters in Washington.[39]

The skill demonstrated in the Carter news strategy, in other words, lay not so much in his advisers' choice of local coverage over national news, but in their ability to diagnose their circumstances and make the most of them. Many other campaigns in similar situations pursued the national media with little success. However, as Carter emerged as the frontrunner, his access to national news outlets increased. The press corps traveling with the candidate expanded dramatically after his New Hampshire victory. Four years later, George Bush's success in the Iowa caucuses produced a similar result. When the candidate reaches the threshold of primary success, the campaign organization, now virtually guaranteed national news coverage, can focus once again on local papers and broadcasters. Local papers that normally only run wire service stories about the campaign then give headline coverage to serious contenders visiting their city; likewise, local television stations that rarely have footage from the campaign trail race to cover successful candidates.

Type of News Coverage. Another difference in campaigns' news strategies is their focus on different media. Some may emphasize television reporting, while others direct their attention primarily toward columnists; still others focus on the leading political reporters for the nation's major dailies.

Again, these variations depend on the candidate's political prospects. During the preprimary period, for example, campaign events may attract more political reporters from major newspapers and fewer from television networks. The work of print reporters can be more useful in attracting support among political activists than among voters. Every campaign treasures favorable stories written by a recognizable reporter or columnist.

> You've just got to sit down with Broder [and] James Reston. We'll go up to New York to the *New York Times* editorial board. While we're there we'll stop at *Newsweek*. . . . The list goes into the scores of people we saw one by one over the months of 1978 and 1979. . . .[40]

These stories are clipped, reproduced in volume, sent to supporters or potential supporters, and forwarded to local journalists in the hope they will follow the lead of the national media.

As the primary season opens, however, successful campaigns may shift their focus to nationwide television coverage. At this point, the campaign's goal becomes a building mass name recognition. As Gary Wills once quipped, "Each campaign day is sure to include a 'photo opportunity' but never a 'typewriter opportunity,' "[41] Print reporters complain that catering to the television news has been increasing in recent campaigns:

> The cold essence of presidential campaigning has become the television camera lens. . . . Reporters for newspapers and magazines have been nudged, literally and figuratively, to the back of the bus by the steady, inexorable encroachment of television.[42]

But from the campaign's viewpoint, television offers the best opportunities for reaching voters.

> A lot fewer people read columns, go all the way back to the editorial page, than read the news articles. It's infinitely better to have a news article. . . and it's all that much better to be on TV news. It's not until you are a lead story on all three networks a number of nights successively that you finally are hammered into the consciousness of your average voter. Getting James Reston columns is very helpful in educating the opinion leader set in Washington and maybe that will be helpful down the road. That will pay dividends, but it doesn't make you famous.[43]

Recently, some campaigns have assigned key operatives to handle the special demands of network reporters:

> The attempt to work with the broadcast journalists was always handled by the press secretary of the other candidates. The point, I guess, was that there's no difference between Stan Cloud, Bill Plant, and Carl Leubsdorf; [they're] all doing the same thing which is covering the news. [That] would be the generally accepted notion about reporters, although everybody knows that there's a different deadline situation, there are different mechanical functions. In my view, that's a simplistic understanding. . . . The differences between the people who are involved in magazine, periodical journalism and wire service journalism or daily journalism and *television* journalism are profound because their decision-making processes are very different. The assumptions are different.[44]

To a degree, White House press office has the resources to handle both print and broadcast reporters, unlike many nonincumbent campaigns. However, the Carter campaign of 1976 staffed up to develop TV coverage. In February 1976, press secretary Jody Powell hired Barry Jagoda who had worked as a television news producer for both NBC and CBS. Jadoga described himself as:

> somebody who was involved in the decisionmaking process in television news, as opposed to being a reporter or researcher in television. . . . I really understood how the bureaucracy works in television. I understand media politics extremely well; I'm a specialist at it.[45]

Jagoda, who designed the campaign's plans for making Carter available to network journalists, had a subtle relationship with his former colleagues. "I was never asked to stage anything," he recalled, "of course, then again I didn't need to be; I knew what they wanted." Jagoda understood the technical demands of how networks put together their regular evening news and their election specials:

> When I call my friends at NBC and say "Hey, look it's Monday and tomorrow's a primary night and we've got a half hour and let's figure out how we

can use Carter and, you know, what are you going to do?" And somebody would say, "Well, look, we're going to do an 'ethnic purity' segment in the last fifteen minutes, 'cause he screwed up on that last week." And I'd think about that for a while, and I'd say, "If we have Carter there in the first fifteen minutes then he'll get on live and talk about how nice it was to win. But if we have him there in the last fifteen minutes, he can do that too, and dominate the ethnic purity discussion." Now, that can be construed to be media manipulation . . . [but] it can also be construed as helping to participate with the producers in the structure of their broadcast, so that the broadcast would facilitate their own program objectives and goals.[46]

Organizational Centralization. Campaigns also varied in the degree to which contacts with newsmen are centralized. In some organizations, the national press office held the most significant responsibilities; in others, state officials were given wider latitude in responding to journalists' inquiries. Here, campaigners did exercise a higher degree of choice in devising their news strategy.

Local–national organization of press interactions takes three forms—decentralization, centralization, and confederation—reflecting differences in the power arrangements within the entire campaign structure. Some campaigns allowed a relatively autonomous organization to coordinate their political support within a given state. Such campaigns, including their press responsibilities, resembled a confederation of state-level organizations. Resources were distributed by the national organization to the local and state-level officials, who then could decide how to distribute these resources within the state. For example, the candidate would be sent into a state for a given number of days and the state organization would make the decisions as to what he would do and whom he would see.

A cleavage in the state party may affect the structure of a presidential campaign. If one faction becomes allied with one candidacy, immediately the other faction joins the opposition. In 1980, when Mayor Byrne of Chicago endorsed Kennedy, she drove her local opponents, including the late Mayor Dailey's son, into supporting the Carter candidacy.[47] In effect, the national campaigns contracted out their organizing efforts within the state to local political forces. In North Carolina in 1976, to cite another example, Ford's campaign was chaired by Governor James Holshouser and conducted by his supporters, while Reagan lined up the forces of Senator Jesse Helms. The Reagan press secretary in North Carolina, Carter Wren, was really a Helms functionary, not a Reagan operative.[48] Again, the presidential contest in North Carolina, in short, was projected upon an intraparty dispute.

Campaigns built as confederations may be anachronisms, however. Under the impact of the campaign finance legislation, which requires full disclosure of the flow of money and limits the amounts that can be spent, campaigns are increasingly becoming independent from local factions.

Although the tendency is definitely toward centralized organization, some candidates have given wide latitude to the personnel they send into primary states. Once in place, the state campaign organization is independent of local political forces, and the national campaign is itself decentralized. Like the confederation model, local campaigners have a good deal of autonomy in deciding how resources—money, candidate time, even the emphasis given to policy issues—will be used. For example, in 1976, Fred Harris's populist theme naturally led to a belief that local campaigners would know best how to maximize support within their state.[49] Unlike the confederation model, the people working at the state level are sent in from outside and owe their primary allegiance to the national organization.

A decentralized model, of course, is probably associated with a higher level of intraorganizational conflict. The perspectives of the national office and the local committees naturally differ. Therefore, most recent national campaigns have used the finance laws to justify tightening their control over local decisionmaking. The drift is certainly toward a close watch over the local organizations by the national campaign headquarters.

Actually, most campaigns follow somewhat more mixed patterns of press interactions. These simplified types imply and should be classified as mixed models. The state press secretary is normally responsible to the state coordinator, and the state campaign functions as an autonomous unit. Nevertheless, the state press secretary is very likely to have been hired, trained, and sent to the state from the national office; he or she may even remain on the national office's payroll. These people will, most likely, be interested in moving on to other primary states, a fact which further cements their allegiance and subordination to the national staff.

Servicing the Media. In 1976 the presidential campaigns did vary in the degree to which they tried to facilitate the tasks of newsmen. In 1980, however, all the campaigners interviewed accepted the value of orchestrating news coverage by being as helpful as possible to the traveling journalists. Of the approximately twenty-five candidate organizations observed in these two elections, only the Wallace campaign of 1976 studiously avoided efforts to facilitate news coverage. The candidate's posture toward the Washington political establishment also became manifest in mutually hostile relations with much of the national press corps.[50] Instead, Wallace's operatives pursued a distinctly local news strategy, ignoring the national news media from which they felt under attack.[51] For example, although schedules of the candidate's appearances were available upon request, newsmen were expected to make their own arrangements for travel, accommodations, and filing reports.

Most other campaigns tried to aid the news-reporting process to varying degrees. Bush, Connally, Kennedy, and Reagan had enough of a press entourage to charter an airplane on a permanent basis.[52] Anderson joined the club during his general election campaign. Carter, as the incumbent president, was able to use Air Force One during the campaign. Four years earlier, only Carter, Ford, and Reagan chartered planes on a permanent basis. The use of an airplane enhances the campaign's flexibility in scheduling, ensures that journalists will always be on hand for the candidate's statements, and increases control over the flow of information into the press corps from external sources.

Campaigns also vary in the degree to which they are genuinely friendly with the press corps. Simply because they make an effort to assist journalists in conducting their work does not imply that they are all equally helpful. Not surpisingly, reporters have valid complaints about how helpful modern campaigners really are when they do such things as limiting sharply the amount of direct access journalists have to the candidate or fostering competition by favoring some journalists with exclusive information.

Organizational Dynamics

Political competition in the past three presidential races has been surprisingly similar. Since 1972, large fields of candidates have contested the nomination of the party not holding the White House. In 1976 and 1980, incumbent presidents were challenged within their own party by candidates generally perceived as articulating policies more in line with the party's professed ideology (see table 4-2).

Table 4-2
Competition by Party in Nomination Contests since Expansion of Primaries and Rule Reforms

	1972		1976		1980	
Incumbent Party	Nixon McCloskey Ashbrooke		Ford Reagan		Carter Brown Kennedy	
	(n = 3)		(n = 2)		(n = 3)	
Nonincumbent Party	Bayh Harris Hartke Humphrey Jackson Lindsay	McGovern Mills Muskie Sanford Wallace Yorty	Bayh (Bentsen) Brown Carter Church Harris	Jackson (Sanford) Shapp Shriver Udall Wallace	Anderson Baker Bush Connolly Crane	Dole Fernandez (Pressler) Reagan (Weicker)
	(n = 12)		(n = 12)		(n = 10)	

Note: Candidates whose names appear in parentheses withdrew before the primaries actually began.

In the "out party," a number of ambitious politicians, apparently enticed by the absence of a heavily favored frontrunner and the openness of the nominations process, have thrust themselves forward as potential nominees. Initially, these races included mostly candidates who were not well known by the public at large. But, in the past three out party races, the number of potential nominees fell precipitously after only a few primaries (see figure 4-1). One of the candidates quickly jumped out ahead and most of the others quit the race, leaving the frontrunner with only one competitor from the original field. Democrat Udall in 1976 and Republican Bush in 1980 were the only unsuccessful candidates to enter primaries in the out party race during the entire prenomination period. In 1972 and 1976 as a front-runner emerged, new competitors entered seeking—but failing—to block his nomination. The evidence from 1976 and 1980 suggests that by the end of the primary season the out party has been generally reconciled to one candidacy. In these years, party leaders and activists staged their nominating conventions as coronations designed to demonstrate party unity against an incumbent; in both cases, the incumbent was defeated in the general election.

Although the number of candidates challenging the renomination of an incumbent has been smaller, competition within the in party has been, if anything, more vicious and divisive. In our interviews, both the Kennedy strategists in 1980 and Reagan's advisers in 1976 underlined the difficulties

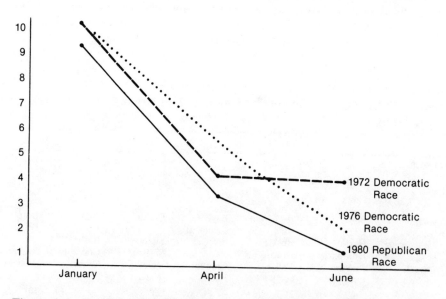

Figure 4-1. Candidates Contesting "Out-Party" Nomination in Early January, April, and June (1972, 1976, and 1980)

of challenging an incumbent within his own party. Both assumed that it could only be undertaken successfully by an established politician supported by a disaffected segment of party activists.[53]

At least four stages can be isolated in the growth of a candidacy, judging from the last three races.[54] From unknown hopeful, a candidate may move up in status to be considered one of a handful of possible nominees. If he wins the early primaries, he will quickly be considered the frontrunner or the probably nominee (assuming the funds continue). After the nomination, the successful candidate is pitted against his counterpart from the other party in the general election.

Challenges to incumbents are truncated contests that begin with candidates already at the second, or even third, stage. Out-party races, on the other hand, include the full range of candidates and are, therefore, more interesting to observe when examining changes in the relationship between campaigners and the media.

Given their experiences with the Democratic contests in 1972 and in 1976, campaign reporters were generally unwilling to write off any of the active Republican candidates in 1980, even though Reagan was always described as the likely nominee. Other than Reagan, the Republican politicians in 1980 began their campaigns, like all Democrats in 1976, under conditions that required diligent efforts to achieve even a meager amount of news coverage. In this preprimary period, the relationship between politician and journalists resembled a courtship of the reluctant media by many ardent suitors.[55] Even after extensive political coverage began in January, the candidates were still scrambling over each other for the attention of journalists. The aspirants found themselves campaigning for support from three separate spheres: the electorate (for name recognition, favorable reactions, and votes); the party activists (for volunteer efforts, public support, money and delegates); and the journalists (for sheer news volume as well as for favorable coverage).

Along the route from unknown hopeful to party nominee, the relationship between news-reporting organizations and the successful candidates changed markedly. The first Carter campaign and Bush's and Anderson's organizations of 1980 underwent a profound transformation in their structural interaction with journalists during the primary months. Their experience was a byproduct of their political success; given primary victories, any of their competitors would have evolved from nearly complete isolation from the national press to a complex and daily exchange of goods and services with a large, traveling press corps.

Growth

During the preprimary period, candidate organizations are normally staffed by a very few individuals, each taking on a large number of broad campaign responsibilities. A national press secretary may write, type, photocopy, and distribute daily press releases without help. As the campaign succeeds in developing political support, volunteers and staff are recruited at the national office and at the state level. Gradually, responsibilities are delegated to an expanding staff and authority within the campaign becomes increasingly stratified.[56] At the same time, growing political support results in an increasing number of demands for access to the candidate and his upper-level staff by both politicians and journalists. The press secretary at this stage no longer answers his own telephone; instead, two or three layers of assistants screen the increasing number of telephone calls. As a consequence, the decisionmaking circles of the campaigning becomes progressively more insulated and difficult for journalists to reach.

The press corps of journalists assigned to travel with successful campaigns expands dramatically. Once the field is reduced to a handful of competitors—after the Florida primary in both 1976 and 1980—most regional and national papers and the weekly news magazines had at least one reporter traveling permanently with the remaining candidates. They joined the film crews from the networks, the wire service reporters, and photographers.

The Bush campaign chartered its first airplane in January when the Iowa caucus results produced an infusion of journalists as well as money to pay for the plane. Mark Bisnow, John Anderson's press secretary, recalled the building of the momentum:

> The Iowa debate . . . was January 6th, that was the first specific thing, then I'd say "Saturday Night Live," then the Doonesbury comic strip, and then, to a much lesser extent, that Bill Moyer's thing, and then the overall accumulation of good press. . . .that all kind of jelled in Massachusetts. . . .[57]

At the same time that the press was writing more about Anderson, more reporters were joining the candidate on the road until the explosion after the Massachusetts and Vermont primaries, when fifty to sixty journalists signed on. And four years earlier, the Carter press entourage built rapidly after his New Hampshire victory and hit a plateau after Pennsylvania. The Carter press corps expanded again for the fall campaign, when two airplanes were required.[58]

The process works just as well in reverse. For Anderson, Bush, and Kennedy, the number of traveling journalists dwindled with their electoral prospects. Bisnow noted that the number fell in rough correspondence to Anderson's poll ratings: "a point every week and a half; from 25 percent in late April to 7 percent on election day."[59]

The number of newsmen traveling rises when those who allocate resources for news-reporting organizations believe that the candidate has a good opportunity to emerge victorious. From the perspective of campaigners, however, this process is cyclical—more reporters guarantee a flow of news and generate an aura of excitement around the candidate in turn leads to a greater ability to orchestrate news and thereby attract support among voters.

The criteria the media use to determine whether a given candidate is likely nominee or president, however, are often questionable. As discussed in the last chapter, ambiguity clouds the task of predicting outcomes. This occurs, moreover, at precisely the point at which newsmen feel most keenly the need to move to candidate coverage—that is, after the candidate has demonstrated some progress but before he becomes insulated by a growing campaign staff. Editors and producers must make these decisions based on shared beliefs about the progress of the race, rather than on objective or ironclad measurements. Being both competitive and bureaucratic organizations, the media also respond to the assignment decisions of other news organizations. To a degree, therefore, the increase of newsmen traveling with the perceived winner stimulates itself.

Interaction

In later stages, the stratification of authority within the campaign and the resulting insulation of the candidate and upper-level personnel affects the work of some journalists more than others. Those planning a single-shot feature story on the candidate may experience considerable difficulty in arranging the necessary access. But journalists working for prestigious news outlets assigned to travel permanently with the candidate will have continued contact with at least the press secretary, if not the candidate. Less prestigious reporters will experience greater difficulty, unless, perhaps, their state is strategically important to the campaign.

Inevitably, a larger number of journalists implies a greater number of competitors for access to the candidate and top campaign aides. Such access can range from exclusive interviews to mere opportunities to pose questions at news conferences. Direct access to the candidate is at an increasing premium, particularly because an increasing number of journalists must compete with an equally increasing number of politicians.

In short, clustering of journalists around successful campaigns changes the terms of trade between them and the politicians. No longer are campaigners pursuing reluctant journalists for news space. Coverage is guaranteed. In effect, the reporter's job constitutes a demand on the campaign—a demand to provide a sustained flow of events and statements that can be reported. Campaigners think it is better to give journalists something to report rather than have them digging around for potentially harmful material.[60]

In summary, the balance of power and control shifts from the reporter to the campaign as primary successes fan the media's interest in his candidacy.

The campaign's dependency fades as its political strength increases. Eventually, campaigners can decide what information to feed to the clamoring reporters. With this shifting relationship also comes a change in the campaigner's goal from quantity of coverage to quality. The issue for the campaign press office is no longer to get coverage but to get the right kind of coverage.

The Effects of Travel

The candidate's travel schedule also represents a shift of control from the media to the campaign. In the early stages of the race, an unknown competitor will travel out of his way to meet with the editorial board of a major news outlet, or would fly to New York just to appear on a morning news show. Later, once reporters have signed on to travel continuously with the candidate, campaigners can influence the substance of what is written about the campaign by controlling the travel schedule. Constant movement also limits the journalists' direct or indirect access of sources of information outside the campaign. As a result, the traveling reporters and correspondents are forced to rely more completely upon a pool of information which the campaign can heavily influence.

> The rules were brutally simple: buses waited for no one. So reporters had to forget about wandering off into the crowd for interviews, or seeking out local officials, or finding out how well organized the local Right-to-Life Group was. If you indulged in such wanderlust, you might be left behind in Abilene, Texas, with no commercial flights scheduled to leave until the next day.[61]

Campaigners understand how the location can influence a journalist's work. For example, faced with a question of how much effort to put into the Wisconsin primary with Pennsylvania three weeks away, the Kennedy organization knew that if it campaigned exclusively in Wisconsin, the press would begin to see that as a must-win state. According to Paul Kirk, it wanted to avoid that impression:

> We didn't want to get backed into a situation where, all of a sudden after the New York and Connecticut win, that Wisconsin then became the next "only if Wisconsin" hurdle. We'd been through that enough. Therefore, I think if we had another day to spend, we decided that we'd go with Pennsylvania, as planned.[62]

In 1976, the Carter campaign used the candidate's location to influence news coverage at least twice. On May 25, Carter was entered in six primaries, three on the West Coast (Oregon, Idaho, and Nevada) and three in southern border states (Kentucky, Tennessee, and Arkansas). The outcome of the Oregon race was perceived as uncertain; therefore, most media speculation centered on that contest. On the night of May 24, however, Jimmy Carter was not in Portland but in New York—in the eastern time zone. He was available for quotations after the results from the southern primaries became available, but his schedule that day ended at 11:01 P.M., just after the West Coast polls closed.

Stories from the press traveling with him emphasized the southern victories and mounting delegate tallies. For example, Jules Witcover's front page analysis in the *Washington Post* was headlined "Carter Takes 2: Southern Strength"; R.W. Apple's equivalent piece appeared under the headline "Ford Tops Reagan in Kentucky Race; Carter is Victor."[63] Although these stories may have been influenced by East Coast press deadlines, the analysis by George Skelton on the front page of the *Los Angeles Times*—"Carter is Easy Winner in 3 States in South"—was not.[64] Skelton gave the results from all six states, but focused on the eastern victories.

Of course, Carter's efforts were not totally successful in obscuring his triple loss on the West Coast, but they did deemphasize them. By morning, Carter's comments could stress the combined results of the six primaries and the necessity to "look at the overall national performance."

Three primaries in California, New Jersey, and Ohio were scheduled to elect delegates on June 8. The Carter campaign, realizing it was safe only in Ohio,[65] scheduled Carter's travel to highlight the significance of the Ohio primary. During the last two weeks of the primary season of campaigning, Carter campaigned two days in California, made appearances in New Jersey on four days, but devoted seven days to Ohio—a state he knew he would win. With great fanfare, the campaign staff canceled a final swing into California, giving the time over to campaigning in Ohio. During the week before the last three primaries, most analyses were describing Ohio as the critical battleground.[66]

Conclusion: Causes or Effects?

The changing nature of campaign contacts with the media documents the role of political success in determining a campaign's ability to conduct its news strategy. The more reporters assigned to cover a candidate, the more leverage the campaign has in influencing the range of stories that will be reported. The more reporters there are, the more the campaign is virtually guaranteed regular flow of news reports, if only to satisfy the pressures within the news organization to justify the commitment of these scarce resources.[67] Campaigners are then able to play one reporter or one news corporation or one type of medium off against its competitors. At the same time, increased political support gives campaign strategists greater control over the very phenomenon reporters seek to cover. They can coordinate the behavior of other politicians for a concerted effort to generate the right kind of headlines.

As a result, skill is less of a factor in implementing the campaign news strategy than might be supposed at first. To be sure, candidates, campaign managers, and press secretaries vary considerably in their ability to handle reporters so that *their* story, rather than the reporters', becomes the news of the day. But the most powerful tools available for influencing news coverage fall into the politician's hands as a result of political successes.

The reverse is also true. Success in implementing a news strategy can be a powerful ingredient in political victory. On the broadest plane, the truth of this assertion must be demonstrated in the substantive messages a campaign wishes to communicate to the voters. Politicians run for office by communicating ideas, whether genuine beliefs or cynical responses. The election process involves both having a convincing message and being able to transmit it effectively through the news channel, as discussed in the next two chapters. Suffice it to say that success in the news strategy is both an effect of political success and a cause of it.

Writing about press coverage of the 1972 presidential race, Timothy Crouse argued that journalists use the campaign's efficiency in organizing its news operation as a measure for the political effectiveness of the entire organization.[68] The conduct of the news strategy is the most direct test reporters have of whether the campaign organization is functioning efficiently. Better organization of the news strategy leads to favorable press coverage and in turn promotes the political success of the campaign (again, assuming that news content shapes voters' evaluations).

One reason why there is little evidence to support Crouse's argument is rooted in the responsiveness of campaigners to the assumptions of journalists. No sooner did Crouse argue that the press operation was for journalists an indicator of likely success than his message was assimilated by politicians and incorporated in their news strategies. Press secretaries interviewed in 1976 and 1980 asserted as an article of faith that they had to be extremely careful in the mechanics of moving the press around. Once each campaign was aware of this standard, it became more difficult for journalists to differentiate between strong campaigns and weak ones on the basis of their ability to organize their press operations.

Looking back to the periods before the news media were so essential to campaigning, it is doubtful that presidential candidates have ever had very extensive direct contacts with voters. Before modern transportation made barnstorming possible, all candidates used an equivalent of the modern

Rose Garden strategy. They would act presidential by remaining aloof from the grubby business of asking for political support. Modern campaigning facilitated by rapid transportation and the news media have given voters a greater opportunity to hear and see the candidates.

All this constant and rapid travel in pursuit of news coverage does impose certain costs on the politicians. For one thing, it limits their full appreciation of local problems and issues; more seriously, it erodes their ability to form strong coalitions during the election campaign. During the nineteenth century, presidential candidates remained at home, while voters, activists, politicians, and journalists traveled to meet them. The candidate's pace was more leisurely, providing ample time for discussion, negotiation, and coalition building.[69] Electoral support could be exchanged for any number of promises—from patronage to public policies.[70] Such politics were certainly an elite game, although they did serve to build coalitions that enhanced presidential power once in office.

Although today's candidates travel to more places, shake more hands, and are seen by more people, they do not have enough time to engage in the laborious process of coalition building.

During the 1976 and 1980 campaigns, in contrast, neither the incumbent candidate, nor their out-party challengers spent much time bargaining with party leaders. Recognizing that state leaders can no longer deliver important blocs of voters, and avoiding making commitments to activists where none were required, Ford and Carter used their presidencies to communicate through the Washington press corps with the voters. Their challengers, competing for news space, moved rapidly around the country hitting as many as three media markets a day. Neither had time to play the elite game of coalition building.

Of course it might be hoped that, while the candidates are out campaigning, their staffs are busily engaged in coalition building. But since reporters and correspondents wish to maintain their contact with the campaign's most important decisionmakers, the effects are felt here as well. During our interviews, campaign managers frequently lamented the amount of time they had to spend answering the inquiries of journalists. While recognizing that media exposure was their bread and butter, they nonetheless felt that dealing with the press diverted them from planning and managing the campaign.[71]

Obviously, journalists neither desire nor abet this result. Yet it occurs. Newsmen worry less about the impact of their industry upon the campaign process and more about the degree to which politicians are able to manipulate the news. But a natural consequence of organizational symbiosis is reciprocal influence, as the examination of campaign-media interactions in the next two chapters indicates. The persuasive messages campaigners seek to transmit to the voters are examined in chapter 5; the struggle to define the perceptual environment that gives meaning to campaign events is described in chapter 6.

Notes

1. William L. Rivers, *The Adversaries: Politics and the Press* (Boston Beacon, 1971). James Perry, *Us and Them* (New York: Clarkson Potter, 1972).

2. Jules Witcover, *Marathon: The Pursuit of the Presidency 1972–1976* (New York: Viking, 1977), p. 557.

3. Note the contrast of presidential politics and state-level campaigns in this regard. See Mary Ellen Leary, *Phantom Politics: Campaigning in California* (Washington, D.C.: Public Affairs Press, 1977).

4. This conclusion runs throughout our interviews with journalists. Sigal discusses how news organizations must determine in advance which news events demand coverage. Leon V. Sigal, *Reporters and Officials* (Lexington, Mass.: D.C. Heath, 1973).

5. Arthur Hadley, *The Invisible Primary* (Englewood Cliffs, N.J.: Prentice-Hall, 1976); Witcover makes the lengthy preprimary campaign a major theme of *Marathon*.

6. Personal interview with Jean Westwood, campaign manager to Terry Sanford, July 9, 1975.

7. Arnold Steinberg, *The Political Campaign Handbook* (Lexington, Mass.: D.C. Heath, 1976), p. 9.

8. Personal interview with Richard Stout, press secretary to Morris Udall, January 21, 1976.

9. Personal interview with Paul Clancey, press secretary to Terry Sanford, July 7, 1975.

10. Personal interview with Peter Kaye, press secretary for the President Ford Committee, January 1976.

11. Joel Swerdlow, "Decline of the Boys on the Bus," *Washington Journalism Review* (January/February 1981), p. 16.

12. Personal interview with Joseph Fishera, Connecticut advanceman for the Carter campaign, October 12, 1980.

13. Shulman's remarks quoted from Swerdlow, "Decline of the Boys on the Bus," p. 16.

14. Personal interview with Patrick Caddell, February 1978. Thus, Lilian Carter, Billy Carter, Amy Carter, or Ruth Carter Stapelton, seemingly by chance, became available to the press for feature stories over the length of the primary campaign.

15. Personal interview with Lynn Nofziger, Reagan's director of communications, December 6, 1980.

16. Personal interview with Hamilton Jordan, Carter's campaign manager, July 1975.

17. This observation agrees with Kayden's assertion that campaigns involve a high degree of fluidity in decisionmaking structures; see Xandra

Kayden, *Campaign Organization* (Lexington, Mass.: Lexington Books, 1978).

18. Personal interview with William Wise, press secretary to Birch Bayh, July 10, 1975.

19. The only competition to Jackson in this regard was Ted Kennedy during 1979. One Kennedy aide counted twelve network news stories in 1979 through September. Carl Wagner, remarks made to a conference sponsored by the Democratic Agenda, January 16, 1981, Washington, D.C.

20. Jackson was able to achieve widespread news coverage during 1975 on such issues as detente, antagonism to Kissinger, Middle East settlement, Vietnam policy, the ineptness of the drug agency, oil prices and energy, uranium exports, and busing.

21. Robert A. Fein conducted the research on newspaper coverage of Jackson. His counts neglect stories in which Jackson's remarks were mentioned in passing in the middle of a report focused on another political actor.

22. The analysis of Jackson's network coverage was undertaken by Roberta E. Pearson using the videotapes from the Vanderbilt University tape library.

23. Interview with Wise, July 10, 1975.

24. I am indebted to Robert Kazdin who led a team of students in observing the Bayh campaign in Massachusetts.

25. These observations on the press treatment of Kennedy's statement were made by Carl Wagner at the Democratic Agenda's conference, January 16, 1981, Washington, D.C.

26. Similar reservations were expressed by Morris Udall's brother and campaign manager, Stuart Udall, in an interview on July 8, 1975. Mo Udall capitalized on an ongoing story by being the first mainstream candidate in 1975 to condemn the Wallace candidacy.

27. See the discussion by Patrick Caddell, Carter's pollster, and Tim Kraft, his campaign director, of the Wisconsin announcement in *Campaign for President: 1980 in Retrospect,* ed. Jonathan Moore (Cambridge, Mass.: Ballinger, 1981), pp. 79–81.

28. Caddell, ibid., p. 90.

29. The Ford strategy book is quoted in Witcover, *Marathon,* pp. 530–542.

30. Teeter in Moore and Fraser, *Campaign for President* (Cambridge, Mass.: Ballinger, 1978), p. 118.

31. Personal interview with Mark Bisnow, campaign press secretary for John Anderson, July 9, 1981.

32. Personal interview with Brian Corcoran, press secretary to Henry Jackson, June 30, 1975.

33. Interview with Bisnow, July 9, 1981.

34. Personal interview with Paul Clancy, press secretary to Terry Sanford, July 7, 1975.

35. Personal interview with Corcoran, June 12, 1975.

36. Jody Powell quoted in Witcover, *Marathon,* p. 195.

37. Personal interview with Jody Powell, July 22, 1975.

38. Ibid.

39. Interview with Jordan, July 22, 1975.

40. Interview with Bisnow, July 9, 1981.

41. Gary Wills, meeting sponsored by Harvard's Institute of Politics, October 1976.

42. Swerdlow, "Decline of the Boys on the Bus," p. 15.

43. Interview with Bisnow, July 9, 1981.

44. Personal interview with Barry Jagoda, adviser to Jimmy Carter, about television news, January 7, 1977.

45. Ibid.

46. Ibid.

47. See the discussion between Kennedy and Carter operatives in Moore, *Campaign for President,* pp. 68-70.

48. Personal interview with Carter Wren, Reagan's press secretary for the 1976 North Carolina primary, March 23, 1976.

49. Personal interviews with James Hightower, campaign manager for Harris, July 8, 1975, and Frank Greer, Harris's press secretary, July 8, 1975.

50. Personal interview with Charles Snider, campaign manager for George Wallace, July 24, 1975.

51. Personal interview with Joseph Azbell, Wallace's advertising manager, July 25, 1975, and Billy Joe Camp, Wallace's press secretary, July 24, 1975.

52. In addition, Howard Baker occasionally chartered a plane for campaign swings out of Washington.

53. Interview with Wagner, February 3, 1980; interview with Nofziger, December 5, 1980.

54. A slightly different scheme can be found in Carl Leubsdorf, "The Reporter and the Presidential Candidate," *Annals of the American Academy of Political and Social Science,* 427 (September 1976), pp. 1-11.

55. The image was suggested to me by Richard Neustadt in his comments concerning a similar finding by the California study; see Leary, *Phantom Politics.* Neustadt's remarks were made at a conference on the California study's results.

56. Burdett Loomis, "Resources into Results?" Unpublished doctoral dissertation, University of Wisconsin, 1974.

57. Interview with Bisnow, July 9, 1981.

58. These estimates were provided by Jordan (December 3, 1976) and Walt Warful (telephone conversation, April 1978), one of Powell's assistants.

59. Interview with Bisnow, July 9, 1981.

60. See Swerdlow, "The Decline of the Boys on the Bus."

61. Ibid., p. 15.

62. Paul Kirk, chief political adviser to Senator Kennedy, in Moore, *Campaign for President,* p. 82.

63. The Witcover and Apple stories were printed on May 26, 1976.

64. George Skelton, "Ford Tops Reagan in Kentucky Race; Carter is Victor," *Los Angeles Times,* May 26, 1976; another story ran on the same front page entitled "Ford Wins Kentucky. He and Church Take Oregon," by Ken Reich.

65. Martin Schram quotes Hamilton Jordan on this point in *Running for President* (New York: Stein and Day, 1977), p. 176.

66. For a typical example, see Jon Margolis, *Chicago Tribune,* June 1, 1976.

67. "Print reporters, whose employers paid up to a thousand dollars each day traveling with the candidates, were reluctant to tell their editors that nothing interesting had happened." Swerdlow, "The Decline of the Boys on The Bus," p. 17.

68. Timothy Crouse, *The Boys on the Bus.* (New York: Ballantine, 1973), chap. 1.

69. The best descriptions of bargaining between party leaders and candidates is found in the writings of Nelson Polsby and Aaron Wildavsky, *Presidential Election* (New York: Scribner's, 1980).

70. An affirmation of the virtues of this bargaining system can be found in Terry Sanford, *A Danger of Democracy* (New York: Westview, 1980).

71. Interview with Jordan, July 22, 1975; personal interviews with Robert Keefe, Jackson's campaign manager, June 12, 1975 and John Gabusi, Udall's campaign manager, on August 8, 1975.

5 Campaign Themes: Character, Issues, and Images

Election campaigns are primarily battles of words. Campaigns seek to communicate messages to a variety of audiences: potential voters, contributors, party activists, public officeholders, delegates, and even their own staff members. The thoughts expressed may be precise or deliberately vague. Statements by the candidate may be extemporaneous, carefully prepared in advance, or repeated by rote. The ideas may be preached to a multitude or whispered among a few. Ultimately, however, campaigns are efforts at persuasion to develop and maintain support.

If campaigners' words are essentially persuasive, news reporting remains descriptive. Reporters seek to present their version of the meaningfullness of candidates' thoughts and actions, but as description, not persuasion. The task of the campaign news strategy, therefore, is to frame events so that news descriptions convey an element of the campaign's persuasive appeal. Campaigners call this process the projection of a campaign theme.

More is involved than just a struggle between campaigners seeking to use the media for their purposes and journalists seeking to guard their objectivity. The functioning of the electoral institution requires candidates to communicate with citizens. Campaigns use several means to communicate: paid advertising, direct mail, door-to-door canvassing, polling, and campaign appearances. Politicians consider these channels inadequate, however, and turn to the news-reporting process through which most citizens acquire their political information.[1] To be informed, citizens must be exposed to both objective descriptions and the persuasive appeals of candidates.

This chapter is the first of two in which I discuss the substance of presidential campaigns, the ideas that campaigns seek to project about themselves, and the words that newsmen produce in response. I focus on the themes that campaigns have developed to attract support and the images that journalists attached to different candidacies. The next chapter discusses the dialog over the horse race.

Generally, campaigners develop arguments on themes that attempt to justify a particular candidacy as well as appeal for political support. During a campaign, candidates and supporters may articulate a multitude of specific reasons for supporting a given candidacy. However, a campaign theme, although it surely comprises some specifics, is a simplified and generalized basis for political support, the essential message a campaign wants to convey to activists and voters.

Conceptually, campaign themes may have both positive and negative dimensions. The positive aspects provide voters and party activists a rationale for supporting a particular candidacy. Campaigners use negatives to differentiate themselves from their opponents and, in some instances, to derogate their opponents' qualifications or policy views.

Campaigners believe that the difficulties of communicating with potential voters require simple themes. Two assumptions underlie this belief. First, many voters are uninterested and uninvolved in electoral politics. Frequent repetition of a few, uncomplex ideas is required to break through these barriers. Conversely, complex policy stands or a lengthy inventory of issues will only create confusion about the candidate and his campaign.[2] Second, because news reporting requires simplification and condensation, campaigners think that they can more successfully influence the content of campaign news by limiting the messages they attempt to convey to voters.

Campaigners' emphasis on repetition runs directly counter to the journalist's quest for novelty. In the last chapter, I stressed the compatibility of goals sought by news and candidate organizations. When we turn to the substance of the campaign, the story is quite different; the objectives of campaigners and reporters are incompatible. At the most basic level, the persuasive designs of politicians are resented by journalists who see news as objective description. Although campaigners want to repeat their messages to drill home the point, reporters operate under the presumption that "old news is no news." Politicians want to communicate primarily reasons why voters should support their candidate; journalists are more interested in the horserace elements of the campaign—that is, in the process of building or losing support rather than in the content that binds voters to candidates.

By examining the themes selected by candidates and their advisers, the outside observer can gain a number of valuable insights into the constraints on the range of ideas candidates feel they can communicate, into the ways in which political circumstance and history affect their selections, and into the degree to which general notions about candidates are mutable once they have become widely accepted.

Campaigns are not always able to orchestrate news coverage to communicate their selected theme to the voters. According to the model of news organizations developed in chapter 3, journalistic reaction to repetitive campaign efforts at theme projection should be predictable. Shorthand notions about the contestants—their policy stands and characteristics—are conveyed by journalists as candidate images. This observation leads to questions such as, why do certain images develop in the press coverage of the presidential race? What is the relationship between the themes projected by candidates and the images transmitted in news reports?

Varieties of Campaign Theme

Descriptively, the candidates who entered the presidential contests in 1976 and 1980 sought to project very different ideas about themselves and their policies. These differences originated in their diverse backgrounds, skills, philosophies, and political circumstances. Analytically, the different appeals were rooted in distinct models employed by campaigners to understand voting behavior. Politicians have different visions of the basis upon which voters choose candidates.

For example, some politicians may propose that public policy should be directed in preferred directions. These candidates view election contests as a response to pressing issues; campaigners seek office to promulgate their solutions over other alternatives. This conception of the electoral process is rooted in traditional democratic theory. However, not all election campaigns are inherently issue-oriented. In both 1976 and 1980, campaigners may not be very specific about the governmental policies they will pursue once they have secured public office. Instead, they may appeal to voters by using such personal attributes as intelligence, integrity, experience, or abilities as the campaign theme.[4]

We asked each campaign manager and press secretary interviewed to identify the theme they were trying to communicate to voters. Although there were minor differences, most members of the same staff made highly consistent statements about the essential message of their campaign. Three categories of themes were mentioned repeatedly: issues, character, or the candidate's electoral prospects. Of course, each campaign projected elements of every category, but most campaigns emphasized one category.

The Issues Campaign

According to the traditional conception of democratic theory, elections should guide the policy choices of political elites. It follows that voters must be able to discover and understand the policy proposals offered by the contenders and that candidates have a duty to tell the voters forthrightly what they seek to accomplish once in office. The thinking of 1976 campaigners who selected policy themes are illustrated by the following responses to our interview questions:

> I think the voters in the Republican Party, because they have a degree of frustration that has existed in society, will be responsive to a candidacy [Reagan's] that is willing to take the risk of saying specific things about specific long-term problems and present a picture of the ultimate resolution of them. At this particular time, you know, these are the basic issues: the issues of inflation; the tremendous size of the deficit; the issues of

deciding American influence and power. . . . [The] matter really of big government, of intrusive government. . . .[5]

We have about four or five major things . . . that we will be stressing that make Udall different from the others. . . of these progressive candidates, he was the first to come out against the war. This is still important to liberals. . . . 2. He was the first to say that he would not accept Wallace on his ticket. . . . 3. Corruption in government . . . twelve years ago, or however long it was, when it wasn't popular to do so, he was disclosing all his assets, all his finance. . . .[6]

I think the biggest thing right now, the biggest thing that we get from the majority of our people [Wallace's] is the economy. And they blame the economy on the bureaucracy, the red tape, the overspending, the giveaway programs, and this sort of thing. You can talk about national defense. . . .[7]

He [Sanford] was genuinely talking about some concepts in this country that we fought the Revolution over. And those are the concepts of individual rights, human dignity, individual opportunity. That applies to virtually everything, whether it's foreign policy or domestic employment policies. . . . Ultimately, politics ought to get down to the individual; and if you're not talking about the dignity of the individual, then you don't deserve to be President.[8]

He's [Harris] willing to raise the sort of issues, and, I think, would do in the Presidency what has to be done, what I believe has to be done in this country. . . . not just an extension of liberalism, not just going to be Lyndon Johnson, Great Society, New Deal, warmed over—and just more money involved in another Liberal program—but, in fact, [he] is talking about fundamental reform, about a fairer distribution of income and power in this country. . . .[9]

The stress on policy issues in 1976 can be largely attributed to George McGovern's success in capturing the Democratic nomination in 1972. McGovern was perceived to have run on the issues, organizing party activists and attracting voters by his clearly stated opposition to the war in Vietnam. McGovern's campaign had a very potent influence as campaign managers and candidates began to plan their strategies for 1976.

In defining the content of their campaigns, Sanford, Udall, Harris, Brown, Wallace, and Reagan turned to policy questions as the source of their political support. As the preceding quotations indicate, each had very different constructions of which policies were appropriate for governmental action and which positions would galvanize a sufficient number of activists and voters to produce victory. Despite these differences, this set of politicians shared the assumption that electoral contests are arenas in which voters and party activists can be induced to support candidates because of perceived congruities in their policy preferences and those of the candidate. (As used here, policy preferences are both the desired outcomes and the priorities to be placed on social problems.) Politicians seek to highlight certain policy areas as definitive issues at stake in the election. The desires of citizens for certain policy outcomes are to be fulfilled by the candidate upon securing office.

However, the policy stands of an issues-oriented candidate are not necessarily any better articulated than the positions of candidates using other appeals. Rather, it is the symbolic identification of the campaign as issues oriented and the candidate as liberal, populist, progressive, moderate, or conservative, that becomes the substance of the campaign theme.[10] These ingredients provide the campaign with a recognizable cast that will draw supporters, differentiate the candidate from his opponents, and, not to be downplayed, allow reporters to categorize its appeal into an existing pigeonhole.

Anderson's candidacy illustrates the symbolic power of running on issues. Anderson obviously felt that important questions of public policy were at stake in the election. His campaign manager stated:

> Our particular strategy at the beginning of the year had less to do with the mechanics than with ideology. . . . We viewed, and I think properly so, the distinction between John Anderson and all of the rest of the candidates as principally ideological.[11]

Accordingly, Anderson's campaign strategists were anxious to have their candidate seen repeatedly speaking out candidly on his policy positions because they assumed that the contrast with other candidates would prove attractive:

> The theme was really a function of the disenchantment of large numbers of voters with the way the process of selecting candidates for office had been operating in recent past. . . . There was a way to take advantage of that ennui, and to turn it to our advantage because we happened to have a candidate who was very forthright and was not afraid to say what he stood for.[12]

> Intellectual honesty—Anderson is willing to say unpopular things; he'd rather be right, than be President. . . . The "tell it like it is" candidate . . . a candidate who said what he thought. . . .[13]

In short, the image of being precise on policy statements gave the campaign the means of differentiating the candidate from his opponents. Anderson's press secretary illustrates how news reporting can be used to project a campaign theme:

> The day after the Massachusetts primary at the Sheraton Boston there was a great big room full of reporters; they'd all gathered because this was the first chance to interview him after his great victory. . . . He got up there

and he said, "I want to make a comment on the election that was held yesterday," kind of paused for effect, and said, "in Zimbabwe."

He wanted to make a statement on a very solid, if somewhat esoteric, subject to show people that despite all this political stuff, he was still the one candidate who was really interested in issues. . . . And, I think the press perceived that. And they in turn projected that. If they didn't do a story on a particular comment, at least their reporting was very sympathetic."[14]

The Character Campaigns

Anderson and his campaigners' expectations that their theme would set his candidacy apart from the competitors was quite reasonable given their competition. Campaigns on the presidential level are increasingly mounted on other bases than appeals to the policy preferences of the electorate. In planning for the 1976 campaign, a number of politicians based their pitch for political support on voters' concerns about the personal attributes of the man occupying the White House. Campaign planners were particularly aware of how the events leading to Nixon's resignation highlighted this factor for voters. Instead of issues, some campaign advisers spoke of integrity, competence, trust, effectiveness, and so forth.

By 1980, Carter's 1976 success in deemphasizing his policy stands while promoting his personal attributes provided a model adopted by many other candidates. The substance had changed slightly as campaigners spoke of "competence" and "leadership":

We pinned our campaign to John Kennedy's famous quote about new times and new problems requiring a new generation of leadership. Phil Crane would provide young, vigorous, attractive leadership, new vision, a good sense and feeling about the country. . . .[15]

The values that people are making for electing a president are really taken all off of the Ford-Carter Presidencies, which means that they're looking for competence; they're looking for leadership; they're looking for decisiveness; they're looking for all of those strengths and kinds of qualities that are missing in Ford and Carter. . . . You talk about *competence*; we know how competent Jimmy Carter is going to be; he is what he is. . . . And, the reverse of it is that Edward Kennedy is what *he* is, and I think those are qualities which America needs at this stage of the game.[16]

We found that there was a sense of malaise among many people in America. Nevertheless . . .[Reagan] could counter it strongly by speaking rather hopefully about an America that can deal with its problems if challenged and if led by leaders who were strong. Very early, then, we sounded the theme of leadership. . . .[17]

With John Connally the force of personality is the obvious one that you are going to use . . . sheer contrast of force and personality. If you accepted at that time that a dominant issue in the campaign was the subjective issue of leadership, then John Connally personified leadership to many different people. . . .[18]

The theme of the campaign really was Jerry Brown, what Jerry Brown's all about. He's a very different kind of politician than what you're used to . . . representing a very different way of analyzing the problems facing the country. He has an ability to attract people into the political process and to government. We had a strong belief that the difference of Jerry Brown would be positive and something the country might well be ready for.[19]

Here is a guy [Carter] that's, first of all, he's honest and clean, and that sort of thing. Then, also that he's tough and competent, and has done things successfully that you, the voter, would like to see done in your government. And finally, that here is a man with some feeling or some soul or some empathy, that he understands how you feel and why you're discouraged or frustrated or upset and has had a taste of some of that himself. . . .[20]

[the] chemistry of the candidate, does he inspire confidence, does he sound like he knows what he's doing, is his head screwed on right—to put it bluntly. Do I feel, you know, that this is the man that really knows what the economy is all about. . . . Our theme [Bentsen] is competence, ability to make things work, moderation, a good decision-making process, physical appearance.[21]

We're hopeful of getting across the fact that Jackson is an effective man, who tells things straight, and you won't always agree with him on everything, but you'll recognize the fact that makes his judgments based on some thought and effort. And he's honest . . . also, that he cares about people, he's concerned about prices, he wants to get people to work and he has some ideas on how to go about it.[22]

Howard Baker is never going to be outspoken on the issues; he's not going to be an ideologue. . . . If we could get to the point where the voters would seriously consider him, then we'd argue that this time it takes somebody who knows Washington, rather than take the outsider's line.[23]

I think this country wants and deserves somebody of great integrity. . . . That's one of his [Church's] great assets. He's an honest man. He's an honest politician. And, there are several facets of his character that I think would be useful. For instance another is his mind. He has an extraordinary mind, not just a very bright man. . . .[24]

Character appeals are justified by the argument that policy issues are ephemeral and, therefore, of less concern to voters. A major question today may be resolved or less important in a year. At the same time, these campaigners argue that policy stands can create enemies as well as supporters, whereas few voters would disagree with the need for honesty or competence in officeholders. Finally, we were told repeatedly that policy stands could lead a candidate into severe trouble. Although George McGovern successfully ran on the issues to capture the 1972 Democratic nomination, he was hurt badly later in the general election campaign, when reporters began to press him on the details of his positions.[25]

Specific policy proposals offer journalists an opportunity to probe for inconsistencies or lack of in-depth knowledge. This was dramatically illustrated early in the 1976 campaign, when Reagan's proposals on social security and federal government programs became the subject of intense questioning and news reporting.[26] In 1980, Reagan's advisers ran into similar trouble in the first week of the general election campaign when reporters began to focus their stories on some controversial aspects of his proposals for a stronger defense posture.

Campaigners find it harder to dramatize a character theme than asking the candidate to repeat his policy proposals in press conferences or prepared speeches. Although paid commercials can use words like "honest," or "experienced," or "compassionate," orchestrating the news so that these words appear or are implied is quite a trick. Even so, campaigners do have some success in using the news process to convey impressions about the personal characteristics of their candidate. For example, Reagan argued vociferously for allowing all the candidates to appear at the Nashua, N.H., debates, which allowed him to portray simultaneously his strength, determination, and fairness.[27]

Just before the start of the 1976 general election, the Carter campaign's plans to allocate rationally the available money and campaign days received widespread discussion in the press.[28] These plans were based on highly dubious assumptions and were, in fact, never actually implemented.[29] As it turns out, a prime reason why the Carter strategists' motivation for formulated (and publicly discussed) plans was to convey the image of candidate Carter carefully and rationally approaching the general election problems.[30] News reporting of the plan would directly project Carter's effectiveness in approaching difficult and complex problems and indirectly reinforce these images in the minds of journalists, a perception that would affect their future reporting.

The Winning or Coalition Campaigns

The third variation in campaign themes suggests that the candidate's position within the party and electorate makes victory not only possible but likely. Group support for the candidate implies that he can put it all together, and go on and win; that he alone will be able to stitch together the coalition necessary to unify the party for the general election.

The electability appeal is not entirely free from issues and policy stands, although they remain in the background. The campaign theme is based on the assumption that activists and voters would prefer a candidate from their party that can win. As such, this type of theme is primarily—though not necessarily exclusively—directed at a prenomination audience. These themes are based on the assumption that party members generally agree on policy stands. The nomination task, therefore, is viewed as finding a standardbearer who is most likely to win the election. Party supporters should rally to this candidacy because he will win both the nomination and the general election.[31]

During the 1980 Republican primary campaign, George Bush and, to a lesser extent, Robert Dole developed appeals based on their prospects to unite the party and go on to defeat the Democratic candidate:

> There are probably three ways that you can establish that uniqueness. First you may have some candidates who just simply by the force of their personality may be unique and different from all the others. Second, you may have a candidate who has a unique message. . . . The third way, the real way to do it, was to win some early caucuses and early primaries, and that alone would break you away. Almost the entire [Bush] effort was to build some kind of an organization that would allow you to do that. . . .

> We had felt that there was a group of voters out there who had not yet identified themselves with any candidate—more or less a coalition of voters that could very personally identify with Dole, such as farmers and veterans that he had worked with on a one-to-one basis over the years legislatively and from a personal standpoint as well.[83]

The appeals of these two candidates differ slightly. Bush's campaign news strategy emphasized the seductiveness of being on the winner's side, whereas Dole's attempted to rally constituent groups for whom he supported beneficial legislation over the years, much like the Bayh campaign which used this type of appeal in 1976:

> I think that most Democrats who are concerned about presidential policies would see the ideal candidate as a person who would be able to reach out to both the traditional elements within the Democratic coalition—the most important being organized labor—and to the other side of that coalition, being liberal activists, blacks, and women.[34]

> Bayh has, in my judgment, probably the best opportunity to get the nomination . . . for a couple of reasons. One, I think that Bayh has the potential to pick up significant labor support. . . . But also he has very good liberal credentials and has managed to pick up significant support there. If you can start with labor and move left in terms of gaining support then you can put it together, then you've got the nomination.[35]

The electability or coalition theme is reminiscent of the politics of an earlier era when party organizations had more power. Concerns over uniting a party behind a candidacy or electing the ideal candidate are more likely to enter the calculations of those deeply committed to and actively involved in party affairs. These messages also carry a sense of constituency, of longstanding rapport with the leadership of particular interests within the party, of mutual support and working relations. During the years when party leaders could direct convention outcomes, such appeals may well have been more effective and sufficient in themselves.

To a degree, all campaigns seek to project an image of their candidate as a winner, and, conversely to avoid being tagged a loser. Campaign advisers pace the frequency of events so as to build to a crescendo just before election day, assuming that the idea of a growing political movement will itself prove contagious to voters.[36] Usually these substantive messages are directed toward inspiring political activists, interest group leaders, party officials, or other politicians rather than to the rank-and-file voters.

Selecting Campaign Themes

The themes developed by the twenty-three campaigns studied in two elections illustrate how campaigners decide the substance of their persuasive efforts. Two decisions are involved: the type of appeal called for in a particular election and the specifics of what should be stressed. The latter—the details of which issues, characteristics or coalitional elements to emphasize—attempt to differentiate each candidate from his competitors. The degree to which politicians are guided by opinion polls and voter surveys varies enormously. For some, personal conviction or discussions with other politicians can be the compelling basis that substitutes for polling research.

On the level of specifics, it appears that the little-known politician has an advantage. Candidates without broad public visibility have greater flexibility in choosing what to highlight and what to ignore. Of course, they are bound to a degree by their past history. Anderson's candidacy, for example, was plagued by questions about his political conversion from a conservative philosophy. But to the extent that they have been less visible in the past, unknown candidates can maneuver the substantive ground of their appeals. At the opposite end of this spectrum lie incumbent presidents who have vast visibility and recognition as well as an administration to defend. In 1976 and 1980, Ford and later Carter focused on altering their opponents' public and press images in both the nomination and general election contests. Incumbency and wide name recognition have very definite advantages, among them a capacity for making news by attacking the opponents' policies. But in terms of campaign themes, these candidates enjoy far less latitude than unknown contenders in choosing the substantive ground on which their campaign will be fought.

There exists a strong tendency to duplicate the ingredients of victory perceived in recent successes, providing a retrospective quality to the development of campaign themes. I have already noted how, after Carter made it to the White House by emphasizing character and avoiding specific programmatic commitments, most candidacies in 1980 were staked upon an effort to project personal characteristics.

Each of these varieties of campaign theme—issues, character, and coalition—can draw upon some support in the voting literature produced by political scientists. Consider, for example, the issues candidate. Political scientists have found that indeed some voters do respond to the domestic and foreign policies proposed by competing candidates.[37] One analysis of the 1972 election by a team of scholars at the University of Michigan indicated that the perceived issue positions of the candidates—particularly as they become reduceable to a simple liberal-to-conservative continuum—can even override partisan identifications in determining voting preferences.[38]

The available evidence also indicates that campaign themes based on the candidate's character can be an important determinant of voting.[39] Particularly when asked to select a nominee from a large number of relatively unknown candidates, primary voters probably do examine individual attributes and heed campaign messages about attitudes and personalities.

Finally, even though coalitional themes may appeal mostly to party activists, such appeals also influence voters' attitudes toward how well their particular reference groups are represented by the political party. The campaigns employing this theme argue that the nominee ought to reflect the largest elements within the party coalition, and that electability should mobilize partisan loyalties in a primary electorate. Political scientists have produced some evidence that the behavior of primary voters and party activists is influenced by voters' perceptions of which candidate seems most likely to win the nomination.[40]

In summary, campaigns either implicitly or consciously adopt a model of voting behavior to develop their substantive appeals to the electorate. These models may not be based on the paradigms of voting behavior developed in the literature by political scientists however. Rather, campaigners more often rely on their own poll data, emulate recent successful campaign themes, and make assumptions about what will induce attitude change and generate political support. The difficulties of reaching voters, either through the news process or by other means, necessitate that these models be rather simplistic. That they work at all may be more a reflection of the restricted choice offered the electorate (in terms of the number of competitors) than a demonstration of the wisdom of campaigners in correctly formulating a model of how voters choose presidential candidates.

Media Reactions to Campaign Themes

The examination of campaign themes leads inevitably to a basic incompatibility between campaigners and journalism. This is not to suggest that whereas campaigners wish to simplify the discourse of an election race, journalists wish to portray the full range of complexity. Reporting itself demands that information be condensed and simplified. Rather the basis of the clash stems from the fact that journalists are not in business to pass on to their viewers and readers the persuasive appeals designed by politicians. Nor are they content to describe where the candidate went and what he said. Perhaps the public relations efforts of politicians have produced an unwillingness among journalists to relay campaign themes uncritically. Perhaps it derives from the Johnson administration's attempts to sell the Vietnam war or Nixon's problems with the press during Watergate. For whatever reason, reporters and correspondents simply are uncomfortable with allowing politicians to reach voters unmediated by explanations or interpretations provided by the journalists themselves. Individually and collectively, they develop and convey their own views about the realities of a presidential campaign.

Contemporary politicians are frequently criticized as offering voters only images of themselves and their programs, highly idealized representations of the citizenry's deepest needs or highest expectations.[41] Witness, for example, the reliance on character themes and in the symbolic quality of issues campaigns. The fault does not lie totally with campaigners, however; newsmaking also involves the use of images about the candidate—images systematize, explain, and reduce the information reported.

The study of images is hardly new. As long ago as the early 1920s, journalist Walter Lippman observed that rather than dealing with complex realities, individuals reconstruct the world into simplified stereotypes.[42] Kenneth Boulding, in a more recent study, argued that people respond to perceptions, images that they believe to be true.[43] Subjective truth, rather than the real world, is the necessary basis of human behavior. Nimmo and Savage have gone a step farther, applying images to election campaigns and voting behavior. They treat images as "a human constant imposed on any of the perceived attributes projected by an object, event, or person."[44] Their definition calls attention to the relationship between the images held by individuals and the messages projected, intentionally or not, by its source. That is, an image not only affects how the source is perceived, but is also influenced by the messages projected by that source.

In studying the contribution of images to voting behavior, Nimmo and Savage explore widely-shared opinions or "public images" about candidates. In contrast, this book is concerned with "press images," beliefs about the candidates widely shared and used by political journalists. These labels categorize the campaign organization or staff, the candidate, his personality traits or abilities, his positions on public policy issues, or the nature of his political support, whether organized groups or segments of the electorate. The use of labels or images in response to the themes of campaigns—and to the reaction of activists and voters to those themes—is an essential ingredient of campaign journalism, brought on more by the economics of the news industry rather than by malice or bias among reporters.

The definition here is even narrower; it is the campaigners' perception of their candidate's press image. A rigorous content analysis of news reporting would be required to document that these images actually pervaded campaign coverage.[45] Although none of the campaigns studied conducted such analyses, we found numerous instances in which politicians adjusted their substantive messages in reaction to perceived problems with the press.

For example, interviews with Senator Jackson's advisers are replete with references to his press image as a "dull" campaigner. Yet, his press coverage seldom made explicit charges of dullness. No reporter wrote "Dull Senator Jackson brought his listless campaign to X today, and. . . ." Rather, coverage of themes and the transmission of images is indirect, as the following examples demonstrate:

> One of Senator Henry M. Jackson's close friends, deploring articles that say Jackson is capable but dull as dishwater, tells the story about. . . . [The] story illustrates a central problem facing him. His supporters insist the product is solid. But will the voters like it any more than they did in 1972, when they yawned and turned up their noses *en masse*?[46]

> His long-time press secretary was praising him for some new passages on the need for "competence" in the White House that he had adroitly worked into his standard off-the-cuff speech. . . .

> "The charisma of competence," he said with a chuckle, "That's it."

> Charisma, or rather the repeated assertions of his critics and acknowledgments by his friends that somehow he lacks it, has haunted him ever since he decided to run for President.[47]

Political correspondents are primarily engaged in explaining the success or failure of candidates. They discuss images, therefore, when they are useful to this explanatory task, when a link can be established between an image of a particular candidate and his electoral prospects. In the preceding quotations, for example, the stories do not simply imply that Jackson was dull, but that his presumed dullness would harm his nomination effort.

Because of the consensual nature of news reporting, images of the candidates eventually become diffused throughout the press corps. Because all journalists are under the same pressure to condense and simplify, there is something of a collective search for a label that captures the essence of a candidate's political problems or strengths. As the campaign continues, events that reinforce that image are reported with that interpretation. It follows that such images become linked to numerous events and are exceedingly difficult to shape. Once a particular label becomes accepted by political reporters, contrary evidence is likely to be dismissed as a campaign ploy.

I do not argue that journalists' images are fabricated; reporters are shrewd observers of politicians and are obliged to report on both the nature and limitations of their appeal.[48] Moreover, since the 1976 race, news organizations have been well armed with systematic public opinion data.[49] However, press images sometimes precede the development of negative images among voters. Many campaigners argue that one is a causal effect of the other. As a result, campaigners try to influence reporters' beliefs about the candidate and the candidacy.

The substance of election campaigns remains a complex discussion between competing candidates, party elites, political activists, and voters. Many campaigns also appeal to journalists on a separate dimension apart from generating votes, support, or funds.

Campaign-Media Interaction over Themes

Both well-known and less-familiar candidates find it necessary to adjust their themes as their press images develop during the campaign. In many cases, these adjustments are nearly continual as the following examples indicate.

George Bush: The Long Shot

Early in the 1980 nomination race, George Bush scored some remarkable successes, most notably his first-place finish in the Iowa caucuses. Long before Iowa, however, many political journalists had compared Bush's efforts to the successful strategy that brought Jimmy Carter from obscurity to nomination victory in 1976. Bush's campaign was perceived in the press as building the same momentum ("big mo" as the candidate called it after Iowa).[50] However, although Bush did win some subsequent contests, in retrospect it seems likely that his campaign peaked on the very day he was proclaiming the importance of momentum. In explaining this collapse, Bush's campaigners discuss their failure to change their news strategy to coverage of his character and policy views:

> That [the first] phase should have ended the evening of the Iowa caucuses. The George Bush who came out the next day, and the next week, and the next month leading into New Hampshire should have been the George Bush of Phase II of the campaign, who would be a more substantive candidate, who having got the attention of the public would then explain why it was that he ought to get their vote. That was something that did not happen. . . .[51]

Bush's advisers blame themselves. With the limelight directly on their candidate, they failed to shift substantive ground and yielded to the temptation to keep on doing what had worked so well.[52] They began to discover a discrepancy between the campaign day they experienced and the news coverage of their candidate:

> We had an insufficient appreciation of what it was that the general public was seeing on the evening news during those first three months, even though we should have known. You don't watch it. You see your candidate out there all day, doing all the things that he does and the press is following him around, you say, "Good. That was a good day; he got this in and that in, and the other in." But he really didn't because what he got in was the seven seconds they picked out.[53]

> [Bush] would tell us when we raised that point, "I'm talking about issues more than anyone, I'm answering questions, I'm out there everyday, I've spent more time in the field than any of these candidates, I've talked to more people, I've addressed myself on Iran and all of these things every single day. Ronald Reagan hasn't done that. No one else has done it. So how can you possibly tell me I'm not talking about the issues?" He's right. But nobody except the people he was meeting one-on-one knew that because that wasn't the story of George Bush. . . .[54]

David Keene, Bush's campaign manager, argued that the press's image of Bush determined what aspects of his activities would become news, rather than the campaign itself:

> If the story of your candidacy is the story of the horserace, and, in his case it was, because of where he came from and because of comparisons to Carter, then it doesn't matter if you make a half hour statement to the press on Iran and 30 seconds on how you're doing; the only part that's going to be shown, is going to be clipped from the 30 seconds. The rest of it's irrelevant!

> It's because that's what fits *the* story. . . . Once that story line becomes ingrained, it becomes ten times as difficult to change it.[55]

The Bush example illustrates some of the problems campaigners have trying to project their messages through the media. Once the press image of the Bush candidacy had been developed, his advisers found that news reporting reflected that image no matter what they did during a campaign day. After his loss in New Hampshire, Bush decided to refuse to answer all questions about the progress of his candidacy. Then his refusal, rather than his answers to substantive questions, dominated the news about his campaign that day.[56]

Shifting Left: Kennedy and Udall

In other cases, news reporting stimulates the revision of campaign themes as Morris Udall's effort in 1976 and Kennedy's campaign in 1980 illustrated. Both campaigns started off with attempts to stake the campaign on matters of character; both ran into trouble. The campaign strategists then tried to emphasize liberal policy positions to draw support from party activists. In both cases, the decision to move left was in part attributable to the campaign's interactions with journalists.

In developing a coherent theme during the formative stages of his campaign, Udall argued that he was "a party unifier," a "compromiser of differences," and "man of integrity" with the abilities needed to govern the country. The earliest news reports of his candidacy reflect this message. For example, Helen Dewar wrote:

> In the wake of the '72 Democratic disaster, his unity pitch appears to have broad-based appeal. He avoids specific, detailed programs, saying this helped torpedo McGovern. Instead, says Udall . . . the country is looking for intangibles like character, integrity, and [the] ability to make the right, crucial decisions.[57]

She also noted that his decision not to adopt the liberal orthodoxy entailed political problems: "liberals bristle at his refusal to endow unconditional amnesty for Vietnam veterans."

Over the next year, however, both the campaign's message and Udall's press reports evolved toward an issues appeal to the party's left. By the time the primaries began, Udall had become the leading liberal, projecting an issues-oriented campaign. During this time, Udall constantly received conflicting advice; a split developed within the organization over the campaign appeal:

> We were concerned from the beginning with the question of whether it was a contest of issues or candidates. How should our candidate be projected? What was his constituency? . . . [We] had a television piece showing our candidate's home town and pine trees, and him walking around the forests, that was pure candidate. Throughout the campaign we were in dispute about whether the candidate should be projected this way or through issues.[58]

[There] was a problem around the imagery. We had a fundamental split in the policy side of the campaign as to what image Mo should have created. . . . There was a group of us that wanted to push that notion of Mo Udall as a person, and the guy who was a leader, and characterize those strengths. A whole other side said that our problem was getting committed support. . . . They said we had to go get the McGovernites, as they put it. We had to go get those activists who win elections in primaries. The way you do that is programatic issues . . . you define your constituency by an issue orientation.[59]

Udall's news exposure ultimately resolved this internal dispute. On February 2, 1975, R.W. Apple wrote in a background report that although Udall was the logical champion of the left, he would avoid specifics in his campaign.[60] The next month, Christopher Lydon noted that Udall's lack of commitment to ideological issues had become a problem in developing liberal support.[61] The press began to perceive a growing and troublesome press image that they moved to counter:

Johnny Apple traveled with him to Atlanta and up to Boston and . . . came away thinking that Mo wasn't precise enough in the responses to the groups and that he was kind of fuzzy, and that was a difficult one to shake once that came out. Then everyone picked it up—you know, it was Crouse's "pack journalism."

Then he had to really confront that and so we'd better really hit hard on particular issues and come up with specific notions.[62]

While this internal debate continued, the press began to respond to the efforts of the issues operation by the campaign press office. The press image of Udall as an issues candidate did not gain complete dominance until the primaries began. Although David Broder described Mo Udall as a compromiser and unifier, his analysis was mostly a restatement of the character theme.[63] With the exception of Broder's profile in the *Washington Post,* however, most reporting followed the issues theme. Four days later, the *New York Times* noted that Udall's goal was to dominate the "liberal pack" by speaking out on the issues.[64] Not until January 21 in the aftermath of the Iowa caucuses did the *Post* stories begin to reflect the issues theme.

During the 1980 campaign, Kennedy's theme underwent a similar transformation. In a strong speech delivered at Georgetown University on January 28th, Kennedy enunciated his policy differences with Carter.[65] At the time, his political problems were quite real; he had lost the Iowa caucuses and was running behind Carter in the polls. In addition, the campaign's situation had a press image component to it.

A common part of the press view was that it [the campaign] was politically and intellectually insolvent. There was an argument as to what course the campaign would take after Iowa. Whether we would continue stressing what I would basically call "the leadership alternative to Jimmy Carter," which was the tone that the campaign tried to set up through Iowa as opposed to the thought that the campaign had to depart radically in an issues sense from the President's campaign. [The debate] was over the direction Kennedy *should* go in what eventually became the Georgetown speech.[66]

The press view of the Kennedy candidacy began to develop shortly before he officially announced. In a broadcast of a long interview with CBS's Roger Mudd, Kennedy appeared unable to articulate a well-reasoned argument for challenging Carter. At the same time, his failure to provide concise answers were symbolically highlighted by the hesitant nature of his replies, and the label "inarticulate" began to crop up in press commentary.

[The Mudd interview] was well circulated in the written press and it gave somewhat of a license, I think, to the electronic media to focus on a perceived inarticulateness. There were only some muffed lines by Kennedy . . . but those verbal flubs were the things that ended up on the news, and, I think, they became self-perpetuating for a while.[67]

The decision to fall back on issues grew out of the campaign's political problems; the decision to cast that appeal first in a decisive, rousing speech came in response to the campaign's problems with news reporting. Although Kennedy had started to step up his attacks on Carter about a week before, the Georgetown speech was notable because Kennedy's campaigners advised the press it would signal a shift in campaign strategy.[68]

Carter's Theme and Developing Image

In 1976, Jimmy Carter and his campaigners projected a character image and avoided policy positions. He repeatedly asserted that the federal government needed reorganization but failed to identify specific agencies or functions, saying that the matter needed intensive study which could not be undertaken in the middle of an election campaign. This call for government reorganization served as a means to appeal for votes of those vaguely dissatisfied with the drift of national policymaking, and project Carter's theme of personal competence.

The decision to call for vague reforms was deliberate. Carter's advisers believed that policy questions would not attract votes:

There is much more in this election year than a desire to see a person's personal character or strength demonstrated along the campaign trail as opposed to where does he stand on this and where does he stand on that.[69]

In addition, Carter's advisers felt that specific proposals would be the wrong tactic with the press:

> Generally, with the issues, McGovern got bogged down in the details of what you would do. When you start talking about tanks and missiles and numbers and so forth, you're lost. . . .[70]

Both Jody Powell and Carter expected the criticism they received for lack of specific proposals. In response, Powell scheduled private meetings with small groups of reporters, specifically so that Carter could delve into the complexities of policy questions off the record. Public pronouncements would be designed to reinforce the character theme portrayed principally through the campaign's advertising on television. Unlike Udall's advisers, the Carter campaign operatives were willing to live with criticisms of vagueness until they became certain their campaign theme was costing them votes.

Not surprisingly, the press image of Carter as vague in policy stands began to develop shortly after the start of the election year.[71] After his victory in the Iowa caucuses, an assertion that many Catholics had been misled by his abortion stand sparked several articles suggesting he would have to be more specific.[72] In addition, a widely quoted article in *Harper's* set off a barrage of criticism about Carter's inconsistent stand on policy issues before different groups, thus expanding his image problem.[73,74] According to Martin Schram of *Newsday*, Scoop Jackson was the first to label Carter as "fuzzy" during a debate sponsored by the League of Women Voters.[75] Both his opponents and journalists picked up this image and it endured right through to the general election.

> There was no way on God's earth we could shake the fuzziness question in the general election, no matter what Carter did or said. He could have spent the whole campaign doing nothing but reading substantive speeches from morning to night and still have had that image in the national press.[76]

Carter's polls, however, did not identify the spread of his fuzziness image to the electoral level until its analysis of the Wisconsin primary. In a memo to upper-level campaign staff, Pat Caddell analyzed the growing problem of Carter's press image:

> The leading Carter negative on open-ended responses was the category "not specific, wishy-washy, changes stands," which went from 3% in our first poll to 11% in the last survey. Also, the agreement to the projective statement: "Jimmy Carter always seems to be changing his positions on the issues" rose from 23% in survey 1 to 33% in survey 2. . . . The CBS poll indicates that 43% of the voters agree to a question similar to ours that Carter was not specific enough and vacillated on the issues.[77]

Caddell noted that if unchecked the image could grow into perceptions of Carter as "untrustworthy" or "dishonest."

Carter and his staff then moved to defuse the image. State press secretaries sent out issues brochures to major media outlets.[78] In the two weeks between the Wisconsin and Pennsylvania primaries, Carter outlined his health insurance plan on April 16[79] and explained his "comprehensive" economic policy on April 23.[80] In the middle of the furor over his statement on "ethnic purity," he endorsed the Humphrey-Hawkins full employment bill.[81] Speech writers and issue experts who had worked in previous campaigns were given greater access to the candidate.[82] Finally, Jerry Rafshoon, his advertising consultant, added new introductions to paid TV advertisements: "Jimmy Carter on the issue of. . . ." and conclusions "If you see this critical issue the way Jimmy Carter does, then vote for him."[83]

The Carter staff also began to complain to journalists that their candidate was being treated unfairly. First they argued that journalists themselves are not really interested in covering specific policy statements. One of Carter's key staff aides asserted that when candidates provide detailed issue positions,

> they get nothing. They get ripped apart or they get no coverage. I have been in two-hour forums, that one in Boston, for example, when I went out, the group that were on the press bus with us, they were all out in the lobby, bored: "When are we going to leave" . . . they didn't want to hear all the details of his positions.[84]

Second, they believed the root cause of the fuzziness charge lay in Carter's refusal to allow himself to be categorized simplistically on a liberal-to-conservative continuum:

> He has opinions on both sides of the fence, but he waffles no more than anyone else. It's just that they manage to use it. . . . Some of his positions are liberal and some are conservative; but he's just as liberal with a conservative audience with those issues as he is conservative with a liberal audience about others. And, I think that's where the "wishy-washy" image got started.[85]

The fuzzy image persisted despite all campaign efforts, primarily because it was a natural outgrowth of Carter's initial character theme. Both his news and advertising strategies eventually reverted to that original theme.[86]

> Whenever we tried to react to this lack of specifics through our paid media, we got burned. . . . I think that fuzziness issue was a catchall for not liking Jimmy Carter. Not knowing enough about Jimmy Carter, you could say he was "fuzzy."[87]

Reagan's Weekly Theme

In planning a strategy to defeat Carter, Reagan's advisers in 1980 confronted a situation similar to Carter's 1976 problem. Having based their primary campaign on Reagan's personal qualities, they came to believe that Reagan was perceived by voters and journalists as possessing only superficial knowledge of policy matters. Accordingly, they decided that each week he would concentrate his speeches upon one policy area, starting with military policy.[88] Addressing the Veterans of Foreign Wars, Reagan attacked Carter for failing to understand the grand design of Soviet strategy and blamed a "Vietnam syndrome" for allowing defense expenditures to lag. Reagan called Vietnam a "noble cause."[89]

Two days later, speaking to the American Legion, Reagan accused Carter of falsifying military statistics.[90] By then, however, his running mate's statements appeared to contradict his strategic policy. That same week, George Bush visited Japan and China where Reagan's policies toward Taiwan raised great apprehension. Although Bush tried to reassure the Chinese that Reagan would not recognize Taiwan, the Chinese leaders were not mollifed.[91] In response, Reagan accused the press of being "more interested in something sensational than in printing the facts," and his advisers complained that the peace aspects of his peace-through-strength speeches had been underplayed.[92]

Reagan's campaigners then dropped their plans to highlight one issue in succeeding weeks. The campaign's focus on a single issue resulted in a mounting series of demands by reporters for clarifiction and amplification. Substantively, the week's events set back the campaign's efforts to portray Mr. Reagan as a centrist on policy matters.

Ford's Image

Gerald Ford entered the 1976 campaign with a severe image problem. Opinion polls revealed that the public questioned his capacities, while journalists openly discussed his competence. He became universally symbolized by his physical clumsiness on one or two occasions. Ford was portrayed in many news reports as something of a "bumbler." Nor did some of his chief aides and close friends do much for his press image.[93] One Ford supporter remarked, "The country still views him as the guy who is filling the gap between Watergate and the next election."[94] In a December, 1979 cover story entitled "Ford in Trouble," *Newsweek* captured the president's press image in two quotations from Ford aides:

> Ford, conceded one troubled counselor, "is coming across as Bozo the President." . . . "We can put together the finest organization on earth," said one weary Ford trooper. "But the President has to shape up."[95]

The repeated use of stories illustrating the president's apparent clumsiness also demonstrates the inertial nature of news reporting. These stories became legitimized during 1975. Every reporter covering the president knew immediately that any mishap would be accepted as newsworthy by every editor and TV producer. As a result,

> the White House suffered through pictures of the President falling down an airplane ramp at Salzburg, Austria. Then came other embarrassments. Mr. Ford bumped his head on the side of a pool while swimming in Florida and banged the top of his head while boarding the presidential helicopter at the White House.[96]

To the Ford campaigners and White House staff, the press image generated by these stories became the principal reason that Ford was in jeopardy of losing the nomination. In late December 1975, widespread news distribution of a presidential spill while skiing in Vail, Colorado provided an opportunity for the White House to attack the press image directly. Noting that falling down is part of the sport, Ron Nessen categorized the reporting as "unfair," implying, of course, that all stories about Ford's mishaps were unjustified.[97] As the *Wall Street Journal* noted, Nessen's statement took what was essentially a joke and turned it into a serious matter.[98]

As later described by Larry Speakes:

> We sort of made a turn-around in that image area, when Ron, out in Vail, commented about [Ford's] skiing, and said, you know, "What difference does it make, if he stumbles or bumps his head? That's not a job qualification!"

> It made the press at least take notice of what they'd been doing. . . . At first I was under the impression that it was maybe a mistake that Ron did that—it only made a second day story out of a spill on the ski slope—but (now) I think it's had a positive effect.[99]

Whether because simultaneously they began to curtail situations in which these mishaps could be recorded or because of the Nessen frontal assault on the press image, commentary about Ford's physical prowess all but ceased until much later in the campaign.

The attempts to alter Ford's image went beyond complaints about his press coverage. In January 1976, his advisers embarked

> on an ironic exercise: striving to modify Gerald R. Ford's nice-man image. . . . Polls have not convinced Mr. Ford's strategists that the image has a paradoxical drawback. It has reinforced many voter's perceptions of Mr. Ford as . . . a man who . . . lacks the leadership to be a good President.[100]

To achieve this transformation, Rogers Morton was brought into the White House and charged with examining all aspects of administration policy from the perspective of the election effort. For example, Morton was to ensure that Ford's policy statements were not attacked by his cabinet officers. Because Ford could not compare to Reagan as a campaigner, his advisers planned only a few trips into primary states. Rather, he would stay in Washington and rely on the White House press corps to dominate the news headlines.[101] In his public speeches, Ford would not attack Reagan directly but leave this task to surrogates speaking on his behalf.[102]

During the primary months, the White House and campaign staff gradually learned how to use the presidency to convey their character theme. Initially, they began using the power of the incumbency rather clumsily; for example, Ford virtually promised the citizens of St. Petersburg, Florida, a new Veterans Administration hospital during one campaign visit.[103] Gradually, they learned that the White House itself provided the most appropriate setting from which to project presidential competence, seeking to increase coverage of his presidential duties rather than his campaign activities.[104]

The division between the White House press staff and the campaign press office also provided Ford's strategists with an advantage. The White House could address Mr. Ford's own image problems, while leaving campaigns free to organize the attack upon his opponents. In effect, the two Ford press offices were dealing with different journalists. The campaign communicated a daily "talking point" to each of the speakers appearing on behalf of the president. Thus, in different parts of the country, Ford spokesmen were supposed to make essentially the same criticism of the president's opponent.[105] The press never did report the degree of coordination exercised by the Ford campaign over these attacks.

The Ford campaign's attempt to make Reagan look like Goldwater was built into the campaign's news strategy, not the White House strategy:

> We want to explore in depth his real record in California as Governor, and to take the points that he emphasizes as his strong points and tell what the situation really was. . . . Obviously, we need the press to carry the message. Now we're doing something a little different from past campaigns with an incumbent president. The President himself will carry his own message, but on a limited basis. . . . We will have advocates speaking for the President in big primary states. . . . We're using local spokesmen, legislators, mayors, county commissioners. . . . Mr. Reagan's record is that of a Governor, so he would be best examined by people on that level.[106]

Reagan's proposal to cut federal outlays by $90 billion through transferring programs to the state governments provides a good example of how this strategy worked.[107] Peter Kaye, the campaign's national press secretary, arranged to have the ranking New Hampshire Senate and House members hold a press conference during Reagan's first trip into New Hampshire. The Senate president and House speaker denounced Reagan's plan (which he had enunciated months earlier in a Chicago speech). At the same time, press releases were handed out to the Washington press corps and the journalists arriving with Reagan in Manchester, New Hampshire. As a result, Reagan spent most of his first campaign tour of New Hampshire defending his proposal and trying to defuse the issue. The vast majority of the news reports were focused on that topic. Similarly, Ford's strategists provoked the press into examining Reagan's position on Social Security:

> We had to work hard to get that story planted. We wanted to start the Social Security business in New Hampshire, where there are a considerable number of retired people. But Cleveland (Ford's N.H. chairman) stopped us from using it in New Hampshire. Then Lou Frey wouldn't say it in Florida. . . . Finally, the Minority Leader of the Massachusetts State Senate, John Parker, put his name on the thing. We took that and used it in Florida.[108]

Ford's pollster, Robert Teeter, later commented on the success of these tactics:

> We proved the benefit of some kind of attack in a campaign. . . . You can create the issue, you can affect the perception of the individual, and you put that campaign under some pressure. They've got to spend time and effort figuring out how to react to what you're doing. And when they're under that pressure, you begin to see they're making more mistakes.[109]

All these efforts did show some positive results. By the end of April, the public perception of Ford's competence had shifted markedly. In an analysis of the CBS/*New York Times* national survey, Robert Reinhold offered this assessment of the changes in Ford's image:

> [Ford] . . . seems to have translated Presidential incumbency into very substantial political strength among the American people. . . . He also seems to have largely dispelled the many doubts about his competence and abilities as a leader. . . . Along with other indicators, this improved view hints that Mr. Ford, the butt of many derisive jokes about his ability, will be anything but a pushover. . . .[110]

During the general election campaign, however, two events renewed the issue of Ford's competence. The Secretary of Agriculture, Earl Butz, resigned after his disparaging remarks about blacks were widely publicized.[111] For a critical week, Ford vacillated over whether he wanted Butz's resignation. Second, during the second televised debate with Carter, Ford made a tactical blunder by declaring that Eastern Europe was not under the domination of the Soviet Union.

After the second debate, perhaps we shouldn't have lingered as much as we did—both writing reporters and television—on President Ford's remarks about Eastern Europe. Well, I think . . . that controversy had nothing to do with Eastern Europe, that controversy had to do with Ford's competence, which had been raised about him from the very beginning.[112]

Newsweek appeared on the newstands the next week with Ford on the cover and the headline "How Good a President?"[113] After a year of campaign efforts to manage the President's press image, that question would not go away.

The 1980 election revealed that incumbency alone cannot guarantee an ability to attack one's opponents effectively and with impunity through the news process. Reagan and Carter both tried to base the voting choice on an advantageous question. Reagan's pollster Richard Wirthlin remarked that while Reagan wanted voters to concentrate on their economic condition ("Ask yourselves, 'Are you better off now than four years ago?' "), the Carter campaign wanted citizens to wonder whether Reagan would involve the country in an unnecessary war.[114] Clearly, the Carter game plan failed,[115] even though the president and his cabinet members sought repeatedly to question Reagan's judgment on defense and foreign policy matters.[115] In fact, these questions were only raised in news coverage by Reagan's own decisions to spend a week talking about defense policy.

The Content of Media Campaigning

The examples considered in this chapter point toward some general propositions concerning the effect of media politics on the content of presidential election campaigns. By their nature, images are simplistic representations based primarily on perceptions that may or may not exactly capture realities. Journalists who rely on images do not traffick in bias or deliberate distortion, however. The news-reporting process is inherently selective; journalists have no alternative to using a shorthand notation for the complex political problems facing a presidential aspirant.

The media, nevertheless, do have an obligation to test continually the accuracy of such labels. There is considerable inertia in press images once they become widely adopted. Politicians find them difficult to change or shake. Because of this selectivity, journalists may ignore or dismiss as political posturing more important aspects of the candidacy.

Because campaign themes dominate the substance of news coverage, much media attention is given to the ingredients of electoral success. Political reporters tell us who is likely to win or lose an election and why; they are not in the business of telling us which candidate would be better for the country by virtue of his personal character or policy proposals. Accordingly, the images and labels emphasized in campaign reporting relate to perceived electoral strength or weaknesses. Press images tell us more about the political prospects of the contenders than they provide cues for assessing future performance in office.

Modern political journalists face a real conundrum: the fundamental incompatibility between the values of the news-reporting industry and the requirements of campaigners and of electoral politics. Politicians seek to persuade; voters need to be exposed to those persuasive arguments. Those reporters who would genuinely like to report the policy stands of the candidates must recognize the instrumental purposes that undergird campaign issue positions. If they merely report what the candidate said, reporters become a vehicle of persuasion, compromising their professional integrity. By examining and reporting the potential for electoral success, journalists hope to unmask what is political in a candidate's words from what is genuine. But if a candidate comes close to the objective truth that the journalist has in mind, the journalist is likely to disclaim it as an instance in which good politics and good policy coincide. Inevitably, explaining why a candidate is emphasizing a given issue stand provides the reporter with a more neutral vantage point than would examining the merits or shortcomings of a given position.

As a result, reporters sidle up to issues, treating them as sources of or limitations on electoral strength. For example, Ronald Reagan's conservatism or age can be safely discussed as potential barriers to his electoral success. President Carter's plea during the televised debate that voters consider the alternative futures promised by the two candidates is analyzed as a subtle effort to play upon fears that Reagan might involve the nation in war.

Contemporary campaigners believe that detailed presentation of policy views will lessen their prospects of victory. While many of those interviewed asserted that the voters are themselves not interested in issue discussions, many more pointed to campaign reporting as lowering the advantages of articulating their stands on issues. These politicians repeatedly stated that the press would not report their policy pronouncements. More to the point, they viewed the press corps as demanding specifics while waiting eagerly to rip apart any inconsistency, misstatement, or uncertainty. Many campaigns have been thrown onto the defensive in their relations with journalists over some detail of the candidate's position. The unfortunate result is that campaigners avoid laying out their policy proposals during the election contest.

Comparatively well-known candidates have relatively little choice in selecting campaign themes; either they continue to develop images consistent with their past public life (Reagan in 1976) or they attempt to eliminate preestablished images (Jackson and Ford in 1976; Carter and Reagan in

1980). Less-familiar candidates have greater latitude in selecting themes they believe will successfully appeal to voters and activitists. These themes are based at first on models of voting behavior—that is, whether they assume citizens vote on the basis of policy stands, candidate characteristics, or likelihood of victory—and modified as images develop in citizen thinking and reported news. However, the images contained in news become increasingly solidified, so that in the end neither campaigners nor dissenting journalists can alter the consensus. As unknown candidates succeed and consequently become better known to both journalists and citizens, their freedom in selecting and modifying campaign themes is constrained.

Given the difficulties that established political leaders have in altering their press images, the political system may be able to adjust to the emergence of new configurations of public sentiment only by recruiting political unknowns. In the media age, new problems demand new leadership. A politician might be fortunate enough to develop an image that becomes current at a later date (a person whose time has come); but almost by definition that politician will not command access to the media in the period before his stance becomes relevant to current national issues.

The finding that campaigners believe they must simplify their messages to receive news coverage leads to a disturbing conclusion. In most instances, the electoral process should involve more substance than just one or two themes. The electoral machinery ought to encompass a range of policies integrated by a public philosophy.[116] Instead, candidates who run without the underpinnings of a party coalition hammer away at a few simple ideas that they believe will energize voters. The demands of media politics, as they perceive them, do not allow them to develop and communicate a broad range of appeals. Enduring party organizations are no longer there to expand on the appeal and incorporate diversity. Perhaps one reason for the declining voter turnout rates is that no candidate has yet found an issue or a personal appeal that triggers a response from anything like a majority of the eligible voters; both Carter and Reagan were elected by approximately 27% of the citizens entitled to vote.

Finally, this analysis raises questions about the impact of campaign reporting on the citizenry. The persuasive messages of politicians are frequently broadcast with implicit warnings that their purpose is to win votes ("Searching for blue-collar votes, Reagan today attacked . . ."). Campaign themes become interpreted solely as means to acquire votes. As a result, this perspective suggests that politicians do not articulate genuine convictions or visions of better public policies; rather, they verbalize only what they perceive as aiding their electoral prospects.

Could all this skepticism about the motivations of campaigners be related to the rise of cynicism about government and politics that has been evident in public opinion surveys? Unfortunately, the research on this point has been sketchy, and the data are not persuasive.[117] But it is clearly a matter that should concern journalists. Many of the campaigners interviewed experienced difficulties in news coverage that resulted from this "objective and critical" perspective of contemporary campaign journalism.

This matter could be considered from a slighly different vantage point. Election campaigns require that politicians make commitments to the voters; the media have become the mechanism of enforcement. Journalists continually press to get the candidate on record as opposing or accepting given policy proposals. In recording these commitments, reporters scrutinize their speeches for changes, extensions, or inconsistencies with previous statements seeking something new that can be reported. While holding the politician's feet to the fire may strengthen the commitment process, it also reduces the enthusiasm of campaigners for detailing their proposals.

News reporters cannot fully enforce the policy commitment process in the same way that was sometimes accomplished through intraelite bargaining in strong party institutions.[118] Journalists can prod and criticize; they cannot, support or promote policies. Although reporters may serve as the instrument through which candidates become committed to given policies, the public pronouncements of media politics do not alone provide politicians with the strength they require to accomplish or implement their policies once they hold office. That strength comes rather from compromise and coalition-building. Campaigning at the presidential level, therefore, has become somewhat divorced from the process by which the means to govern is secured.[119]

Notes

1. The actual information derived through television news, however, is in dispute. See Thomas E. Patterson and Robert McClure, *The Unseeing Eye* (New York: Putnam, 1976), and *Political Advertising: Voter Reaction to Televised Political Commercials* (Princeton, N.J.: Citizens Research Foundation, Study 23, 1974).

2. On the level of sophistication among voters, see Philip E. Converse, "Mass Belief Systems," David Apter, in *Ideology and Discontent* (Glencoe, Ill.: The Free Press, 1963). For a discussion of how candidates frame their policy views, see Benjamin Page, *Choices and Echoes in Presidential Elections* (Chicago: University of Chicago Press, 1975).

3. Remarks by Ann Lewis, national political coordinator for Birch Bayh, at a conference sponsored by the American Assembly, Mt. Kisco, N.Y., May 1978.

4. Detailed research, on the degree to which voter choices involve assessment of such short-term forces as candidate characteristics, is still in its

infancy. See Donald R. Kinder and David O. Sears, "Political Psychology," in *The Handbook of Social Psychology*, ed. G. Lindzey and E. Aronson (Reading, Mass.: Addison-Wesley, 3rd edition, forthcoming); or Dan Nimmo and Robert Savage, *Candidates and Their Images* (Pacific Palisades, Calif.: Goodyear, 1976).

5. Personal interview with Lyn Nofziger, press secretary to Ronald Reagan, August 6, 1975.

6. Personal interview with Richard Stout, press secretary to Morris Udall, January 21, 1976.

7. Personal interview with Charles Snider, campaign manager for George Wallace, July 24, 1975.

8. Personal interview with Paul Clancey, press secretary to Terry Sanford, July 7, 1975.

9. Personal interview with Jim Hightower, campaign manager for Fred Harris, July 8, 1975.

10. Samuel Popkin and others stress the importance to voting of these labels in "What Have You Done for Me Lately: Toward an Incentive Theory of Voting," *American Political Science Review*, 70, 3 (September 1976), pp. 779–805.

11. Michael F. MacLeod, campaign manager for Anderson's National Unity Campaign, remarks at a conference held at Harvard University's Institute of Politics, December 5 and 6, 1980; see *The Campaign for President: 1980 in Retrospect* ed. Jonathan Moore (Cambridge, Mass.: Ballinger, 1981), p. 5.

12. Personal interview with Michael MacLeod, campaign manager for John Anderson, December 6, 1980.

13. Personal interview with Mark Bisnow, press secretary to John Anderson, July 2, 1981.

14. Ibid.

15. Personal interview with Laura Broderick, campaign press secretary to Philip Crane, September 7, 1981.

16. Personal interview with Peter Hart, pollster to Edward Kennedy's presidential campaign, February 2, 1981.

17. Remarks of Richard Wirthlin, Ronald Reagan's campaign pollster, in Moore, *The Campaign for President,* p. 39.

18. Remarks of Eddie Mahe, Jr., campaign director for John Connally, in Moore, *The Campaign for President,* p. 4.

19. Personal interview with Tom Quinn, campaign manager for Jerry Brown, December 6, 1980.

20. Personal interview with Jody Powell, press secretary to Jimmy Carter, July 22, 1975.

21. Personal interviews with Ben Palumbo, campaign manager for Lloyd Bentsen, July 8, 1975 and with Robert Healy, campaign manager for Bentsen, January 22, 1976.

22. Personal interview with Brian Corcoran, press secretary to Henry Jackson, June 12, 1975.

23. Personal interview with Doug Bailey, advertising manager for Howard Baker, December 5, 1980.

24. Personal interview with William Hall, press secretary to Senator Church, July 26, 1975.

25. For an account of the events of the 1972 campaign, see Theodore White, *Making of the President, 1972* (New York: Atheneum, 1973) and James Perry, *Us and Them* (New York: Potter, 1973).

26. The fact that Reagan was placed on the defensive by his statements on transferring $90 billion in federal programs to the states is amply demonstrated by the news coverage he received. See the *New York Times*, January 6, 7, 11, 13, 16, 26, 29, and 31, and February 5 and 21, 1976. The bulk of Reagan's coverage during his January swings into New Hampshire was on this topic.

27. For accounts of the Nashua debate, see the *New York Times*, February 22, 24, and 25, 1980; or the *Washington Post*, February 24 and 25, 1980.

28. See, for example, *Newsweek*, August 23, 1976.

29. This conclusion was supported by research conducted on national-level decisionmaking in the Carter campaign and in a case study of the general election campaign in Ohio. Larry Bartels and Henrietta Wright conducted these research projects.

30. Interview with Patrick Caddell, Jimmy Carter's pollster, by Henrietta Wright, March 1978.

31. A desire to be on the winning side has been recognized as an important motivation of party elites by Nelson W. Polsby and Aaron B. Wildavsky in *Presidential Elections*, 4th Edition (New York: Scribner's, 1976). Thomas Patterson extends the concept to primary electorates in *Mass Media Elections* (New York: Praeger, 1980) and "Press Coverage and Candidate Success in Presidential Primaries: the 1976 Democratic Race," a paper presented at the 1977 annual meetings of the American Political Science Association, Washington, D.C., September 1 and 4, 1977.

32. Remarks of Robert Teeter, pollster for George Bush in Moore, *The Campaign for President,* p. 3.

33. Remarks of Jo-Anne Coe of Senator Robert Dole's office, in Moore, *The Campaign for President,* p. 5.

34. Personal interview with Jay Berman, administrative assistant to Birch Bayh, August 8, 1975.

35. Personal interview with William Wise, press secretary to Birch Bayh, July 10, 1975.

36. For the pace of campaign events, see the advice offered in Arnold Steinberg, *Political Campaign Management* (Lexington, Mass.: D.C. Heath, 1976).

37. Sidney Verba, Norman Nie, and John Petrocik, *The Changing American Voter* (Cambridge, Mass.: Harvard University Press, 1975).

38. Warren Miller and others, "Majority Party in Disarray: Policy Polarization in the 1972 Elections," *American Political Science Review* 70, 3 (September 1976), pp. 753–78; Warren Miller and Terrasa Levitan, *Leadership and Change* (Cambridge, Mass.: Winthrop, 1975), pp. 11–20; and Nimmo and Savage, *Candidates and Their Images.*

39. Robert Reinhold, "Poll Finds Voters Judging '76 Rivals on Personality," *New York Times*, February 13, 1976; Popkin and others, "What Have You Done for Me Lately"; Nimmo and Savage, *Candidates and Their Images*; Page, *Choices and Echoes.*

40. Thomas Patterson, *Mass Media Election* (New York: Praeger, 1980).

41. In addition to the academic literature found in Larry Sabato, *The Rise of Political Consultants* (New York: Basic, 1981); Nimmo and Savage *Candidates and Their Images,* or Page, *Choices and Echoes;* James Perry *The New Politics: The Expanding Technology of Political Manipulation* (New York: Potter, 1968); Joe McGinniss, *The Selling of the President 1968* (New York: Trident, 1969); Tony Schwartz, *The Responsive Chord* (New York: Doubleday, 1974); and Schwartz, *Media: The Second God* (New York: Random House, 1983).

42. Walter Lippman, *Public Opinion* (New York: Macmillan, 1922). The following discusson relies heavily on Nimmo and Savage, *Candidates and Their Images*, pp. 7–9.

43. Kenneth E. Boulding, *The Image* (Ann Arbor, Mich.: University of Michigan Press, 1956.

44. Nimmo and Savage, *Candidates and Their Images*, p. 8.

45. Patterson has undertaken some of this analysis in *Mass Media Election*; for the 1980 campaign see Michael Robinson and Margaret Sheehan, *Over the Wire and on TV* (New York: Russell-Sage, 1983). Also see David Paletz and Robert Entman, *Media Power Politics* (New York: Free Press, 1981).

46. Jules Witcover, "Senator Jackson: Conscientious Loner," *Washington Post,* December 21, 1975, pp. A1 and A6.

47. Douglas E. Kneeland, "Jackson Views the Issues as Ability, Not Charisma," *New York Times*, December 28, 1975, p. 10.

48. For a discussion of the obligations of campaign journalism, see the chapters by James David Barber in *Race for the Presidency*, ed. J.D. Barber (Englewood Cliffs, N.J., Prentice-Hall, 1978).

49. See the chapter by William Bicker, in Barber, ibid.

50. See Bush's comments in Martin Schram's "Iowa Vote: The Strategies," *Washington Post*, January 23, 1980 and David Broder's "Bush Still Faces a Long Haul," *Washington Post*, January 25, 1980. Other ar-

ticles on the significance of Bush's win in Iowa can be found in the *Washington Post*, January 14, 20, and 21, 1980, and Broder's piece comparing Bush to Carter in 1976, *Washington Post*, January 27, 1980.

51. Personal Interview with David Keene, national political director for George Bush, December 5, 1980.

52. Personal interviews with David Keene and Robert Teeter, pollster for George Bush, December 6, 1980. See also their comments at the Harvard Conference, Moore, *Campaign for President* p. 94–100.

53. Interview with Teeter, December 6, 1980.

54. Interview with Keene, December 5, 1980.

55. Ibid.

56. See *Washington Post*, March 14, 1980, p. A16.

57. Helen Dewar, "Udall Knows He's Long Shot for '76," *Washington Post*, October 17, 1974, p. A2.

58. Remarks of John Gabusi, campaign manager for Morris Udall, in Jonathan Moore and Janet Fraser, *Campaign for President* (Cambridge, Mass.: Ballinger, 1978) pp. 89–91.

59. Personal interview with John Gabusi, campaign manager for Udall, December 10, 1976.

60. R.W. Apple, Jr., *New York Times*, February 2, 1975.

61. Christopher Lydon "Democratic Left is Standoffish on Udall's Candidacy," *New York Times*, March 24, 1975.

62. Personal interview with Robert Newman, press secretary to Morris Udall, June 12, 1975.

63. David Broder, "Udall Encourages Conciliator Image," *Washington Post*, December 18, 1975.

64. Douglas Kneeland, "Udall Seeking to Outstrip 'Liberal Pack.' " *New York Times*, January 1, 1976.

65. Drummond Ayres, "Kennedy's Campaign Shift: New Strategy, Disputing Carter on Foreign Policy and Veering Back to the Left, is Viewed as Risky," *New York Times*, January 30, 1980, p. 18A.

66. Remarks by Richard Stearns, delegate selection coordinator for Kennedy, in Moore, *The Campaign for President,* p. 61.

67. Remarks by Paul Kirk, national political director for Kennedy, in Moore, *Campaign for President*, p. 49. The "Mudd interview" was taped in August and broadcast November 4, 1979.

68. Personal interview with Rick Stearns, delegate selection coordinator for Ted Kennedy, February 2, 1980.

69. Interview with Hamilton Jordan, July 22, 1975.

70. Ibid.

71. Christopher Lydon, "Carter is Vague on the Issues," *Atlanta Constitution*, January 13, 1976.

72. Rowland Evans and Robert Novak, *Washington Post*, January, 1976. A number of pieces across the country specifically repeated the Evans and Novak charge; c.f. *Miami Herald,* January 26, 1976. Christopher Lydon, "Carter Now a Target of Criticism," *New York Times,* January 19, 1976; James Wooten, "As Carter Moves into the Limelight, He Becomes Highly Visible and Vulnerable," *New York Times*, February 4, 1976; "Carter's Campaign Program Contrasted with His Record on the Issues while He Was Governor of Georgia," *New York Times*, February 18, 1976; Jules Witcover, "Carter Finds His Words Are Watched," January 27, 1976; George Shelton and Bill Boyarsky, "Carter must Pay Price of Victory: Added Demands Seen for Platform Specifics," *Los Angeles Times*, January 21, 1976.

73. Steven Brill, "Jimmy Carter's Pathetic Lies," Harpers, March, 1976; see also James Ridgeway and Alexander Cockburn, "The Riddle of Jimmy Carter," *Village Voice*, January 12, 1976.

74. *St. Louis Post Dispatch*, April 6, 1976; John Margolis, "Jimmy Carter's Many Faces," *Chicago Tribune*, March 31, 1976.

75. Martin Schram, *Running for President* (New York: Stein and Day, 1977), pp. 30-31.

76. Remarks by Powell, in Moore and Fraser, *Campaign for President* p. 131.

77. Excerpts from the Caddell memo can be found in Schram, *Running for President* p. 120-121.

78. Personal interview with Charlotte Scott, Jimmy Carter's Pennsylvania press secretary, April 22, 1976.

79. Stuart Auerbach "Carter Unveils Health Plan, Denies DC Local Squabble," *Washington Post*, April 17, 1976.

80. David Broder, "Carter Details Economic Plan," *Washington Post*, April 24, 1976.

81. Roland Evans and Robert Novak, "Jimmy Carter's Tactical Problems" *Washington Post*, April 14, 1976.

82. David Broder, "Carter Re-Gears His Campaign" *Washington Post*, April 26, 1976.

83. Remarks by Gerald Rafshoon, in Moore and Fraser, *Campaign for President*, p. 99; see also Schram, *Running for President*, p. 121.

84. Rafshoon interview, March 21, 1976.

85. Personal interview with Charlotte Scott, press secretary for Jimmy Carter in North Carolina, Pennsylvania and California, April 22, 1976.

86. Interview with Rafshoon, December 3, 1976.

87. Ibid.

88. Howell Raines, "Reagan Campaign Runs into Unexpected Obstacles," *New York Times*, August 24, 1980, p. 28.

89. Howell Raines, *New York Times*, August 19, 1980, p. 1.

90. *New York Times*, August 21, 1980.

91. *New York Times*, August 24, 1980.

92. Howell Raines, *New York Times*, August 24, 1980.

93. Vic Gold discusses the growing openness of campaign advisers in discussing the image problems and thematic strategies in *PR as in President* (Garden City, N.Y.: Doubleday, 1977).

94. Christopher Lydon, "Ford's First National Campaign: Incumbent In The Role of Underdog," *New York Times*, December 22, 1975, p. 1.

95. Tom Matthews, "Ford in Trouble," *Newsweek*, December 22, 1975, pp. 20-23.

96. *U.S. News & World Report*, January 12, 1976.

97. Ron Nessen asserts that his outburst over Ford's news coverage was not a calculated effort to diffuse the image; see *It Sure Looks Different from the Inside* (Chicago: Playboy, 1978), pp. 167-170.

98. *Wall Street Journal*, January 14, 1976.

99. Personal interview with Larry Speakes, deputy White House press secretary, January 22, 1976.

100. Dennis Farney, "President's Strategists Polish His New Image: No More Mr. Nice Guy," *Wall Street Journal*, January 14, 1976, p. 1.

101. See R.W. Apple, Jr., "New Hampshire Voters Get a Clear View of Ford," *New York Times*, February 22, 1976.

102. Dennis Farney, *Wall Street Journal*, January 14, 1976.

103. James Naughton, "Aides Call President 'Amateur Campaigner,' " *New York Times*, February 22, 1976.

104. Personal interview with Peter Kaye, press secretary to President Ford Committee, January 13, 1976.

105. Personal interview with Rob Quartel, acting research director, President Ford Committee, April 1977; see also Nessen's description of coordinating surrogates attacks on Carter, in *It Sure Looks Different from the Inside,* pp. 253, 255-256.

106. Interview with Kaye, January 13, 1977.

107. Witcover, *Marathon*, pp. 373-397.

108. Remarks of Peter Kaye at conference sponsored by American Assembly, Mt. Kisco, N.Y., May, 1978.

109. Teeter's remarks are quoted in Witcover, *Marathon*, p. 385.

110. Robert Reinhold, "Poll Finds President Strong as Candidate," *New York Times*, April 23, 1976.

111. Witcover, *Marathon: The Pursuit of The Presidency, 1972-1976* (New York: Viking, 1977), pp. 590-591, describes the incident, noting that it knocked coverage of Carter's problems created by his *Playboy* interview off the front page of most newspapers.

112. Tom Wicker of the *New York Times* made these remarks on *NBC Forum on the 1976 Presidential Elections*. Access to the transcript obtained courtesy of Stan Losak (New York: NBC News, 1977).

113. October 18, 1976. The article was undoubtedly prepared before the second debates. The Carter profile four weeks earlier was entitled "Sizing Up Carter," *Newsweek*, September 13, 1976.

114. Remarks of Richard Wirthlin, Reagan's pollster at the 1981 American Political Science Association panel on Pollsters and the 1980 Elections, September 6, 1981, New York.

115. The exit polls conducted by both ABC and CBS demonstrated that each campaign had succeeded in communicating these concerns to their supporters. Carter failed to convince enough voters that this was a sufficient concern to vote against Reagan.

116. See the report of the American Political Science Association's Committee on Political Parties, "Toward A More Responsible Two-Party System," *American Political Science Review* (September 1950), supplement; E.E. Schattsneider, *Party Government* (New York: Rinehart, 1942); Effron Kirkpatrick, "Toward a More Responsible Two-Party System": Political Science, Policy Science, or Pseudo Science," *American Political Science Review*, 65:4 (December 1971), pp. 965–990.

117. Michael J. Robinson, "Public Affairs Television and the Growth of Political Malaise," *American Political Science Review*, 71, 2 (June 1976), pp. 409–432; and Robinson, "American Political Legitimacy in an Era of Electronic Journalism," *Television as a Social Force,* eds. D. Cater and R. Alder (New York: Praeger, 1975).

118. For a forcefully argued view that intraelite bargaining occurred during nominations before media politics and is missing today, see Terry Sanford, *A Danger of Democracy* (Boulder, Col.: Westview, 1981).

119. For a more complete argument on this point, see Nelson W. Polsby *The Consequences of Party Reform* (New York: Oxford University Press, 1983).

6

The Horserace:
Scenarios, Standards,
and Benchmarks

The existence of the press is why I have always been such a believer in trying to divine what I refer to as "motion" or timing aspects to a campaign. If you can keep your motion, keep it moving, you'll be written off as a winner all the time just by virtue of that. . . . A lot of the importance of that has to do with the press; if it weren't for the press, that wouldn't be that important. —John Sears

It seems to me that this campaign has been more tactically dominated than any that I can remember going back to 1960. Not to say that all those other campaigns were all that rich with substantive issues, but this one especially. And that seems to me to be somewhat paradoxical: The expression on the part of everyone is we really want to know about these candidates and their issues, but, in fact . . . the news is results. —Ed Kosner, *Newsweek*

At its most basic level, campaign reporting is the story of electoral success or failure—"the thrill of victory and the agony of defeat." Campaign news might provide the electorate with the means for making an informed choice about the candidates' abilities, character, policy questions, and supporters. As argued in chapter 5, policy questions or character stories most often require a direct link to the candidate's electoral prospects for journalists to perceive them as newsworthy. News coverage sheds more light on topics that may make an electoral difference rather than on substantive policies. Both the news-reporting process and the strategies of campaigners contribute to this narrowing of news content.

Reporting the progress of the presidential horserace constitutes the second major topic of the substantive interaction between campaigners and journalists. Predicting outcomes and interpreting electoral events occupies much of the attention of politicians, reporters, and, presumably, voters. Not only are journalists interested in these aspects, campaigners firmly believe that this reporting directly affects their electoral success; they become preoccupied with ensuring that journalists view their candidate's electoral prospects as credible.

Unfortunately, untangling the purely political calculations of campaign decisions from considerations of how events will be interpreted by reporters is almost impossible. Each campaign's plan for achieving the nomination inherently involved both political considerations of how to acquire support and estimates of the effects of news reporting. The last two presidential campaigns did include documentable instances in which projected news reporting was the dominant factor in campaign decisionmaking.

Horserace reporting may consist of statements about the progress of the various candidates on three different conceptual levels. From the most general to the more specific, journalists discuss their general view of the race's progress ("scenarios"), the mileposts candidates pass along the way ("standards"), and measurements of how each competitor is faring at different points ("benchmarks"). On each plane, journalists describe the candidates' progress, while campaigners seek to influence both the content of campaign news reporting and the perceptions of those working in the news industry.

At the most general level, campaign journalism contains notions about the dynamics of the race as a whole. For example, a nomination campaign may be seen as a long, drawn-out struggle in a divided party or as a brief competition between several contenders in which one will break out of the pack rather early. A frontrunner may survive challenges to his claim to the nomination and move on to unify the party. General elections may be cast variously as a referendum on the incumbents' first term or as a choice between two equally unattractive candidates or as an ideological crusade by an improbable contender. An independent or third-party candidacy could be described as a noble challenge to electoral politics as usual, or it may be cast as a spoiler, drawing votes and possible victory away from one of the legitimate contenders.

Different scenarios highlight the importance of different standards which can be used to gauge the progress of the race. The wide selection of possible indicators available to journalists and other observers greatly complicates the task of predicting presidential election races. Thus, horserace reporting also involves a search for appropriate standards with which to assess and compare the performance of the contending candidates. For example, the emphasis placed upon victory in early primaries may differ, depending on whether one believes that a dark horse candidate will emerge to eliminate his competitors or that support within the party is so fragmented that a multiballot convention will be required.

Finally, journalists develop specific benchmarks to rate the progress of each candidacy along a projected trajectory to the nomination. Given the ambiguity of the selection process, agreement on appropriate standards will not suffice. Journalists must also judge what level of performance on those indicators is adequate for each candidacy. For example, Kennedy's campaign managers complained that, at several points in their nomination quest, news reporting assigned must-win status to an upcoming primary.[1] Before the start of the primaries, to cite another example, news reporting may attach great importance to an unexpectedly strong showing in a straw poll among party activists in a given state.

Once widely disseminated and accepted, scenarios, standards, and benchmarks combine to establish the strategic environment within which campaigns compete. These propositions are likely to be linked—the acceptance of one scenario will lead to reporting focused on certain standards with implicit benchmarks for each competitor.

As evidence in this chapter documents, campaigners compete at each level to promote the acceptance of propositions favorable to their campaign. In a two-candidate race, for example, the initially favored campaign will advocate a scenario postulating a "quick kill"—early primary results will determine the nomination question. Their opponents will most likely argue for a long, drawn-out conception of the race. The financially secure campaign will point to the importance of money as a standard to predict electoral victory, while others will contend that zealous volunteers make the difference.

The role of media politics in the conduct of presidential campaigns is revealed not simply by the efforts of politicians to maneuver perceptions surrounding the progress of the race; it is more consequential in campaigners' efforts to accommodate political strategies to journalistic consensus, once it becomes established. On horserace questions, our interviews uncovered abundant evidence of influence in both these directions: campaigners arguing for their construction of events to be cast as reality in news reporting, as well as conformity to journalists' perceptual consensus.

Strategies and Scenarios

Each presidential campaign develops an elaborate scenario according to which its candidate will secure the nomination or win the election. These scenarios can be partially distinguished from actual political strategies. Scenarios are made public and intended by campaigners to influence the perceptual environment of the campaign and the interpretations of objective campaign events. Scenarios serve both as the basis of appeal to party activists and voters motivated by prospects of electoral victory, and as an effort to convince journalists that the campaign has serious prospects of victory.

Despite the possible gap between public scenarios and clandestine political strategies, the former is something of an approximation of the campaign's true design.[2] A scenario must accord, to a large degree, with observable campaign behaviors because reporters are almost certain to notice if campaign actions are at variance with their verbal descriptions. For example, early in the 1976 campaign, Udall's strategists repeatedly told the press that the New Hampshire primary would be the real starting point of their campaign, thus attempting to obscure their extensive effort in the January Iowa caucuses. Most of the national headquarters staff was trans-

ferred to Iowa, but the Washington headquarters took telephone messages
for those working in Iowa as if they had just stepped out of the office for
lunch. Of course, the national press soon uncovered the attempt and concluded that Udall had made an all-out effort and failed badly.

> [T]here's no sense to play games with them; they see through it . . . . We
> were trying, for a while I guess, to keep quiet how much help [from the na-
> tional headquarters] we'd sent out there in way of bodies. And [Witcover]
> walked into the [state] headquarters and began asking, "Where are you
> from?" and that kind of thing. Pretty soon he had a pretty good grasp that
> "God, there's a sudden influx out here!"[3]

From the perspective of campaigns that rely on media politics, scenarios
serve multiple purposes. At the simplest level, they provide calculated—not
casual—answers to persistent questioning by journalists about the campaign's progress. To a varying extent, the scenarios were discussed and
agreed upon by top-level campaign management, especially in those critical
elements where the public scenarios differed from the actual political
strategy. News coverage of a campaign's blueprint for electoral victory may
reach political activists from whom the campaign seeks to attract support,
volunteer efforts, and money. A plausible scenario may also heighten the
interest of reporters and generate greater news coverage. Finally, although
voters may not be aware of the details of political strategies, campaigners
hope to project through the news a general perception of serious prospects for
electoral victory. Campaigners want their candidate to look like a winner.

Like campaign themes, scenarios are not free of external constraints.
The number of competing candidates, the themes of political support of
competitors, the number and order of primaries, the level of financial support, and the interest groups supporting a particular candidate are the
political realities that campaigners must consider when developing their
political strategies. The scenarios they articulate to the news media are versions of these strategies, versions especially tailored to projected news
coverage of campaign events.

Both campaigners and journalists bring to their work assumptions as to
how the political process will evolve. They are formulated, in large part, out
of past experiences, particularly the immediate "last war." Because these
presumptions are shared, campaigners are able to plan their political and
accompanying news strategies with reasonably accurate expectations as to
how the journalists will initially view the election dynamics. As a result,
estimates of reported news are so ingrained in the covert strategies and
public scenarios developed by campaign operatives that it is difficult to
isolate the independent impact of media considerations.

However, 1980 was not a carbon copy of 1976, nor 1976 of 1972. In
each year journalists were forced to change their assumptions about the dy-

namics of the race. When these changes became clear to campaigners, the resulting adjustments in campaign strategies provide graphic illustrations of the media's impact on contemporary campaigning.

Varieties of Scenarios

As discussed in chapter 2, the nomination portion of the election year is much more indefinite and subject to interpretation than the general election period. Therefore, this discusssion of scenarios will concentrate almost entirely on the nomination process. We asked our campaign informants to describe their plans for gaining the nomination before the primaries actually began and obtained their projections of the unfolding of future events. For the most part, these scenarios reflected the logic campaigns used to convince political journalists of their seriousness. These political strategies fell into distinct battle plans depending on estimates of the major factors shaping nomination politics.

In examining the strategic options available to presidential candidates in 1964, Polsby and Wildavsky contrast the public front-running aspirant who contests primaries in the hope of securing sufficient delegate strength with the dark horse candidate who hopes that no frontrunner will emerge and the convention will have to turn to other candidates who can unify the party.[4] After the 1976 and 1980 campaigns, this neat dichotomy appears too limited. On one side, the possibilities of a dark horse strategy appear to be seriously eroded by the volume of news coverage currently devoted to presidential campaigns.[5] One cannot organize and escape notice; examination of one's strategy by political reporters initiates the same benchmarking process that determines whether active candidates are viewed as serious threats. For example, on March 1, 1980, the *New York Times* published a story in which Gerald Ford revealed his view that Reagan would prove an unelectable candidate and mused that he himself might be forced to enter the race.[6] The article touched off a period of intense activity by Ford and his 1976 political advisers. Their deliberation and the reaction of others were fully covered over the next week in the press, which increased the pressure on Ford to make a definitive statement that he would not be a candidate.

A similar instance occurred in April 1976. The press analysis of the Pennsylvania primary results primarily concentrated upon how they affected Humphrey's noncandidate strategy. The volume of speculation eventually forced the noncandidate into announcing that he did not plan on campaigning for the nomination—an explicit recognition that a dark horse strategy was no longer viable.

In the other half of Polsby and Wildavsky's dichotomy, an even more significant change has occurred. Major differences can be detected in the political strategies of active candidates.

The "Outright Win" Candidate. Two important changes have occurred in nomination politics since 1968. The number of primaries has expanded and changes in party rules have produced a greater correspondence between the presidential preference of voters or caucus participants, on the one hand, and the delegates awarded to the competing candidates, on the other. Primaries are no longer important strictly for their demonstration effect. Although potential nominees could once enter primaries mainly to impress local and state party leaders who controlled the decisive delegate votes, now presidential aspirants enter primaries to elect a majority of the convention votes.

Despite the expenditure limitations of the Federal Elections Campaign Act of 1974, seven candidates in 1976 and 1980 planned at various stages of the race to enter enough primaries and caucuses to capture the nomination outright.

In 1980, Carter's manager was most explicit:

> Our strategy was to run everywhere. What that really did was have a balancing effect both in terms of our political strength and winnability, from start to finish, across the board. . . . We had more of a national campaign than the Kennedy campaign did. . . . So by virtue of this gradual ball control, delegate accumulation sort of thing, we were never led to believe that "we would blow it." I mean, not even "Super Tuesday" and losing five out of eight scared hell out of us at that point because we knew we had the delegates.[7]

While favorable poll rating for much of 1979 may have tempted Kennedy's advisers into hoping that they would win handily, the initial strategic plans of his campaign were laid assuming a drawn-out race, as had occurred on the Republican side in 1976:

> I don't think we ever felt that we would adopt an early knock-out strategy when you had an incumbent President. . . . Early on, there was a feeling that it would not be a cinch in the primaries at all, that it might well be a long, protracted struggle.[8]

After Kennedy's initial setback in Iowa, Carl Wagner, the campaign director, envisioned a long-run shift in his favor:

> President Carter was better off yesterday than today; he's better off today than tomorrow. . . . From a delegate perspective, you could write the January, February and March primaries either way—Carter wins or Kennedy wins. The point is that in the middle of March probably less than two hundred or three hundred delegates will separate the candidates.[9]

Both the Wallace and Carter campaigns in 1976 opted for win-outright strategies:

We are going to run in all the primaries with the exception of, possibly, New Hampshire. . . . We'll be in there because under your proportional representation law . . . you get that number of delegates directly proportional to the vote. You know, we would be foolish not to, because, I think, the Governor is good for a pretty good chunk of the vote in most any state in this country. . . .[10]

The sequence of the primaries, from our point of view, dictates that you establish yourself in that first period when there are, granted, not that many votes, delegate votes, at stake. If you get through that first period, you've then got to put it together and get, you know, those 1,500 votes. . . . I feel like we're the only campaign that's trying to win the nomination before the convention. . . . Everybody else has developed a very coy strategy for kind of trying to end up at the convention with enough votes that they can parlay into the Presidential nomination.[11]

In 1980, John Connally initially planned long efforts to contest every possible delegate vote with frontrunner Ronald Reagan. Connally's manager, Eddie Mahe, argued that it would not be sufficient to defeat Reagan in one or two primaries; rather, Mahe thought it would be necessary to beat him all the way to the convention:

We felt we had to take Ronald Reagan on more head-to-head at some point because his base and our base were too much the same. . . . We tried to do that at a national level. We could not attempt to take him on just in Iowa. . . . We had to take Governor Reagan on nationally. . . . John Connally had to be a national candidate.[12]

This calculation led to Connally's decision to decline public funding and avoid the expenditure limitations of the long campaign.

In 1976, after Ronald Reagan won the North Carolina primary, both the Reagan and Ford staffs recognized that neither would concede defeat until the other controlled a convention majority. They were forced to struggle over every delegate vote, a possibility which they had envisioned earlier but hoped would not be necessary:

You wanted to do well in the primaries under the old system because it gave you something to talk about in the convention states. It gave you the ability to say that your man could win, whether he was a good campaigner, and a number of other political arguments. . . . But now, you're not in the primaries really for that purpose; you're in there to secure delegates. So it isn't a matter any more of selecting which ones you're running in; you have to examine them all from a delegates standpoint, and decide, more on a piecemeal basis, to what degree—not whether you will or not, but to what degree—he will participate in just about all of them.[13]

The early primaries will be very important, particularly New Hampshire and Florida. But, if they're close, then we'll move on. . . . If Illinois stays close, we then move on again. It's almost a one-at-a-time situation.[14]

The similarities among these campaigns reveal at least two reasons why campaigns envision the race as a long siege and plan to run in as many primaries as possible. First, most faced a major opponent with perceived staying power: Carter versus Kennedy, the Ford-Reagan contest of 1976, and Connally's challenge to Reagan's dominance in 1980. Second, as party outsiders who could not expect to persuade large elements of the party establishment to support their candidacy, Wallace and Carter both planned to seize the Democratic nomination in 1976 on their own. But these factors do not completely determine the campaign's strategy. In early 1980, George Bush was in the first position and John Anderson second, yet neither opted for an outright win battle plan. Campaigners do exercise some choice in the selection of political strategies.

The "Winnow In" Candidate. A second nomination blueprint assumes that while mobilizing sufficient resources to elect a convention majority is simply impossible, the primaries will yield a conclusive result. Some time before the conventions in July and August, party leaders and uncommitted delegates would throw their support behind a clear choice as determined by victories in contested primaries.

According to this scenario, the early primaries narrow the number of realistic candidates sharply and force the survivors into a critical test. From this primary (or finite set of primaries), one obvious frontrunner emerges, while the other candidacies are damaged beyond repair. At that point, the frontrunner may be far short of a convention majority, but he will gradually acccumulate support for a first-ballot victory. In the words which campaigners use to describe this process, the competition is "winnowed out"; the survivor "winnowed in."[15]

This nomination strategy is underlined by a heavy emphasis on the impact of the perceptual environment and effects of news commentary. Throughout the nomination battle, journalists will be looking for critical primaries that eliminate candidates. Interpretations of these pivotal contests disparage the nomination prospects of candidates making poor showings, thereby weakening their capacity to mobilize resources for subsequent primaries. The media are expected to designate the key contests on which the nomination hinges and to winnow out the losers.

The political strategy of the Kennedy campaign evolved considerably over the course of the 1980 primaries, shifting principally on the basis of its declining fortunes. With the resurgence of Carter's popularity accompanying the events in Iran, Kennedy was forced to fall back upon a subset of primaries to be held in the large industrial states, the strongholds of the Democratic party:

> In terms of delegate counts, there really are two major blocks of states that
> must be won to win the nomination. There are five industrial states in April

and May. . . . These are those states which constitute almost 25 percent of the convention. And there are the June 3 primaries; 22 percent of the delegates are chosen on the last day of the race. . . . The election will be resolved in the major industrial states.[16]

By winning in these states, Kennedy's campaign hoped to demonstrate Carter's weakness and either force him from the race or convince enough delegates to come over to Kennedy's side: "If the president is upset there, momentum will roll against him." Of course, by the end of the primaries, Kennedy's only hope was that somehow the Carter delegates would desert him.

On the Republican side in 1980, most of the contenders saw their race as boiling down to a few key states that would decide the contest. In most cases, their plans, based upon a misreading of Carter's success in 1976, focused on the value of early primary victories in eliminating all other contenders. Robert Teeter, Bush's pollster, explained the initial strategy:

We simply followed the rules that everyone has come to know that [early] primaries and early caucuses are far and away the most important—they're everything now. . . . to some significant degree the Bush campaign was the Carter campaign of 1976.[17]

As the campaign progessed, Teeter argued that the dynamics of the race hinged on a few specific events:

He wins in Iowa; he either wins or does very well in New Hampshire; probably wins in Vermont and Massachusetts; does very well, or wins, in the Southern states; and, I would think, wins or does very well in Illinois. One of two things happen . . . he continues to beat Baker quite badly and then he beats Reagan and, therefore, he finishes in first place and he is well on his way to being nominated by Illinois. The second possibility is that he continues to beat Baker and runs essentially even with Reagan, and . . . he and Reagan get into a relatively protracted fight and he wins at the convention.[18]

Meanwhile, the Baker strategy was essentially the same but the results were reversed:

Howard Baker couldn't become nominated unless he beat Ronald Reagan. Howard Baker couldn't beat Ronald Reagan unless the field was winnowed down to Baker and Reagan. He had to stop Bush. . . . [Baker] was absolutely confident that the winnowing out process would be pretty quick.[19]

Both Bush and Baker sought to replicate only the early-primary part of the strategy that achieved victory for Carter in 1976. In fact, all the Republican candidates, except Reagan and Connally, believed that the race could be won by victory in a finite number of state contests. Phil Crane adopted a similar strategy, hoping that if he could keep his campaign alive,

Reagan's mantle would fall on him should the frontrunner falter in the early stages.[20] Meanwhile, Anderson focused on states in which Democrats could cross over or in which independents could vote in the Republican primaries. Dole looked to states with a substantial farm population.[21]

Some contenders for the 1976 Democratic nomination adopted similar strategies. Rather than envisioning the winnowing primaries piled up at the beginning, however, they counted on critical contests occurring throughout the primary season as the field progressively narrowed:

> We're really looking at the industrial north, and it starts in Massachusetts—which we think we can do very well in Massachusetts—down through Rhode Island and New York, New Jersey, Pennyslvania, Ohio, Michigan, Indiana and Illinois right across there. That's our area . . . and California, that's our target area.[22]

> the brokering will occur well into the late primaries, when it's obvious that some of the candidates are not going to have the strength going into the convention, and there's going to be a single person. Then, the brokering will go from the secondary candidates who will have delegate strength and they'll . . . release their delegates. . . . [I]t will be a first ballot.[23]

> So Fred Harris, the dark horse of the campaign, the populist, etc., etc., comes in the top three, and, I think, in the process of coming in the top three knocks out some of the liberals . . . the middle primaries—Wisconsin, Pennsylvania, or whatever—we hope to be in the top two, and, continuing to winnow out the field. And by California I think there will be two candidates . . . going into California I think that there'll be a conservative . . . and Fred Harris.[24]

The "Brokered Convention" Candidate. A third strategy was followed by some campaigns in 1976, based upon their assumption that the primaries would yield an inconclusive result. These campaign tacticians supposed that the primary process was too fragmented to produce a single choice, because no single candidate could hurdle the financial and organizational barriers posed by the large number of primaries. A large candidate field would split up the delegates into small groups. No candidate would have an incentive to drop out of the race early because proportional representation would guarantee weaker candidates at least some additional delegate strength and federal subsidiaries would allow these candidates to stay active.

In short, some Democratic campaigners calculated that their party's convention would require more than one ballot to award the nomination and planned their strategy so that delegate support would flow to them after the first ballot. However, in most statements of the "brokered convention" strategy the campaigners were generally vague about who would do the brokering—whether state party leaders, candidate organizations, ascriptive groups like the black caucus or the labor caucus, or party chairman Robert Strauss.

Note that under the brokered convention formula, extreme fragmentation would return primaries to their previous role of providing a demonstration of vote-getting ability. Candidates would enter primaries representing a variety of electoral settings: northern industrial, midcentral, southern, and western. Late-entering candidates Church and Brown thought that victories in primaries held in May and June would give their campaigns momentum going into the convention whereas the early entrants would be exhausted by then. All expected newsmen to forecast growing support and general election success, thus influencing the behavior of delegates and party leaders:

> There's two keys to it this time, as our strategy sees it. Number one: a winner is not going to emerge in the primaries. . . . This is what Bentsen's trying to do: he's not trying to get a bandwagon going, or knock everybody out of the box except Bentsen. His goal is to pick up delegates in areas of strength; go to the convention with 250 to 500 delegates; [and] be a factor at the convention; be right in the middle of the brokering process.[25]

> No candidate is going to win more than, I'll say, six or eight of the thirty primaries, and [therefore] would you rather go to the convention being the candidate who won the last six or eight or the first six or eight? Because the candidate who wins the last six or eight is, at the same time, defeating candidates who won some of the first ones, so you arrive with momentum as the man of the hour. . . . It's a fact that no candidate under this law can truly afford to spend enough to win in all thirty primaries. So you have to pick your shots; and we're picking late.[26]

> As I read the rules and as I look at the large number of states that are proportional. . . . Then I've just got to assume that nobody can pick up 1,500 votes on the first ballot. [Bayh's] got great skill at brokering; he has managed to do it for some time. He has strong allies among the constitutent groups that are going to be represented at the convention, i.e., blacks, women, labor. . . .[27]

> We made our move right after Florida, prior to Wisconsin and New York and Pennsylvania, and prior to Hubert Humphrey's dropping out of the process. It looked as if Frank Church was going to be in the process, Mo Udall might win Wisconsin, and Scoop Jackson could win New York and Pennsylvania. In such a fractionated process, it seemed possible that a young governor coming out of California and winning maybe one primary outside California might be in a good position.[28]

> Out of a combination of primaries and picking up from people that have folded before the first ballot, there is a possibility of a first ballot: I think that that's a slim possibility, but there is a possibility. Whether it will be multi-ballot or only 2 or 3 ballots is another question.[29]

Categorizing each campaign into a single slot is difficult. For one thing, strategies are adjusted as circumstances change. Ford and Reagan altered their plans; Carter won as a winnow-in candidate. For another, individuals within the same campaign may differ about how their combined effort should proceed.[30] Finally, despite the necessity of planning and the desirability of giving to newsmen the same cohesive scenario, campaigners themselves may not be very clear on the strategy they are pursuing. Despite these difficulties, the interview data and analysis of profile articles in the *Washington Post* and the *New York Times* indicate that the original nomination strategies of the 1980 and 1976 campaign fell into the groupings presented in table 6-1.

The contrast in strategies adopted in 1976 and 1980 indicate the factors that campaigners weigh heavily in their planning to secure electoral victory. The last-war syndrome does appear to explain the disappearance of the brokered convention strategy. But, in 1975 many campaigners were impressed principally by the vast changes that had occurred since 1972: the new delegate selection rules, the imposition of campaign finance laws, and the increased numbers of primaries. They convinced themselves that the race would be different in overall dynamics. Once 1976 turned out like the Democratic race in 1972, the common wisdom in 1980 became a replication of Carter's 1976 strategy, or at least part of it.

The difference evident in table 6-1 between those who attempted to win the nomination outright and those who sought to eliminate their opponents in a series of critical tests, moreover, appears to be related not so much to strategic brilliance as to the resources reasonably foreseeable at the time of planning. Frontrunners or those who could expect success in preprimary fundraising chose to run for as many delegates as possible. The

Table 6-1
Political Strategies of Presidential Campaigns (1976–1980)

	1980	
Outright Win	*Winnowing*	*Brokered Convention*
Early Kennedy	Middle Kennedy	Late Kennedy
Carter	Brown	
Connally	Anderson	
	Bush	
Late Reagan	Early Reagan	
	Baker	
	Crane	
	Dole	
	1976	
Carter	Jackson	Bentsen
Wallace	Udall	Brown
Late Ford	Early Ford	Bayh
Late Reagan	Early Reagan	Church
	Shriver	Sanford
	Harris	

others based their strategy on concentrating their limited resources in a few states.

General Election Strategies

The general election strategies of the two major candidates are less complex strategically. Without the sequential process of the nomination race, plans for winning the general election involve primarily estimates of which states are most likely to produce an electoral college majority. Momentum, however, is still an important concept. Arnold Steinberg, for example, argues that an accelerating pace of campaign activities and television advertising can impart a sense of growth in political support.[31] In both 1976 and 1980, the candidates sought to create the perception of movement in the last few weeks by accelerating the pace of advertisements and campaign events.[32] In both years, poll stories and news reporting generally described the race as difficult to predict because of changes in support in the final week.

Interaction over Scenarios and Strategy

Initial strategies are devised as a response to the political circumstances faced by each candidate, including projected news coverage, as forecast by campaigners. As these circumstances change, the campaign staffs, most often motivated purely by political calculations, adjust their strategies and related scenarios. For example, the changing perception of the 1976 Republican nomination race forced both Ford and Reagan staffers to modify their strategies. The examples that follow however, illustrate the interplay of strategies and journalistic consensus.

Early Losses. Several very different candidacies who failed to win early primaries or caucuses confronted the same strategic difficulty. Reagan and Udall in 1976 and Kennedy and Bush in 1980 all tried to convince journalists to focus on other primaries later in the season and to use those as tests of their viability. In each case, the candidate eventually failed. But in every case the campaigns proved to have a good deal more vitality left than was stated in the premature obituaries analyzing their early losses. Although Udall never did win a primary, he remained in the race until the final week, running second in nine states. Reagan had to endure four losses to Ford before he finally won in North Carolina (March 23). About the same point in the race four years later, Kennedy defeated Carter in New York and Connecticut (March 25). On the Republican side, Bush beat Reagan in the Iowa caucuses (January 21) and the Massachusetts (March 4) and four other primaries, but was in trouble from the moment he lost the New Hampshire primary (February 26).

To a large degree, these politicians got into trouble because they failed to accomplish their own stated objective:

> The campaign was in real peril after we did not do all that well [in Iowa]. But I think the problem was really set by the Senator himself. He had, inadvertently and unfortunately, in the fall, right after the straw caucus in Florida, pointed to Iowa as the first test of the campaign. . . . That set up an expectation for the outcome in Iowa which was difficult for us to escape or explain away when the campaign did not go well.[33]

Because they had explicitly established their initial scenarios in the minds of reporters, the Udall, Kennedy, and Bush campaigns were not very successful in shifting their strategic grounds once their initial efforts failed. Reagan, on the other hand, was able to alter his initial scenario in 1980 and to convince journalists to accept a new game plan:

> With the loss in Iowa . . . the basic strategy of a quick knockout blow setting into force a series of steps that were already being planned could not be maintained. That is, it was agreed, after the New Hampshire primary, that we would not place ourselves in a position of putting all our chips on one state or one event, that we would run the primaries with backup options that would provide us with a way out should events not unfold as we had hoped they might.[34]

The difference between Reagan and those candidates who failed to persuade reporters to adopt a different scenario is attributable to two factors. First, the margin of Reagan's victory in New Hampshire was considerable (50 percent to 23 percent for Bush); his convincing win was in stark contrast to the polls that showed the New Hampshire race to be almost even. Second, in 1976 Reagan established a track record of strong performances in southern and western primaries after initial defeats. Even so, there were some important weaknesses in Reagan's long-campaign scenario. For journalists to accept that game plan meant ignoring a very severe financial problem that began to develop. Reagan's March disclosure statement revealed that Reagan had spent almost three quarters of the permissible funds by the first week of the primary season.

Udall and the Iowa Caucus. Reagan's planners were somewhat caught off-guard by the attention given the Iowa caucus results. They watched with some dismay as George Bush received extensive news coverage that rapidly increased his name recognition.[35] They should not have been so surprised. The level of news attention given to the caucuses in the Democratic races had increased steadily in 1972 and 1976. Back in 1976, Mo Udall's campaign had been significantly affected by this change.

In their initial decisionmaking, the Udall campaigners planned to make their first solid effort in the New Hampshire primary, assuming that, as in years past, the major media would begin nomination coverage with the first primary. Campaigning in New Hampshire, Udall would be able to attract considerable press coverage; winning New Hampshire would catapult Udall into the frontrunner status. It was a familiar route: "Our strategy," explained Stewart Udall, the candidate's brother, "has to be a McGovern/Jack Kennedy strategy in the key states, which are New Hampshire, Massachusetts and Wisconsin."[36] Other interviews confirmed the same strategy. Although Udall did have the beginning of an organization in Iowa, where precinct caucuses were scheduled on January 19, their first major test was planned for New Hampshire.

Beginning on October 27, however, the national political reporters began to devote so much attention to the upcoming Iowa caucuses that it became apparent to the Udall staff that the first big splash of the 1976 race would occur there, rather than in New Hampshire. R.W. Apple's piece in the *New York Times* not only put the spotlight for the first time on Carter's growing strength, but it also signaled the fact that the Iowa caucuses would be an important event from the perspective of news-reporting organizations.[37] As in 1972, Iowa would provide the media's first opportunity to observe which candidates were "emerging from the pack." Reacting to criticism, Witcover justified the reporters' interest in Iowa (emphasis added):

> The media's seizing upon Iowa, though it chose only 47 of 3,008 delegates to the Democratic National Convention, was both understandable and defensible. . . . In 1976, if there were going to be early signals, the fourth estate was going to be on the scene *en masse* to catch them.[38]

Media attention caused Udall campaigners to reconsider their decision to bypass Iowa. As frequently happens, the campaign staff was divided over the best course to follow. Jack Quinn, the campaign political director, argued for making a major, albeit eleventh hour, effort in Iowa. His position was reinforced by Ken Bode, a key adviser who, after an exploratory trip into the state, produced an internal memo:

> Iowa justified the expense. It will be covered like the first primary always has been in the national press. If we can emerge as the clear liberal choice in Iowa, the payoffs in New Hampshire will be enormous.[39]

Despite the argument by others in the campaign that it was too late, Quinn's side won with the additional argument that even if they didn't win Iowa, at least their presence there would keep a liberal frontrunner from emerging in the headlines until New Hampshire. The Udall campaign committed about

$80,000 and, an even scarcer resource, ten days of the candidate's time to the Iowa effort.

While it can never be determined whether this decision to switch resources from New Hampshire resulted in Udall's loss there, it certainly did not improve their New Hampshire prospects. All the Udall staffers we interviewed acknowledge the preeminence of the media considerations in their strategy shift. In retrospect, they felt this change was a major error:

> Iowa was regrettable in that we had no inclination or desire to devote resources and time and money to Iowa. But it became such a media event that I think some of our staff people—national staff and Iowa staff—panicked in the face of it, and we rushed in headlong.[40]

> In 1975, the argument had been made in the press in the spring of that year that they were going to take another look somewhere besides New Hampshire. Well, I never believed that, I believed that the first election where people walked into and pulled the levers, that that was the beginning. . . . I just said we put all our marbles in New Hampshire and we start there. . . . Then when other people who were then in campaign positions began to take the position that the press might do it [in Iowa]. . . . They reversed a decision that had been made and was there for a year. . . . The worst thing that happened was we took ten days away from the New Hampshire schedule, Mo's traveling time.[41]

By any criterion, the change in the status of their effort in Iowa was a major decision; it was primarily motivated by predictions of news reporting rather than by an analysis of delegates to be won, opportunities for success, opponents to be defeated, or organizational support (such as volunteers) to be captured for future primaries.

The Later Democratic Primaries. In the perceptual environment surrounding the 1976 Democratic race, Carter became firmly established as the front-runner after the Florida primary and as the probable nominee after defeating Jackson and Udall in Pennsylvania. By April 27, Carter had finished first in delegate or preference votes in seven of nine primaries.

From that point on, however, his campaign was less successful, losing eleven of the remaining twenty-three primaries. Moreover, Carter lost many of what were seen as key primaries while winning less pivotal states. Each loss was offset by at least one victory on the same day (New York by Wisconsin; Nebraska by Connecticut; Maryland by Michigan; Idaho, Nevada and Oregon by Kentucky, Arkansas, and Tennessee; Rhode Island and Montana by South Dakota; and California and New Jersey by Ohio).

The scenario advanced by Carter's advisers to interpret these events pictured their candidate as running everywhere and gradually building delegate tallies toward a first ballot majority. Carter was the only candidate entered into enough states to win the nomination outright. Therefore, the choice for the Democratic party was, according to this blueprint, between Carter and a brokered convention. When it became clear that even Carter would not finish the primaries with the required 1,505 delegates, their scenario offered various break points above which the remaining delegate votes could be acquired through switches of individual delegates. After a certain level was attained, they argued—whether 1,000, 1,200, or 1,300 delegate votes—it would be suicidal for the party to deny Carter the nomination.

On the other hand, after Pennsylvania, Brown and Church began entering primaries against Carter. They proved quite successful. With one exception, all of Carter's post-Pennsylvania victories were against candidates whom he had beaten in earlier showings. Ten of his eleven losses were to either Church or Brown or some combination of them.[42]

Naturally, Brown and Church saw the dynamics of the last stages of the nomination race quite differently from Carter's staff. Although acknowledging his lead in delegate tallies, Brown and Church argued that primaries were useful as a demonstration of support and vote-getting ability within the party. Carter had peaked midway through the primaries; key contests during the latter half demonstrated his weakness.

Polsby and Wildavsky note that the emergence of a frontrunner naturally stimulates coalitions among other candidates seeking to prevent the nomination of a rival.[43] As predicted, a stop-Carter movement among candidates whose interests coincided came into being during April and May. Carter himself used press conferences to highlight the attempt to deny him the nomination.[44] Far from avoiding the issue and proclaiming the virtues of party unity, the Carter campaign repeated almost daily the charge that unnamed Democrats were seeking to unfairly deprive him of the nomination.

Carter's pronouncements kept the mounting delegate tally as the central question of the later primary race. Discussions of whether Church or Brown were gaining momentum by their critical primary strategies were obscured by the attention given to whether Carter could be stopped. Although this attention was perfectly reasonable, we should not overlook the fact that acceptance of that scenario as the basis for interpreting the post-Pennsylvania competition certainly benefited Carter because it cast Church and Brown in the role of spoilers. Whereas earlier the primary results had been assessed for their psychological impacts, these more nebulous concepts—which could have been read as favoring Carter's opponents—were discarded in the later stages. (How this grand conception of the nomination race affected news coverage is described later in full.) The competing candidate organizations were not only trying to win primaries, they were engaged in a bitter struggle to convince the press to view the basic dynamics of the race according to their own scenarios. Carter was more successful at persuading the press than at winning primaries.

The Debate over Standards

Journalists respond to the ambiguities of presidential selection by continually searching for indicators or standards that allow them to assess the candidates' progress. Their art is to select an indicator and sketch out the logic as to how it might predict the future. If organization is critically important, one might estimate that a given candidate is in the lead. A stronger than expected performance in Iowa might indicate that a different competitor is moving ahead. When delegate votes are the name of the game, still another aspirant appears to be moving forward.

The standards that become established as the consensus of journalists are not manufactured in a vacuum. To a degree, standards are implicit in the scenario adopted to explain the overall dynamics of the race. A brokered convention scenario, for example, will point the observer to results in pivotal primary states. If an unknown candidate is going to leap out of the pack, the first few primaries will be key. In addition, the last-war syndrome influences the thinking of journalists—the lessons of 1976 become the rules of 1980. If Kennedy's weakness against Carter first showed up in the preprimary straw vote in Florida, similar events in 1983 need to be given closer scrutiny for their implication for the 1984 race. Finally, these assumptions can be modified through the continual discussions that journalists have with the competitors themselves.

Here again the influence between campaigners and journalists is reciprocal. Campaigners compete to persuade journalists to adopt standards that benefit their candidacy. At the same time, their initial strategies accommodate the standards established by previous election cycles. Few campaigners, for example, questioned the importance of early primaries. Once certain standards are accepted, campaigns believe that they must compete along those dimensions. Initial strategies have to be scrapped primarily because journalists adopted different, or new, standards between one election and the next.

Because they are short-term, specific indicators, the standards applied to campaigns by journalists change markedly during the presidential election. During the preprimary months, fundraising success and, to a lesser extent, organizational strength are accepted as useful standards for comparing candidates. At this stage, journalists may also rely upon informed opinions of party activists. After the impact of the initial primaries has faded, delegate standings become accepted as the definitive standard against which candidate prospects are rated in the later stages. During the general election, the search for indicators usually fastens upon the public opinion polls, even though the precision of these polls may be confounded by a large proportion of undecided voters.

Interaction over Preprimary Standards

In terms of standards, the impact of horserace reporting on campaign behavior diminishes as the presidential year proceeds. During the preprimary period, the ambiguity of measuring political support places a premium upon the professional judgments of newsmen. As perceived by campaigners, journalists have, during these earliest months, the widest latitude in selecting standards. Those selected, furthermore, will have the greatest impact because they will influence both the coverage patterns and the content of reported news. That is, the imprint of journalists on the perceptual environment of the election contest is greatest when the available indicators are weakest and require or permit the maximum in journalistic judgment and interpretation.

R.W. Apple, for example, used the informed-opinion approach in a front-page story in the *New York Times* January 12, 1976:

> A kind of rough standing among the candidates has suddenly started to emerge in the minds of political professionals around the country. . . . In the group from which the nominee is believed most likely to be selected are Senator Henry M. Jackson of Washington, Senator Birch Bayh of Indiana, former Gov. Jimmy Carter of Georgia, and Senator Hubert Humphrey of Minnesota. In the second, candidates given a conceivable chance of being nominated, are. . . .[45]

Apple referred to visits to 12 states and conversations with hundreds of politicians and activists as the basis for his article. Although journalists must make these judgments in predicting future success and in allotting coverage to candidates with serious prospects, they are unquestionably aware of and uncomfortable with the frailty of the data with which they must work, particularly during the long preprimary period. The Apple story continued as follows:

> Such early calculations are highly speculative. . . . Public opinion polls are of little utility until the electorates in various states get to know the candidates. So most of the judgments are based on instincts—instincts that may be thrown off this year by the unusual size of the field, by the new campaign financing laws and the changes in the number and the order of primaries. But early calculations have a life of their own, because they are the backdrop against which politicians and the media tend to measure the performance of the various candidates in their early confrontations.

Over the period of this study, the institutions of presidential selection have been constantly changing. As a result, the rules have not been entirely clear. For journalists, the uncertainty means difficulty in gauging the progress of the race; for campaigners, it offers an opportunity to promote their own strong points as objective indicators. In both election years some campaigners suggested to journalists that during the preprimary months money in the bank or organizational development constitute the best indicators of progress. The campaign of Senator Henry Jackson was the most vocal in emphasizing the impact of money:

> [T]here was an early recognition of the tremendous importance the new campaign finance laws would have on the strategy and tactics of campaigns. If you didn't raise your money early, and if you didn't develop a structure to keep some funds coming in, if you didn't develop a capacity to reach out for smaller contributions, if you weren't successful in that regard, you wouldn't be able to do it later on.[46]

> It's in our interest to try to get things evaluated by journalists in the way we would like to see them evaluated. . . . We spend a lot of time trying to get them to understand the impact of money. We'll have to develop a strategy and plan. If the press conveys something foreign to that, we'll look silly. So we have to convince them that finance is important. That a candidate with $1,600,000 in the bank is different from a candidate with $20,000; that someone with $20,000 will have a lot to do to catch up.[47]

Other campaigns have sought to convince reporters that the matching provisions of the finance act ensured that most candidates would have an adequate cash flow to survive. The key to projecting ultimate success, they argued, lay not in money, but in the ability to attract party activists and construct a campaign organization. Primaries and caucuses would be won by personally contacting voters, identifying potential supporters, and getting them to the polls. Accordingly, these campaigners urged journalists to compare organizational strength as the standard:

> We try to stress that this is an organization-oriented effort. This is not a fundraising effort, it's not a big-money, free-spending effort. This is a tight, lean, well-arranged effort. . . . The McGovern effort is still fresh in the minds of most of the political press, and they know the importance of that organization in the field. . . .[48]

It is difficult for campaigners to dramatize organizational strength in a way that will make it newsworthy, nor is it easy for the press to observe, certainly not as simple as asking about the campaign's bank balance.[49]

In 1975, Udall's operatives made several efforts to make this standard more concrete to the press. One such attempt was to announce organizing committees in their key states:

> [Take] Mo's real big swing into Wisconsin a couple of weeks ago. . . . He went in there and we put out a news release that had the list of 80

something, 83 people committee to Udall, including the Speaker of the Assembly, 5 of the 7 Democratic Congressmen. And it's that kind of an organization thing that is impressive. And you see it come up in columns and think pieces by political writers. They'll say "Udall's out organizing"—those little key phrases, you know you're doing your job.[50]

A story that we really prized was in late April, when we announced an organizing committee in Wisconsin and a Wisconsin newspaper said "Udall gets a head start." That means something. Now that was a perception of a political reporter in analyzing the 50- or 75-person organizing committee that we put together which was pretty impressive.[51]

In 1979, state parties in Florida and Maine followed Iowa's example and staged straw votes among party activists. These became a means of measuring the comparative strength of candidate organization. The media covered them intensively. By 1983, the straw-vote mechanism had become much more common. In mid-1983, Mondale was trying to convince journalists that money was the important indicator, Cranston was arguing for the straw votes, and Glenn was citing the national opinion polls.

In arguing for organizational strength in 1975, Udall's staff not only tried to provide specific comparisons across campaigns but also to impart a sense of progress and meeting goals:

In December, we laid out, in a set of memos, both the structure we wanted to have by the end of June—operationally what we wanted to have—plus we set out a sense of where we thought we had to be in terms of state organizations and things like that. If you go back and read those memoranda—which I did about two weeks ago—we are exactly on schedule in the operations of the office here and in terms of the personnel we wanted to hire, the number of people, the jobs that needed to be filled. And we have offices open in six states now. . . .[52]

Of course, neither Udall's staff nor the journalists could establish whether those self-generated targets were appropriate; their importance was rather to convey a perception of motion.

The first year in which presidential campaigns were affected by the new finance laws was 1975. Terry Sanford, the former governor of North Carolina, planned to concentrate his efforts on a few early primaries (New Hampshire, Massachusetts, and North Carolina) while relying upon his contacts in North Carolina to provide a financial base. Other funds would be collected by building a financial arm into the primary organizations in states where he would make an effort. Thus, initial money would be raised only in three or four states; later the effort could be extended to the twenty states needed to qualify for federal matching funds.[53]

By the summer of 1975, however, Sanford found his strategy running headlong into the standard of progress adopted by journalists to discriminate hopeless from serious campaigns. Reporters decided that qualifying for matching funds constituted an important test of the candidates' strength. The Sanford staff had difficulties in getting journalists to write about his campaign; some reporters told them explicitly that they would not be covered until they had qualified. As Sanford's press secretary noted:

> That's definitely where the press corps has been known to influence the actions of the campaign, because we, (or rather) Sanford, maintained for a long time that he was not going to waste his energies on getting up political matching funds, and yet, it has become about the only game in town. . . .[54]

During this same period, both Udall's campaign director, John Gabusi, and Jim Hightower, Harris' campaign manager, noted similar pressures from the media:

> The press had decided that's the way they're going to certify who a candidate is, if you raise a hundred thousand dollars. This is ludicrous, but it is a game they're playing. And not only are they trying to do it, but I think they've succeeded; I think we've got to go raise our $100,000 now.[55]

While news organizations identified serious candidates by asking whether they had qualified for matching funds, most campaigners recognized the test was meaningless as a real indicator of political strength. The sarcasm of Hightower's comment was echoed by Sanford's campaign manager:

> Everyone thinks that once you've got $100,000, you're viable. Well, how far does $100,000 go in a national campaign? And you receive no matching money until the first of January no matter how much you raise.[56]

Despite his recognition of the political realities confronting his campaign, Governor Sanford decided he had to conform to the standards set by journalists so that he could have at least some news coverage. At his press conference on July 2, 1975, describing qualification as a "license to practice," he committed his organization to raising the necessary funds within one month. This shift greatly surprised his finance people; it required a different organizational structure and diverted resources and time from the states in which he planned his early efforts—New Hampshire, Massachusetts, and North Carolina. Staff members and Sanford himself would have to be sent into nonessential states to set up fundraisers.

Not surprisingly, Sanford's switch in strategy did not receive a great deal of press coverage. David Broder, summarizing the press conferences of Sanford and Udall, referred to Sanford as "one of five candidates still struggling to cross that barrier (qualification)," and mentioned his hopes to qualify in July. A week and a half later, Christopher Lydon quoted Sanford's "license to practice" in an article on the difficulties of raising money.[57]

By 1980, the influence of money had taken on a new dimension about which campaigners could argue. The campaign finance laws limit what candidates who accepted public funds can legally spend in pursuit of the nomination.[58] In 1976, Ford and Reagan came very close to overspending their limits; by 1980 the ceiling was perceived as more restrictive because the number of states holding primaries had risen and the costs of campaigning had increased more rapidly than the act's inflation adjustment.

Reagan's campaign spent nearly all the permissible level quite early in the primary process. After the initial races, Reagan's opponents attempted to convince the press that the limits would hamper his success in later primaries:

> The second thing you would have to do from the outset is . . . not attempt to run a fifty-state campaign. This magnifies the problem of the frontrunner because the front runner has to almost move quickly everywhere . . . that means you have to spend money on a national campaign before you really want to.[59]

> I don't think the press really understands the function of money. If they had, I think they would have been with a New Hampshire victory. . . . As of election day in New Hampshire [the Reagan campaign] had spent 74% of what they could spend. And that's not including the several million dollars you must have for the convention. . . .[60]

> We were confronted with the same thing the Reagan campaign was confronted with, and we were shocked when they took matching funds. . . . You could see coming up in November and December of 1979 that they were going to soon be in very real difficulties with the overall spending limit.[61]

As the race neared its conclusion, the Reagan campaign did come very close to the spending limits and George Bush was able to target individual states for intense campaigning. Bush was never able, however, to convince journalists that Reagan's campaign would collapse by running out of money.

Interaction over Standards during the Primaries

In the early months, journalists attempt to read psychological impact from primary results. During later stages, the speculation centers around the mounting delegate tallies for the competing candidates. The ambiguities of the preprimary period may lead to an overemphasis on results during the early primary period. Winning and losing in the early caucuses and primaries are seen as the first hard news stories of the presidential race, a perception that almost guarantees such inflation of their significance. Never mind that the indicators are still not very good; they are, at least, solid evidence that the process is underway. The presumption that these early delegate selection events have improved validity over the indicators available during the preprimary season, should not, however, lead one to overlook the unrepresentative nature of the early contest. And it cannot justify the overabundance of coverage devoted to the initial primaries and caucuses and the over-estimation of their insignificance. For example, in a careful count of stories on the network evening news shows and in three daily newspapers during three months before the New Hampshire primary, Robinson and MacPherson reported that fully 54 percent of the print stories and sixty percent of the broadcast time devoted to the 1976 presidential race dealt with the New Hampshire primary.[62] After his early wins, Jimmy Carter received two to three times as much attention as that given any other candidate.[63] After the 1976 Iowa caucuses, the *Miami Herald* awarded Carter the status of frontrunner with a story headlined "Now Jimmy Carter's the Man to Beat."[64] *Newsweek's* analysis was only slightly more cautious:

> But the Iowa caucuses were serious business as well, the first event of the 1976 political calendar and an early litmus test of candidate credibility. And, when all the votes were counted, the caucuses had thrust a fresh new face into the forefront of Presidential speculation: Jimmy Carter. . . .[65]

After the New Hampshire primary, NBC's Tom Pettit described Carter as "the man to beat," while *Time* opined that Carter had the "only campaign that holds real possibilities of breaking far ahead of the pack."[66] Carter was on the cover of both major news weeklies, appearing alone on the cover of *Newsweek* and featured as a caricature astride a donkey being restrained by the other candidates on the *Time* cover.

In the 1980 campaign, the Iowa caucus results had, in the view of many campaigners, a similar, marked influence on both nomination races. Kennedy lost to Jimmy Carter. For Kennedy, the loss was seen as a sharp, perhaps even decisive setback. *Newsweek* ran a story, "Can Kennedy Hang On?" that capsulized the horserace:

> The President buried the senator and the twenty-year legend of Kennedy invincibility under a devastating 2-to-1 landslide. . . . [I]t was big and persuasive enough to propel Carter within dreaming distance of striking up his renomination before Winter is out.[67]

Kennedy's campaigners sought to rebut this shift in their perceptual environment:

The difference in Iowa on a delegate basis is 10 delegates; the difference in terms of press perception and, most importantly, ability to raise money, is, of course, much more dramatic. But the election will be resolved in the major industrial states and the June 3rd primaries.[68]

Kennedy campaigners admitted that the selection of Iowa as a standard against which the Democratic race should be judged was, to a degree, determined by the Senator himself. Rick Smith, political reporter for the *New York Times*, agreed:

I think it was very significant that Senator Kennedy did say before the Florida caucuses that Iowa was the first test. He set that battleground.[69]

For George Bush, Iowa in 1980 looked remarkably like Iowa for Carter in 1976:

There is absolutely no way to measure or estimate the effect of something like what happened to Bush after Iowa.I mean the *Newsweek* piece and the cover, and his face up on the corner of *Time,* and the network coverage he got. There is some evidence that, at least temporarily, Reagan has dropped a measurable degree. . . . Reagan's lost 20 points in New Hampshire![70]

Eventually, Reagan regained his lead in New Hampshire and snuffed out the Bush forest fire. The post-Iowa press commentary, however, scarcely reflects that eventuality.

Jules Witcover reacted to criticism of the emphasis placed upon the 1976 Iowa caucuses:

One unhappy Udall worker later stated in The *Washington Post* that the candidates themselves and the issues were lost in the efforts to draw press attention, and in the reporters' determination to draw significance from an insignificant exercise. "The reality of a presidential campaign," he wrote in a woeful misunderstanding of the dynamics of the system, "is the delegate count, but no significant number of delegates will be selected until March. . . ." The fact is that the reality in the early going of a presidential campaign is *not* the delegate count at all. The reality at the beginning stage is the psychological impact of the results—the perception by press, public, and contending politicians of what has happened.[71]

Witcover's counterargument, however, has three weak points. Establishing "the psychological impact of the results" is an exceedingly difficult judgment. It also is difficult to sustain the argument that voters will weigh the journalists analysis separately from the hard news when the two appear in a single story. The results of early delegate selection events are not described as one candidate obtaining a small plurality in a multicandidate field in the first of a number of similar exercises. Instead, the sequential nature and diversity of the nomination process is too frequently neglected, even though the assumption that early primaries are representative of national sentiment is highly dubious. Finally, to aggravate the impact of these early interpretations, the subsequent behavior of the news-reporting industry itself is directly determined by these perceptions—that is, press coverage is thereafter directed disproportionately toward the winner.[72]

As the nomination race moves into the later primaries, the indicators improve. A narrowing field of candidates, each with enhanced visibility, strengthens the meaningfulness of poll results. The remaining contestants maneuver to force their competitors into critical tests in pivotal primaries. Mounting delegate tallies provide a direct measure of how the nomination race is progressing. Although the improvement in the validity of indicators diminishes the judgmental nature of benchmarking, newsmen must still confront strategic uncertainty and must choose among these indicators, especially if they conflict with each other. For example, during May and June 1980, Carter was losing many of the primaries held in strongholds of the Democratic party, even while he continued to pile up his total delegate strength. Reporting on the likely nominee—Carter versus Kennedy—required a choice between these indicators.

Another example of how acceptance of certain standards can affect candidates occurred in the Jackson campaign during the 1976 Florida primary. In 1972, Jackson's campaign had been heavily damaged by a poor showing (12.5 percent) in Florida where he expected support among Jewish voters. Politically, however, Florida is a hybrid, with its deep South culture in the northern panhandle and its transplanted New Yorkers in Miami and along the coasts. Jackson could expect to do well among the latter voters, but not well enough to compile a statewide plurality against Wallace's reputed strength (42 percent in 1972) and Carter's appeal to stop-Wallace sentiment.

The rules under which Democrats select delegates, nevertheless, provided an incentive for Jackson to enter the Florida primary, at least in the Miami area. In Florida and many other states, delegates were to be directly elected in separate congressional districts primaries; thus, a candidate with a plurality of votes in a given district could expect to elect all the delegates from that district. The Jackson strategists wanted to elect as many delegates as they could from the three districts around Miami, while conceding the rest of the state to the Wallace-Carter face-off.

Their political objectives—to maximize their convention delegates—ran headlong into the journalists' need for a single winner. Jackson would undoubtedly lose in the statewide tally of presidential preference. Thus the Jackson staff set out to convince journalists to view the Florida race as a composite of fifteen primaries, one in each congressional district.

We're looking at Florida, and we're looking at . . . the Tampa area and the Miami area, those two areas represent about 6 Congressional districts. . . . We're definitely interested in certain Congressional districts and we can do it that way. I think we can sell that idea . . . [to the press].[73]

We also have to sell people [journalists] on the fact that there are 400 primaries rather than 30 [because it's run by CDs], that who gets delegates is the key. And that's a foreign notion to the press. . . . You keep repeating it to the press. When we were in New Jersey the other day, a reporter asked, "How many of the New Jersey primaries will you enter?" So we're getting the right questions asked.[74]

Jackson's campaign manager discussed this strategy with Leslie Stahl of CBS, who would report on the Jackson campaign on primary night. Keefe's objective was to focus her report about Jackson's performance in the delegate contest and to convey the Jackson strategy to her superiors.[75] Although a number of preprimary stories on campaign strategies mentioned Jackson's concentration on a few districts, on election night the analyses of the results focused on the statewide totals.[76] Jackson received 24 percent of the statewide votes and 26 percent of the delegation. Jackson could claim victories in those congressional districts that he targeted; he carried the three Miami districts and Fort Lauderdale, but narrowly lost to Carter in West Palm Beach. Nevertheless, the news media applied the statewide results in rating performance. As summarized by Witcover,

Scoop Jackson was a loser again. He had picked up twenty-one delegates to thirty-four for Carter and twenty-six for Wallace, but the press was not in a delegate-counting mood. Winning or losing primaries was still what captured headlines and network television coverage. . . .[77]

Interaction over the Standards of the
General Election

During the general election, the lack of sequential primaries creates strong incentives for reporters and campaigners to manufacture an artificial sequence—and to report the horserace around those events. Campaigners and journalists—each for their separate reasons—cooperate in turning the televised debates into tests of progress. The debates became pseudo-primaries, complete with discussions of strategy, tactics, benchmarks, and victories. The journalists' search for indicators of political support also fastens on the public opinion polls, even though their results are imprecise because many voters do not decide on a candidate until quite late in the race. Polls did provide the drama of a tightening race in 1976 and of a stand off for much of the 1980 campaign. Reporters are also able to describe each campaign's plans for victory in a combination of states to secure an electoral college majority. In 1980, they had polls in many key states to aid their forecasting efforts.[78]

However, the general election campaign generates fewer dramatic moments than the primary races. For two months the candidates travel around making speeches; their advertising program appeals for votes; their organizations endeavor to contact as many voters as possible; and polls indicate how the race is progressing. But they never provide as dramatic an event as a primary victory or defeat.

In this context, candidate debates have a natural attraction for journalists. As head-to-head confrontations, they are less amenable to planning and control by the candidates and their advisers. They can be imbued with the high drama of a shoot-out in which one contender may be mortally wounded. Because they attract huge television audiences, they have the potential to influence the outcome of the election. And, once agreed on by the principals, debates are predictable events and can, therefore, become the subject of considerable planning, build-up and speculation in advance.

The contribution of debates to the general election outcome—even more so than to primaries—is questionable. They are tailormade, in short, for argumentation and influence between campaigners and journalists.

In the news reports of the 1976 and 1980 general elections, the televised debates were viewed as influencing the election outcome substantially: "This first debate would surely be the most critical event of the 1976 campaign, and both candidates knew it," commented *Time*'s Robert Ajemian.[79] Four years later, after reviewing a rostrum of states in which 272 electoral votes were too close to call even in the final week of the campaign, Adam Clymer of the *New York Times* wrote: "These states . . . appear to be so closely contested that they could fall into the column of the candidate who appeared to be the winner in tomorrow's debate, if there is one."[80] The next day, he reiterated the point: "Their only face-to-face exchange of the Presidential campaign was expected to have a decisive impact at the polls next Tuesday. . . ."[81]

For strategic reasons, campaigners are apt to cooperate in emphasizing the electoral importance of the debates. For example, Republican party chairman Bill Brock gave Clymer a quote that set up the tone of his story: "Most of the states are so close that a very strong showing by Reagan could give us an electoral vote landslide."[82]

The debates offer campaigners unparalled opportunities for free media exposure to a huge audience, one reason why they cooperate in giving them a big buildup:

> The debates were the ultimate media event in a campaign filled with media politics—an opportunity for the two candidates for president to present their

views to the American public in a relatively unfiltered way. Unfiltered in the sense that political advertising is not filtered by the journalistic process. Of course, it's filtered and distorted by the advertising and propaganda process, but at least the politicians control the process.[83]

Although they cannot control what eventually happens in a presidential debate, neither side is prepared to leave anything to chance. The negotiations are elaborate; everything from format to podium height can be seen as offering advantages to one side or the other. Candidates are well briefed on possible questions and put through dress rehearsals with surrogate opponents. On both sides, campaigners carefully establish objectives they hope to secure in the debate:

> Our candidate Reagan is a seasoned but strong individual, that he has the ability to assume the Presidency, and people would feel comfortable with him in the White House.[84]

> We hope and we believe that people will look beyond the fact that Ronald Reagan is an actor and an experienced one and will look to the substance.[85]

> We thought that the debates might serve to push Carter into specifics. People tended to think that Governor Carter held the same positions as they did regardless of what their positions were. We felt that if we could push him to specific positions on a number of issues, he had to lose some people.[86]

> We thought the debates would postpone the decisionmaking of undecided voters, as they did, and allow us [Ford's campaign] to get going. On this score, the first debate was seen as particularly crucial to us, because we could create the impression in people's minds that it was almost sinful for them to decide before they'd had a chance to see the two candidates going at each other.[87]

> The debates were an opportunity to remove any growing doubts about Carter, and to devalue to some extent some of the news events that took place.[88]

> It never occurred to anybody that we had the same problem as Jack Kennedy because we were 30 points ahead in the polls. But we had that problem in spades. . . . We wanted a situation in which Carter was seen with Jerry Ford in a position of parity. We wanted Carter and Ford to be two guys asking the American people for their votes, not one President running against a peanut farmer.[89]

Out of their interviews with campaigners, journalists attempt to develop a sense of what is at stake in these encounters. Usually, however, this reporting yields standards that are too complex to be easily or rapidly measured:

> For Mr. Reagan, the challenge was to appear of "Presidential" caliber and to appear reassuring in order to counter the Democratic campaign's efforts

172   Media Politics

to suggest that his election would increase the risk of war, his aides acknowledged.[90]

For Mr. Carter, the occasion was an opportunity to portray himself as
more knowledgeable than his rival. . . .[91]

Given this ambiguity, candidate debates share another characteristic
with primaries. The performance of each candidate can be assessed according to somewhat arbitrary expectations of how each candidate ought to
fare. Campaign advisers, therefore, become interested in shaping coverage
in advance of the debates that might affect the subsequent interpretations.
For example, according to Ron Nessen:

One CBS story that angered the campaign planners . . . reported that the
actor/comedian/producer/speech coach [Don Penny] planned to master
Carter's mannerisms and voice patterns so he could play the part of the
Democratic candidate in dress rehearsals to help Ford prepare for the
debates. . . . The story was potentially damaging to Ford, since a good
showing in the debates might be written off by the press as the result of
careful rehearsing.[92]

In the process of their interaction, campaigners and journalists reduce
the debates to win-lose propositions. However, the ingredients of victory
are certainly not clear. In 1980, according to a CBS-*New York Times* poll
after the Carter-Reagan debate, 44 percent of the viewers felt Reagan had
won, while 36 percent thought Carter won, results which were almost dupli-
cated by Republican pollster Robert Teeter.[93] More significantly, 90 percent
said the debate did not change their vote. As Carter's pollster Pat Caddell
said at the time:

We're all running around playing games—racing around playing "who
won?" . . . The question is who was impacted the most, how were they impacted, and how will it affect the electoral vote if at all.[94]

The discourse between reporters and campaigners takes place at the
perceptual level, where defining a clear winner is viewed as highly consequential. For example, after the second debate between Ford and Carter in
1976, the Ford polls found clear evidence of the impact of news commentary upon the public perceptions of who won the debate. As described by
Robert Teeter:

In the polling we did, starting the last minute of the second debate, between
11:00 and 1:00 that night, the question of who did a better job in the debate

came out Ford 44 percent, Carter 43. Between 9:00 in the morning and noon the next day, it was Ford 32, Carter 44. Between noon and 5:00 in the afternoon, it was Ford 21, Carter 43. Between 5:00 and midnight the day after, it was Ford 17, Carter 62. Reports of the debate had re-emphasized the President as a mistake-prone, inept bumbler, exactly what we had spent six or seven weeks trying to get away from.[95]

Since the criteria for assessing performance in debates are uncertain, journalists often rely on public opinion polls to determine the winner. Teeter's evidence indicates, however, voters' perceptions of the winner may follow the commentary by journalists.

Teeter's data do not, however, provide conclusive proof that news reporting shapes the outcomes of presidential elections. As in 1980, the polls were not able to establish a link between a voter's choice of candidate and his or her beliefs about who won. More likely, by concentrating on the debates, politicians and journalists transform the issue of who won from a judgmental question for each viewer to decide into a perceived factual matter. Just as Ford lost the North Carolina primary, so he lost the second debate.

Finally, journalists have a difficult job covering the general election. The candidates' speeches quickly become repetitive. The narrowing polls stories can only be written so many times and remain interesting. Lacking real events, reporters seize upon the debates as standards from which they can project the eventual winner. Careful survey research has yet to decipher the impact of these events on voters' choices.[96] The emphasis given the Carter-Reagan and the Ford-Carter debates cannot be justified in terms of political impact, rather it was a byproduct of the news strategies of the two campaigns and of the organizationally determined nature of news reporting.

The Application of Benchmarks

At a third conceptual level, campaigners are also engaged in influencing the interpretations journalists give to specific events of the presidential selection process. Particularly during the preprimary and early primary periods, a rather vexing problem for journalists is the estimation of whether objective events portend changes in political support. Political reporters cannot be content merely to describe an event. The importance of each step in the selection process becomes clear only when its long-run implications are traced. Deciphering the growth or decay of a campaign's ability to mobilize resources is particularly crucial.

The Development of Benchmarks

Generally, interpretations of campaign events are developed by estimating the probable consequences of possible outcomes. In the weeks before a given primary, for example, reporters seek to establish a consensus about what different results might mean to individual candidacies. The actual primary results can then be compared with these preestablished beliefs, yielding interpretations of whether the campaign has succeeded or failed and whether the candidate appears to be gaining or losing support.

Central to this benchmarking process is the establishment of expectations as to how each campaign ought to perform. The handiest guide available to journalists is, of course, the scenarios campaigners use to describe their election strategy. Given that these provide a realistic path for securing nomination or electoral victory, they indicate how well the campaign anticipates performing at each stage of the process. At issue between campaigners and journalists then are the questions of whether a given percentage of the vote represents growing political support and, if so, whether that support will expand sufficiently for the campaign to achieve long-run success.

Despite the specificity involved in benchmarking, propositions about the horserace at this level are characterized by a high level of uncertainty. For example, what impact does geographic region have on candidates' performance? Was Kennedy's defeat in New Hampshire a more serious sign of weakness because the state was in his backyard? As a May 1982 *Newsweek* reported a year and a half before the 1984 Iowa caucuses:

> But Iowa, at least in these early days, is clearly Fritz Mondale country. At every stop of his recent tour, Mondale, 54, ran into old acquaintances. "For years Fritz was our only Senator," explains plumber Kent Stafflebeam, a loyal Democrat who recalls the years when both of Iowa's senators were Republicans and Minnesota's Mondale was the closest Democrat.[97]

Even though benchmarks are the most specific and concrete perceptions about the state of the horserace, they are established by an arbitrary process—that is, the result of interaction among campaigners and journalists. Campaigners are likely to understate the level of performance they anticipate. If they convey a modest expected level of performance and if the actual results surpass that level, the resulting perception will be of a candidacy growing in support achieving or overachieving its goals, and successfully pursuing its strategy for nomination or election victory.

> What you're dealing with in a national campaign with the media—the media is so critical—that you're talking about continually overperforming in terms of arbitrary expectations they set for you. . . . We never talked

about winning in New Hampshire. We never talk about winning *anywhere*. We talk about doing well. And so, I think, the candidate and the campaign itself plays a part in establishing this expectation with the media. The media expect not much from us, and we, even to this point, have been able to overperform in terms of what they expect from us and that's going to continue to be the case. . . .[98]

Vote results in given primaries are the most common form of measurement. Before the first primary, few campaigners will publicly avow that their candidate has to finish first in one of the early primaries to be nominated:

We'll always be considered a victor in Massachusetts or New Hampshire if we're up there with the top three, given the crowded field.[99]

We have been concentrating . . . on the first four states, which are Iowa, Mississippi, New Hampshire and Massachusetts. . . . I feel that we will certainly be in the top half to top one third of all the states I just mentioned in terms of returns.[100]

We don't have to finish first, we don't think, in New Hampshire or Massachusetts, but we have to finish ahead of, or right even with, the Progressive Democrats in those two places.[101]

For some candidates, that means they're going to have to finish first in an early primary. For other candidates, I think, they can survive finishing in the "pack," or, you know, first, second, or third without being knocked out. . . . I think Bayh is one of those who doesn't have to win every primary; I mean, he can survive.[102]

The Evolution of Benchmarks

Just as the perceived standards for measuring the horserace have evolved over the course of recent presidential contests, so too has consensus over benchmarks for primary performance. In 1968, Lyndon Johnson defeated Senator Gene McCarthy in the New Hampshire primary by a margin (50 percent to 42 percent) that was perceived by journalists to demonstrate considerable weakness for the incumbent president. In 1972, the Democratic frontrunner, Senator Edmund Muskie, carried New Hampshire with 48 percent of the vote, while George McGovern's 37 percent share appeared better than had been expected before the primary.[103] In both cases, the candidate who came in second was perceived as having demonstrated surprising strength. The people had spoken, and the positions of the frontrunners were not as solid as they should have been.

These interpretations have met with considerable criticism. After all, had not Johnson and Muskie actually won? By 1976, many reporters whom we interviewed were determined to follow what they called "Apple's dictum: winning is winning."[104] Psychological victories were viewed as less defensible than reliance on the strict formula proposed by Apple. In 1980, this same consensus held: first place showings were described as victories. In both years, however, there were exceptions.

The dictum "winning is winning" is most clear cut when applied to the dynamics of a two-candidate contest such as Ford versus Reagan or Carter versus Kennedy. A win for one candidate comes at the expense of the other. Even in a two-candidate race, however, there will remain some ambiguity. For example, Carter's Alabama victory in March 1980 with 82 percent of the vote was not described as a devastating blow to Kennedy, who had not been expected to do very well in that southern state.

The benchmark is even more ambiguous, however, in interpreting results of multicandidate races. For example, when Carter won the 1976 New Hampshire primary with 30 percent of the votes, he was competing against four candidates who fragmented liberal votes. When John Anderson came in second behind Bush in Massachusetts and, on the same day, second behind Reagan in Vermont, his performance was given considerable attention in press coverage. If Kennedy

> loses in New Hampshire or wins New Hampshire by a very close margin, in effect he does lose. . . . If it's very close, he's going to get a very small margin in the delegate count as well. It would be a big setback to him for it to be very close.[105]

Long after the event, journalists and George Bush's advisers were still debating whether his campaign would have been better off if he had narrowly lost to Reagan in the Iowa caucus rather than winning.[106] Among many benefits, the victory inflated expectations about how well Bush would have to do in New Hampshire to be perceived as accomplishing his campaign strategy.

The expectations game implicit in benchmarking poses for politicians an almost irreconcilable conflict between the techniques of political organizing and the requirements of the news strategy. For practicing politicans and activists, being on the winning side can be an important inducement for supporting a given candidacy. Accordingly, campaigners and candidates often inflate their prospects for victory, hoping they will set in motion a self-fulfilling prophecy. In the process, however, they may increase the benchmarks against which reporters will measure their achievements.

Mo Udall's emphasis on the strength of his organization in Wisconsin illustrates this point. Numerous references to the strength of Udall's Wisconsin organization can be found in the preprimary press commentary. A full month before Wisconsin, Witcover wrote:

> The assumption now is that Wisconsin, a progressive state where Udall has done much organization work, can give him his first primary victory. . . .[107]

Politicians' need to overstate their positions and the dangers of raising expectations that the press can use to benchmark the campaign is another discrepancy between political requirements and the demands of media politics.

Organizationally, setting benchmarks as a part of the campaign's news strategy necessitates a high degree of planning and control by the national office. National decisionmakers need to ensure consistent responses from others in the campaign who might be interviewed. In 1972, a low-level New Hampshire campaigner for Muskie told David Broder that the campaign would be in trouble if Muskie did not take 50 percent of the vote. The benchmark stuck and hurt Muskie badly. The statements of the candidate himself must also be controlled. For example, in 1976 when Senator Jackson, enthusiastically discussing his growing support in New York, allowed himself to speculate on a landslide victory. When pushed by reporters to define landslide, the Senator projected that he would capture at least 50 percent of the delegates. Although he decisively defeated his opponents, the final tally was slightly lower than his forecast, and journalists dismissed the significance of his victory.

Interaction over Benchmarks

Candidates interact most often with journalists to establish benchmarks, as numerous examples from the 1976 and 1980 elections attest. However, such examples are firmly rooted in the specifics of a given candidacy at a given moment. Accordingly, this analysis is confined to two major cases, both drawn from 1976. In the first, the campaign was almost eliminated from contention prematurely by benchmark reporting that it had allowed to develop. Certainly, reporters applying these benchmarks had concluded the candidacy was finished. In the second case, adroit attention to the coordination of campaign behaviors led to a benchmark that the campaign staff knew was within its grasp. When the campaign succeeded, the bulk of journalistic commentary awarded the candidate the nomination.

Reagan's Performance in New Hampshire and Florida. In 1976, Ronald Reagan narrowly lost both the New Hampshire and Florida primaries to Ford, but registered strong showings against an incumbent.[108] Unlike those of his predecessors in 1968 and 1972, Reagan's early showings were not described as psychological victories but as major defeats. Because of adverse news reporting surrounding these benchmarks, Reagan staffers believed his campaign was lucky to survive through to North Carolina. Political support was ebbing everywhere, the campaign treasury was near zero, and the cash flow was falling off.[109] The difference between Reagan's situation and the near-wins of earlier campaign is primarily due to the interaction between newsmen and campaigners over benchmark perceptions.

The Ford and Reagan campaigns had managed to work themselves into a zero-sum game before the Florida and New Hampshire primaries. Initially the Reagan campaign, believing the two states would support its candidate, represented the two primaries as an early showdown:

> I have a feeling that if Reagan wins in New Hampshire (which he will), wins in Florida (which he will), and wins in one or two of those other early states, that Mr. Ford may all of a sudden desire or figure out maybe his wife isn't as well as he thought or things aren't as good as he thought, and do us a "Lyndon Johnson."[110]

As a result, most press speculation conveyed the notion of a well-organized charismatic campaigner encountering an unelected, bumbling incumbent. While carefully hedged, the predictions favored a Reagan victory.[111]

At a critical point, Reagan's campaign organization lost control over its strategy of focusing news speculation on "strong showings" rather than "startling victories." New Hampshire Governor Melgrim Thomson predicted Reagan would achieve 55 percent of the vote, a statement that made national headlines.[112] Meanwhile, his campaign manager in Florida, Tommie Thomas, predicted a 55 percent Florida win, a downward revision of his earlier, overenthusiastic claim of a two-to-one victory.[113]

When Reagan failed to poll more voters than Ford in New Hampshire, reporters naturally recalled these preprimary predictions in their discussions of the defeat.[114] John Sears, Reagan's campaign manager, thought the press commentary neglected the strength of Reagan's vote:

> What happens matters less than the perception about what happens. Even though we came closer than anybody else to winning the New Hampshire primary over a sitting President, we were perceived as having lost it. . . . They [newsmen] would go around with Reagan and see that his crowds were enthusiastic and quite large in comparison to previous years. People felt that we had managed to put together an organization in New Hampshire that was broad enough to attract voters from the moderate as well as the conservative sections of the party. All this led people to believe before

the primary was run that if we didn't win it at that point, that we were losers, regardless of how close we might come and regardless of how our performance might stack up against other people's in previous years.[115]

Though some journalists did report the closeness of the voting and did predict a long nomination struggle, the net result was to make the Florida primary perceived as a make-or-break test for the Reagan candidacy.[116,117] When Reagan also lost the Florida primary, news reports then began to speculate on the prospects for his withdrawal for the race.[118] *Newsweek*'s Peter Goldman reported that the Florida results

> brought Reagan's own quick-kill strategy to a dead stop, and left him—not Ford—on the edge of an early-round TKO. . . . [The] spreading view of his peers was that he was finished. . . . The presumption among party insiders was that he would quit in a matter of weeks, or ought to. . . .[119]

Reports of Reagan's pending elimination spread from the national to the local press. When Reagan flew into North Carolina on March 18 to campaign for primary votes for four days, he was continually besieged by reporters' questions about whether he was planning to drop out of the race, particularly by the national press traveling with him.[120] Lou Cannon covered his first day in North Carolina:

> Ronald Reagan brought his fading presidential candidacy into North Carolina today with harsh words for President Ford's campaign committee and a defiant refusal to quit the Republican Presidential Race. Reagan, apparently exasperated with questions about how long he will be able to remain in the race, responded testily in Greensboro when he was asked by reporters. . . . But there were private indications here from some staunch Reagan supporters that the former California governor's campaign is on its last legs.[121]

Only one North Carolina newspaper report had previously suggested that Reagan might be shortly eliminated, but after March 18, such stories began appearing with increasing frequency.[122] Local reporters joining the candidate and the national journalists' tour of the state focused on this topic.[123]

Reagan's campaign coordinator in North Carolina complained that this speculation obscured the attacks Reagan was making against the President's policies:

> That influenced the local press, because in North Carolina there'd been no talk of withdrawal until the national press came in here. What they saw was a strong campaign and everybody was working very hard and aiming at the issues very concretely. . . . Then the local press picked it up and all we had for a couple days, in every evening news the first thing was, "Reagan again today reiterated that he will not withdraw from the race." So it took away from the issues of detente and the economy.[124]

This example also illustrates the interplay between opposing campaigners using reported news to accomplish their purposes. Following the Florida primary, the Ford Committee in Washington coordinated the pressures on Reagan to withdraw. On March 16, a group of Republican congressional leaders asked him to step aside; the next day a group of mayors said he should abandon his race.[125] In North Carolina, Ford's campaign office began putting out several press releases suggesting the time had come for Reagan to quit in the name of party unity.[126] All of these pressures were conveyed to Reagan in the form of news stories or questions from reporters.

Ford's southern coordinator Brad Hays offered the view that the efforts of the President Ford Committee contributed to the journalists' attention on Reagan's withdrawal.[127] Bo Calloway, Ford's national campaign manager, told newsmen that Florida was Reagan's best southern state, even though Calloway knew that was not the case.

> But the press picked up on it, and used it to help paint Reagan as "a loser." The press was beginning to believe, as Callaway was arguing, that when Reagan lost early, he no longer had a chance. . . . If you can get the press to believe what you want, you're in one hell of a position. . . . What the press believes is the biggest determinant of what the people believe. . . . The press viewing Reagan as "a loser," could cripple him. That's immensely important to Ford. . . . They are making Reagan justify his existence.[128]

The Ford campaign's efforts were the only reason for the perception that Reagan was finished. Reagan campaigners themselves sought to portray New Hampshire and Florida as their knock-out blows to Ford. Until North Carolina, both campaigns had been strategically planning upon a short campaign; critical primaries would winnow out the loser. Reagan's advisers conveyed their confidence to the press and failed to curtail the enthusiastic predictions of important local supporters in the two states.

Carter's Critical Test in Ohio. On June 8, 1976, delegates were selected in three large state primaries. The Democratic primary in California was generally conceded to Governor Jerry Brown, although proportional representation meant that strong second- and third-place showings could net some delegates. In Ohio, Jimmy Carter was entered against Mo Udall, a candidate whom he had beaten twice before in major head-to-head contests. In New Jersey, Carter faced a combination of forces that constituted the remaining major threats to his nomination: Jerry Brown, a candidate he had never defeated, running with the support of local party leaders, who had never been won over to the Carter candidacy. In these circumstances, most objective assessments would have placed New Jersey as the most critical test of the three.

Based on polling data, the Carter campaign realized it was going to lose California and the New Jersey delegate race, but would win in Ohio.[129] It therefore needed a means of emphasizing the Ohio results and downplaying their other losses. Their news strategy was to use Carter's traveling plans to highlight the significance of the Ohio primary. During the last two weeks of campaigning, Carter spent two days campaigning in California; he made appearances in New Jersey on four days; and was in Ohio on seven days.[130] To highlight Ohio even further, the campaign staff canceled a final trip to California and spent the day campaigning in Ohio.[131] As Jon Margolis of the *Chicago Tribune* had noted earlier, these last-minute campaign stops by Carter drew attention to the states in which he campaigned simply because the press corps traveling with him was so large.[132] As a result, during the week before the last three primaries, most analyses began to describe Ohio as the critical battleground.[133]

The Carter staff used another technique to ensure that the Ohio results would be uppermost in the journalists' thinking. Success had brought the Carter campaigners a growing influence over other important aspects of the very process on which journalists were trying to report. The day of the three primaries, Carter called Mayor Daley of Chicago, who controlled 86 delegates nominally pledged to Illinois' Senator Stevenson, to tell him that he would lose New Jersey and California, but would win in Ohio. Immediately after his talk with Carter, Daley said at a press conference: "If he [Carter] wins in Ohio, he'll walk in under his own power. . . ."[134] When asked how Ohio became the critical primary on June 8, Pat Caddell recalled:

> We orchestrated that. We were in trouble in New Jersey but we knew we were going to win in Ohio. Then Daley did it. Of course, we orchestrated that too! Jimmy called Daley and said "We're going to lose New Jersey, but we'll win in Ohio."[135]

Carter did well in Ohio. His at-large delegate states won 52 percent of the vote, and 126 delegates pledged to him were elected.[136] Always careful to understate expected showings, Carter had been predicting he would add 200 delegates to his committed support, an estimate based on a better showing in New Jersey.[137,138] Yet his Ohio win brought him 218 delegates for the day.

With Daley's endorsement virtually ensured, the pieces began to fall quickly into place. The three networks carried statements by his Ohio opponents saying they thought Carter would now receive the nomination, an opinion generally supported by the broadcast journalists. Once the nomination victory had been proclaimed over the networks, reality began to catch up with projections rapidly. Early the next morning, George Wallace called Carter to say he was releasing his delegates and urging them to vote for Carter. Daley, having started the bandwagon by helping to focus journalists on a primary that he knew in advance Carter would win, made his endorsement official, and Jackson called to say he would shortly release his delegates. Twenty-four hours later, Carter had a convention majority.

However, Jerry Brown took a very different view of the results. He insisted in live network interviews from Los Angeles the night of the primaries that his California and New Jersey victories meant that the nomination was not secured for Carter. In fact, Brown was quite startled to learn just before an interview with CBS's Walter Cronkite that Carter seemed to have the nomination sewed up. In the following except, JB is Jerry Brown and RW is Richard Wagner of CBS news:

> JB: What are you showing?
>
> RW: Sevareid said he didn't see how Carter could be stopped.
>
> JB: Jesus, he lost two out of three tonight!
>
> RW: Well, say that! Look, here's how it will go. Walter will start the interview. He'll say. . . . Well, with Church, he said—
>
> JB: [interrupting] What did Church say?
>
> RW: He thought it would be hard to stop Carter. . . .
>
> JB: What about Udall, what did he say?
>
> RW: He said it was all over. It's all up to you now. Daley said today, "If Carter wins in Ohio, he has it, and nobody can get it who hasn't run in the primaries." He knocked Hubert right out of the saddle.
>
> Producer: We're coming on.
>
> RW: Look, I may never get a chance to ask a question; Walter may do it all. . . .
>
> CBS Staffer: When it's his show, he runs it.
>
> Brown Staffer: Jerry, your hair's falling down.
>
> Producer: OK, here we come.
>
> [Cronkite asks a long question from election central in New York; not heard in room.]
>
> JB: Well, we're feeling awfully good. We're encouraged by New Jersey. We won two out of three tonight and. . . .

Mickey Kantor, Brown's campaign manager, recalled Brown's campaign's surprise at how fast the support gravitated to Carter:

> We felt we had two weeks to four weeks to affect all this. Things were moving so fast for us. We were concentrating on Oregon, Nevada, Rhode Island, New Jersey, California and how the media was viewing this situation. And then the media turned on the Ohio victory so quickly, it was like being hit in the face with a bucket of cold water.[139]

Regardless of the plausibility of Brown's contentions, the nomination fell rapidly into Carter's hands because his campaign had achieved its news strategy of focusing attention on the Ohio results and the delegate tally. His staff had been able to convince the newsmen that victory in Ohio constituted an adequate benchmark.

Conclusion

Campaigners and journalists devote considerable attention to the horserace aspects of presidential selection. The essence of the campaigner's job is to secure the election of their candidate. The discussion here, however, has pictured campaigners as preoccupied with more than the managing of political factors to achieve victory. The decisionmakers of presidential candidate organizations paid great attention to their perceptual environment, comprised by the body of interpretive statements surrounding objective campaign events. Campaigners base their action on those perceptions, and they attempt to influence the judgments journalists make in linking contemporary events to projected final outcomes.

For journalists, calling the horserace is a major element of campaign reporting. Projecting success and failure provides a continuously interesting story line. In contrast, the other possibilities—such as discussions of the candidates' personality or character, public policy positions, or support groups that may benefit under different presidents—are difficult to report. Horserace questions are ever-changing and exciting.

During the early stages of the presidential selection system, the imprecision of forecasting indicators places a premium on judgment and interpretation. Reporters must use their judgment in describing an overall scenario according to which the race will proceed; in selecting indicators; and applying these standards to the different campaigns to measure expansion or constriction in political support. Campaigners believe that those judgments sharply affect their electoral prospects. The images of serious versus failing candidacy affects both their ability to mobilize resources and their access to news coverage.

As presidential candidates succeed politically, they increasingly gain influence over the substance of horserace reporting for several reasons. Success in the primaries validates the scenarios, standards, and benchmarks promoted by winning campaigners. Carter's campaigners developed and promoted an explicit news strategy to cope with primary losses; the media reports reflected those conceptions.

Successful presidential candidates have the means to orient reporters toward questions which suit their purposes. For example, to make Ohio seem like the critical primary, the Carter campaign coordinated the behavior of other politicians in a manner that might lead reporters to the appropriate conclusions. Furthermore, the large press retinue traveling with Carter became a resource through which the campaign could orchestrate horserace reporting onto advantageous questions. Specifically, the staff kept attention focused on Carter's delegate count while Brown and other candidates argued that journalists should concentrate on the results of competitive primaries.

Thus, these recent experiences indicate that the political relationship between campaigners and journalists generally depends on the candidates's electoral success. Neither Reagan nor Ford could shape 1976 campaign reporting of the horserace to the extent that the Carter campaign could. Stalemate on the strategic dimension implied that the campaigners were unable to promote standards and benchmarks to their satisfaction.

The general election, lacking a sequential nature, is generally devoid of horserace reporting at the level of standards and benchmarks. When broad scenarios of electoral college strategies became quickly exhausted in terms of news value, campaign reporting tends to concentrate on policy questions or peripheral events which might shape the outcome. Coverage has generally been critical, often throwing candidates onto the defensive. In this atmosphere, campaigners reintroduce horserace questions to give journalists something to report upon other than a series of campaign gaffes. The televised presidential debates serve this purpose ideally; they have become transformed into pseudo-primaries.

In asserting that horserace reporting can influence voting, campaigners are really arguing that the impact of journalists lies in communicating perceived factual assertions, rather than opinions or attitudes. They receive some support from a study of voters' reactions to media in the 1972 race. Patterson and McClure distinguished between beliefs and opinions, asserting that campaign advertising through the media was effective in projecting beliefs to attentive citizens.[140] Their work attempted to refine earlier research that tried to measure, without much success, the transmission of political attitudes.

This perceived impact of factual assertions in the news is a variant of the agenda-setting power of mass media. In this case, however, the influence on voters is perceived as originating in the content of news reports as well as in coverage decisions that highlight certain candidates over others.

Media considerations and journalistic consensus play a major—if not primary—role in campaign decision making, at least in the two election years analyzed in this book. This influence seems strongest during the preprimary and early primary periods when the candidates have not yet developed strong political relationships with journalists. Campaigners reported that media considerations often resulted in major changes in their campaign plans. In retrospect, some campaigners complain about not being free to pursue the presidency without the judgments of journalists influencing their strategies and behaviors. In general, though, most take the view that those who live by the sword risk perishing that way as well:

[Y]ou can make those kinds of criticisms, but history proves that it doesn't make any difference: that's how they report it. That's how they've been reporting it. It is bred in the nature of what the press is about. . . . They've got rating problems. They've got to "hype" things. They have to create conflicts to build interest. I mean, you have to do that; that's the business you're in. So, I don't criticize them. They did precisely what we expected them to do. . . . I just wish we'd won one, that's all.[141]

I don't think that we were mistreated by the press in New Hampshire. The press was, perhaps, reacting to perceptions that predated the actual running of the primary. But you can question yourself constantly about what is perception and what is fact, and what responsibility people have to recognize fact as opposed to perception. In politics you reach a point where such distinctions are not possible—not for the press, not for the politicians. . . . There are times when you're helped, and times when you're hurt. That's just one of the facts of being in the business.[142]

Notes

1. Paul Kirk, national political director to Edward Kennedy, in *The Campaign for President: 1980 in Retrospect*, ed. Jonathan Moore (Cambridge, Mass.: Ballinger, 1981), p. 82.

2. At least one observer of 1976 found the willingness of campaign personnel to discuss their strategies openly with reporters quite astounding. See Vic Gold, *PR as in President* (Garden City, N.Y.: Doubleday, 1977).

3. Personal interview with Richard Stout, press secretary for Morris Udall, January 21, 1976.

4. Nelson W. Polsby and Aaron B. Wildavsky, *Presidential Elections* (New York: Scribners, 1976), pp. 165–167.

5. Leon D. Epstein makes a similar observation in "Political Science and Presidential Nomination," *Political Science Quarterly* (Summer 1978), pp. 177–196.

6. *New York Times*, March 1, 1980.

7. Remarks of Tim Kraft, campaign manager for Carter-Mondale Reelection Committee, at the Harvard Conference, Moore, *The Campaign for President,* pp. 76–77.

8. Paul Kirk, in ibid., p. 49–54.

9. Personal interview with Carl Wagner, director of field operations for Edward Kennedy, February 5, 1980.

10. Personal interview with Charles Snider, campaign manager for George Wallace, July 24, 1975.

11. Personal interview with Hamilton Jordan, campaign manager for Jimmy Carter, July 22, 1975.

12. Eddie Mahe, campaign director for John Connally, in Moore, *The Campaign for President,* pp. 4, 41.

13. Personal interview with John Sears, national campaign manager for Ronald Reagan, August 7, 1975.

14. Personal interview with Peter Kaye, press secretary for Gerald Ford's President Ford Committee, January 13, 1976.

15. The phrase "winnowed in" owes its inspiration to candidate Fred Harris. See Donald R. Matthews, "Winnowing: The News Media and the 1976 Presidential Nominations," in *Race for the Presidency*, ed. J.D. Barber (Englewood Cliffs, N.J.: Prentice-Hall, 1978).

16. Interview with Carl Wagner, February 5, 1980.

17. Remarks of Robert Teeter, pollster for George Bush at the Harvard Conference, in Moore, *The Campaign for President*, pp. 3 and 12.

18. Personal interview with Robert Teeter, February 4, 1980.

19. Personal interview with Doug Bailey, communications consultant to Howard Baker for President Committee, December 12, 1980.

20. Personal interview with Laura Broderick, press secretary for Philip Crane, April 18, 1981.

21. Personal interview with Mark Bisnow, press secretary for John Anderson, July 9, 1981; Joanne Coe, campaign manager for Robert Dole, in Moore, *The Campaign for President*, p. 5.

22. Personal interview with Brian Corcoran, press secretary to Henry Jackson, June 12, 1975.

23. Personal interview with Robert Neuman, press secretary to Morris Udall, June 12, 1975.

24. Personal interview with Frank Greer, national press secretary for Fred Harris, January 13, 1976.

25. Personal interview with Jack DeVore, press secretary to Lloyd Bentsen, January 21, 1976.

26. Personal interview with William Hall, press secretary to Frank Church, January 21, 1976. Peter Curtin, political director for Church, denied later that they were planning on a brokered convention, see Jonathan Moore and Janet Fraser, *Campaign for President* (Cambridge, Mass.: Ballinger, 1978), p. 108. But, without assuming a multiballot convention, the Church campaign's actions do not make a great deal of sense.

27. Personal interview with Ann Lewis, national political coordinator for Birch Bayh, January 22, 1976.

28. Remarks of Micky Kantor, campaign manager for Jerry Brown, found in Moore and Fraser, pp. 106–107.

29. Personal interview with Jean Westwood, campaign manager for Terry Sanford, July 9, 1975.

30. Spokesmen for the Church campaign, for example, differed as to the role of a multiballot convention would play in their effort. See note 26.

31. Arnold Steinberg, *The Political Campaign Handbook* (Lexington, Mass.: D.C. Heath, 1976).

32. Remarks of John Deardourff before the American Association of Advertising Agents, New York City, October 14, 1976; and his remarks in

Moore and Fraser, eds. *Campaign for President*, pp. 136–138. Wirthlin, Reagan's pollster, noted that in 1980 the bulk of their resources were husbanded during the last twenty and last ten days of the campaign (see Moore, *Campaign for President*, p. 192) and Peter Daley reported that 40 percent of their ad budget was saved for the last two weeks (see ibid., p. 246).

33. Remarks of Rick Sterns, Kennedy's chief of delegate selection, in Moore, *Campaign for President*, p. 59.

34. Remarks of Richard Wirthlin, in Moore, *The Campaign for President*, p. 109.

35. Remarks of Richard Wirthlin, in Moore, *The Campaign for President*, pp. 94, 97, and 109.

36. Personal interview with Steward Udall, national campaign manager for Morris Udall, July 8, 1975.

37. R.W. Apple, Jr., *New York Times*, October 27, 1975.

38. Witcover, Jules. *Marathon: The Pursuit of The Presidency, 1972–1976* (New York: Viking, 1977), p. 2000.

39. Ibid., p. 204.

40. Personal interview with Robert Newman, January 21, 1976.

41. Personal interview with John Gabusi, political coordinator for Morris Udall, December 10, 1976.

42. Carter lost to Wallace in the latter's home state, Alabama. Ohio was a partial exception since Church placed third (14%) behind Udall (21%).

43. Polsby and Wildavsky, *Presidential Elections*, pp. 106–107.

44. See stories reported by Peterson, *Washington Post*, May 8, 1976; Mohr, *New York Times*, May 8, 1976; *Washington Post*, May 15, 1976; Madden, *Washington Post*, May 15, 1976; Baker, *Washington Post*, May 19, 1976; Dewar, *Washington Post, May 21, 1976; Witcover, Washington Post*, May 28, 1976; Apple, *New York Times*, May 11, and 13, 1976.

45. R.W. Apple, Jr., "Democratic Chiefs Beginning to Rank Presidential Rivals," *New York Times*, January 12, 1976.

46. Interview by Scott Moeller with Sterling Monroe, administrative assistant to Henry Jackson, February 18, 1977.

47. Personal interview with Robert Keefe, campaign manager for Henry Jackson, June 12, 1975.

48. Personal interview with Robert Neuman, June 12, 1975.

49. Hamilton Jordan predicted the difficulties Udall would have selling this indicator to the media in a personal interview, July 22, 1975.

50. Personal interview with Robert Neumann, June 12, 1975.

51. Personal interview with Stewart Udall, July 8, 1975.

52. Personal interview with John Cabusi, July 8, 1975.

53. Personal interview with Paul Clancey, press secretary to Terry Sanford, July 7, 1975.

54. Ibid.

55. Quote from personal interview with James Hightower, campaign manager to Fred Harris, July 8, 1975. Interview with John Gabusi, July 8, 1975.

56. Personal interview with Jean Westwood, July 9, 1975.

57. Broder, *Washington Post*, July 3, 1975; Lydon, *New York Times*, July 13, 1975.

58. For a complete assessment of the effects of the finance laws see *Financing Presidential Campaigns*, a report of the Campaign Finance Study Group to the Committee on Rules and Administration of the U.S. Senate (Cambridge, Mass.: Institute of Politics, Harvard U., 1982).

59. Interview with David Keene, Bush's campaign manager, conducted by Jeff Kampelman, February 14, 1980.

60. Personal interview with Michael MacLeod, campaign manager for John Anderson, December 6, 1980.

61. Remarks of Eddie Mahe, campaign manager for John Connally, in Moore, *The Campaign for President,* p. 41.

62. Michael J. Robinson and Karen A. McPherson, "Television News Coverage Before the 1976 New Hampshire Primary: The Focus of Network Journalism," *Journal of Broadcasting,* 21 (Spring 1977), pp. 177–186.

63. Thomas Patterson, *Mass Media Election* (New York: Praeger, 1980).

64. Lloyd Miller, Jr., "Now, Jimmy Carter's the Man to Beat," *Miami Herald*, January 21, 1976, p. 11A.

65. David Alpern, "Man on the Move," *Newsweek*, February 2, 1976, p. 18.

66. NBC Nightly News, February 25, 1976; *Time*, March 8, 1976, p. 11.

67. Peter Goldman, "Can Kennedy Hang On?" *Newsweek*, February 4, 1980, p. 43.

68. Interview with Wagner, February 4, 1980.

69. Remarks of Hedrick Smith, in *Nominating a President: The Press and the Process,* Ed. The Los Angeles Times Editors, (New York: Praeger, 1980), p. 9.

70. Personal interview with Robert Teeter, Bush's pollster, February 3, 1980.

71. Witcover, *Marathon*, p. 202.

72. Patterson, *Mass Media Election.*

73. Personal interview with Brian Corcoran, June 12, 1975.

74. Personal interview with Robert Keefe, June 12, 1975.

75. Interview by Paul Storffer with Robert Keefe, March 18, 1978.

76. For analysis in advance of the voting see, Witcover, *Washington Post*, March 9, 1976; MacPherson, *Washington Post*, March 8, 1976; Reed, *New York Times*, March 4 and 7, 1976; Rosenbaum, *New York Times*, March 6, 1976. Analysis of the results is found in Reed, *New York Times*,

March 10, 19976; Reinhold, *New York Times*, March 11, 1976; Lardner, *Washington Post*, March 10, 1976.

77. Witcover, *Marathon*, p. 261.

78. For a detailed look at the forecasting problem, see Steven Rosenstone, *Forecasting Presidential Elections* (New Haven, Conn.: Yale U. Press, 1983). The most extensive set of public polls was conducted during the 1980 general election by the *New York Times* and CBS News. Especially during October, analysis of key states can be found on an almost daily basis.

79. Robert Ajemian, "Jostling for the Edge," *Time*, September 27, 1976, p. 11; see also James Wooten, "First of 3 debates by Ford and Carter Viewed as Critical," *New York Times*, September 24, 1976.

80. Adam Clymer, "Carter and Reagan to Meet Tonight in Debate That Could Decide Race," *New York Times*, October 28, 1980.

81. Adam Clymer, "Reagan and Carter Poised for Debate Crucial to Election," *New York Times*, October 29, 1980.

82. Ibid.

83. Personal interview with Barry Jagoda, media adviser to Carter, January, 1977.

84. See Clymer, *New York Times,* October 28, 1980.

85. Ibid.

86. Remarks by Robert Teeter, pollster for Ford, in Moore and Fraser, *The Campaign for President*, p. 142.

87. Remarks by John Deardourff, ibid., p. 142.

88. Remarks by Patrick Caddell, ibid., p. 141. Caddell was referring to the series of news crises experienced by the Carter campaign during the general election.

89. Personal interview with Barry Jagoda, January 7, 1977.

90. Clymer, *New York Times,* October 29, 1980.

91. Ibid.

92. Ron Nessen, *It Sure Looks Different from the Inside* (New York: Playboy Press, 1978), p. 248.

93. See Martin Schram, "After the Debate the Pollsters Scramble," *Washington Post*, October 30, 1980, p. A1.

94. Remarks of Patrick Caddell, Carter's pollster, ibid.

95. Remarks by Robert Teeter, Moore and Fraser, *The Campaign for President*, p. 142.

96. See George F. Bishop and others (eds.) *The Presidential Debates* (New York: Praeger, 1978) or Sidney Kraus (ed.) *The Great Debates* (Bloomington: Indiana University Press, 1962).

97. David Alpern, "Iowa: Off and Running," *Newsweek*, April 24, 1982.

98. Personal interview with Hamilton Jordan, July 22, 1975.

99. Personal interview with Frank Greer, January 13, 1976.

100. Personal interview with Richard Murphy, campaign manager for Sargeant Shriver, January 14, 1976.

101. Personal interview with Richard Stout, press secretary for Morris Udall, January 21, 1976.

102. Personal interview with William Wise, January 14, 1976.

103. R.W. Apple, Jr., "New Hampshire Primary Fades into a Numbers Game," *New York Times*, February 14, 1972. See also the *Washington Post* story on February 3, 1972.

104. Personal interview with Martin Plisner, CBS News, December 5, 1976.

105. Remarks of Jack Nelson, political correspondent for the *Los Angeles Times*, in *Nominating the President*, p. 17. Italics added.

106. See the discussion in Moore, *The Campaign for President,* pp. 95-99.

107. Jules Witcover, *Washington Post*, March 9, 1976.

108. New Hampshire results: Ford: 55, 156 (49%); Reagan: 53,569 (48%). Florida results: Ford: 321,982 (53%); Reagan: 287,837 (47%). See ABC News, *Factbook* (New York: ABC News, 1976).

109. During March the campaign was running a deficit of $1.5 million without much income (Sears, in Moore and Fraser, *The Campaign for President*, p. 43). After North Carolina the candidate went on national television and raised $1.3 million with a single appearance.

110. Personal interview with Lyn Nofziger, press secretary for Reagan (later California coordinator, later convention manager, and still later Dole's campaign manager), August 6, 1975.

111. See the following stories: Thomas Wicker, *New York Times*, January 4, 1976; Warren Weaver, *New York Times*, January 6, 1976; Jules Witcover, *Washington Post*, January 6, 1976; David Broder, *Washington Post*, January 31, 1976, February 6, 12, and 22, 1976; Douglas Kneeland, *New York Times*, February 5 and 7, 1976; James Naughton, *New York Times*, February 8 and 10, 1976; John Nordheimer, *New York Times*, February 13, 1976; and unsigned stories: *Washington Post*, February 11 and 16, 1976; *New York Times*, February 18, 1976. An examination of regional newspapers shows the same pattern of reporting; in the *St. Louis Post-Dispatch*, for example, Reagan's potential victories were noted in stories by Thomas Ottenand, January 18, 1976, February 1, 7, 8, 22, and 24, 1976.

112. Thompson's statement was quoted in many papers repeatedly; see *Washington Post*, February 12 and 16, 1976, or *Miami Herald*, February 16, 1976.

113. See, for example, Roland Evans and Robert Novak, *Washington Post*, January 5, 1976; R.W. Apple, Jr., *New York Times*, January 11 and 28, 1976; Lou Cannon, *Washington Post*, January 12 and 30 and February 14, 1976.

114. For analyses of the New Hampshire defeat see Witcover, *Washington Post*, February 26, 1976; Naughton, *New York Times*,

February 26, 1976; Helen Dewar, *Washington Post*, February 26, 1976; Joseph Kraft, *Washington Post*, February 26, 1976; R.W. Apple, Jr., *New York Times,* February 26,1976; Ottenad, *St. Louis Post-Dispatch,* February 25, 1976; Squires, *Chicago Tribune,* February 26, 1976.

115. Sears, in Moore and Fraser, *The Campaign for President*, p. 35.

116. See the pieces by R.W. Apple, *New York Times*, February 26, 1976; Robert Reinhold, *New York Times,* February 26, 1976; Ottenad, *St. Louis Post-Dispatch*, February 25, 1976; Squires, *Chicago Tribune*, February 25, 1976.

117. For analyses that depict Florida as a critical test for Reagan, see Witcover, *Washington Post*, February 26, 1976 and March 9, 1976; Nordheimer, *New York Times*, February 27, 1976, and March 4, and 6, 1976; *Washington Post* editorial, ". . . and Reagan Prepares for His 'Last Stand', " February 26, 1976; Wicker, *New York Times*, March 2 and 7, 1976; Reed, *New York Times*, March 2 and 7, 1976; Evans and Novak, *Washington Post*, March 6, 1976; Cannon, *Washington Post*, March 9, 1976.

118. Articles from the two national papers which suggest that Reagan was close to being eliminated include those by Apple, *New York Times*, March 12 and 17, 1976; Broder, *Washington Post*, March 12, 14, and 17, 1976; Cannon, *Washington Post*, March 19 and 22, 1976; and Curtis Wilkie, *Boston Globe*, March 10, 1976.

119. Peter Goldman, "Ford's Winning Look," *Newsweek* March 22, 1976, p. 16.

120. Personal observation at Reagan's news conferences.

121. Lou Cannon, "Reagan Assails Ford Group, Refuses to Quit GOP Race," *Washington Post*, March 19, 1976, p. A4.

122. *Charlotte Observer*, "Illinois Victory for Ford Could End Reagan's Hopes," March 15, 1976. Local papers were clipped during the month before the primary and examined for comments on Reagan's withdrawal.

123. Research uncovered two such stories appeared on March 19, two on March 20, four on March 22, and twelve on March 23, the day of the primary.

124. Interview with Carter Wren, campaign coordinator in North Carolina for Ronald Reagan, March 22, 1976.

125. See Cannon, *Washington Post*, or *Charlotte Observer*, March 20, 1976, for discussion of this Ford effort.

126. Report by student observers in Reagan's North Carolina campaign.

127. Personal interview with Bradford Hayes, Southern Coordinator for Ford, March 23, 1976.

128. Ibid.

129. See the account given by Martin Schram in *Running for President* (New York: Stein and Day, 1977), p. 176.

130. Carter's schedule was as follows: May 25: Rhode Island and New York; May 26: New York, New Jersey, and Washington, D.C.; Ohio; May 28: Ohio; May 29: Georgia; May 30: Rhode Island; May 31: Rhode Island, Ohio, and South Dakota; June 1: California; June 2; California; June 3: Ohio; June 4; Ohio; June 5; New Jersey; June 6: New Jersey and Ohio; June 7: Ohio and New Jersey.

131. The decision to write off California was reported by the *Houston Post* (June 5, 1976) as follows: "Powell also announced Carter cancelled a scheduled trip Monday into California. . . . He said Carter would concentrate instead on Ohio. . . ." Helen Dewar reported the extra time would be spent in Ohio and New Jersey: "Carter Pushes Drive in Ohio, New Jersey," *Washington Post*, June 5, 1976, p. 4.

132. *Chicago Tribune*, June 1, 1976.

133. Evans and Novak, *Washington Post*, June 2, 1976; Kraft, *Washington Post*, June 2, 1976; Broder, *Washington Post*, June 3, 1976.

134. For another report suggesting collusion, see Witcover, *Marathon*, p. 349.

135. Personal conversation with Pat Caddell, June 24, 1977.

136. Carter received 83 percent of the delegates because Ohio's delegate selection rules fell under the party rules which provided an exception to the proportional representation rules, the so-called "loophole" primary.

137. Broder, *Washington Post*, June 3, 1976; *Atlanta Constitution*, May 29, 1976; *Miami Herald*, June 7, 1976; and *Newsweek*, June 14, 1976.

138. Associated Press, for example, estimated his New Jersey total might reach 54; he received only 25. "World Series for Candidates in 3 Primaries," *Boston Globe*, June 8, 1976, p. 1.

139. Mickey Kantor quoted in Witcover, *Marathon,* p. 353. Emphasis added.

140. Thomas E. Patterson and Robert P. McClure, *Political Advertising: Voter Reaction to Televised Political Commercials* (Princeton, N.J.: Citizens Research Foundation, 1973).

141. Personal interview with John Gabusi, December 10, 1976.

142. Sears, in Moore and Fraser, *The Campaign for President*, pp. 37–38.

7 Presidential Elections and Media Politics

That presidential campaign organizations should attempt to exploit the mass media is hardly surprising. The political system under which we nominate and elect presidents imposes upon campaigns a heavy burden of rapid and repetitive communications with a large and diverse electorate. Campaigns, being temporary political organizations, are simply incapable of reaching directly the required number of citizens. Moreover, whether through disinterest or hostility to politics, a large number of voters insulate themselves from persuasive messages emanating from politicians. In compensation, campaigners turn to the news-reporting industry with its preexisting, extensive, and credible communication links to the electorate.

The nature of the nomination process itself, moreover, magnifies the importance of media politics for campaigners. Election politics involve a high degree of uncertainty. Public opinion polls, the sophistication of campaign organizations, endorsements by recognized officeholders, support from active interest groups, personal style on television, fundraising success, performance in early primaries and caucuses, accumulated delegates, leadership on public policy questions all provide clues to the ultimate success or failure of the contenders.

At their best, however, these indicators yield only a static picture of the support for each candidate, when what is required is a projection of growth or decline in that support. When combined, moreover, these estimates most frequently render contradictory and confusing predictions. Each candidate is likely to have different strong points. The key to success is obscure. In short, the ambiguities inherent in the political system that leads to the presidency are so manifold as to require considerable judgment on the part of political observers, politicians and journalists.

Uncertainty about the realities of political support, therefore, highlights the importance of those interpretations which are bantered about by campaigners, journalists, and assumedly, voters. These judgments, once they become widely accepted, take on a life of their own whether or not they are defensible conceptions of the status of the race. The perceptual environment within which the campaign is conducted is frequently more important than actual events. Thus, reporters may perceive a candidate's win in a given primary as an indication of declining support if the margin of victory failed to meet media expectations. A narrow loss can be interpreted as a significant defeat; a bare plurality in a multicandidate field might be viewed as a signal victory.

As a result, campaigns struggle to define a perceptual environment that surrounds concrete events. Yet statements by the politicians about changes in their support or that of their competitors are, in most instances, dismissed as self-serving and biased. At the same time, voters give greater credibility to interpretations disseminated through the news media, because they are associated with the norm of journalistic objectivity. Politicians firmly believe that media statements can become a substitute for political reality and have definite consequences for their ability to mobilize support. Naturally they seek to influence the interpretations made by journalists.

Journalists, no doubt, wish that there were fewer uncertainties in predicting electoral success. They would rather call it as it is. Unfortunately, the history of recent presidential campaigns indicates that the realities of political support are not evident until very late in the process. This is not to say that campaign journalism is totally the creation of the reporters' imaginations. Unquestionably, reporters and correspondents are projecting pictures of an ongoing political process of gathering support. It is also true, however, that in so doing, they contribute to that process.

Manipulating the Media?

If it is clear why politicians might wish to shape the content of news reporting, it is equally understandable why career journalists resent overt attempts to influence their work. Reporters, however, face something of a dilemma in their relations with politicians. Undeniably, a presidential race involves events that will affect the life of every viewer and reader. As a result, newsgathering organizations have little choice in whether or not they will cover the campaign, only in how they will cover it. Journalists are, therefore, forced to rely upon campaigners as sources of important news; that reliance exposes them to influence by the politicians.

On face value, it is obvious that campaigners can influence the content of news coverage. Politicians hold much of the initiative in their dealings with newsmen. Through speeches, position papers, press releases, appearances in desired contexts, and other actions, candidate organizations create events that journalists report as the news from the campaign trail.

If the manipulation was limited to this level, it would be trivial. Journalists surround their descriptions with interpretations of the importance of these occurrences of the motivations that underlie the campaign's effort. These statements of interpretation, the perceptual environment within which campaign events occur, become the focus of a struggle between campaigners and journalists.

"Orchestration" rather than "manipulation" is a more apt description of the efforts of politicians to confine the content of reported news to material and observations that benefit their campaigns. Their attempts may be as benign as creating a daily story to fill up the available news space. Campaign activity may be so structured to lead reporters to focus upon one topic and to ignore others. Yet, campaigners sometimes deliberately distort information to mislead journalists.

Obviously, it is difficult to prove conclusively that campaigners have successfully determined the news coverage received by their candidate. Certainly campaigners are not able to dictate stories to the reporters and correspondents assigned to cover them. Overt attempts to manipulate news content are certain to be counterproductive when journalistic norms of independence and objectivity are triggered. Rather, the nature of campaign influence described here consists mainly of attempts to narrow the range of reportable stories.

The examples in previous chapters document that news coverage—particularly that which required a high degree of interpretation and judgment on the part of the journalist—often reflects campaign goals. Even though the campaigners in question claimed to have promoted those interpretations, their claims should not be accepted too readily. These examples do not provide conclusive evidence that newsmen were responding, even unwittingly, to their influence.

With these reservations, the major assertions of the orchestration hypothesis can be stated. First, campaigners are increasingly explicit in their attempts to orchestrate news coverage. They frame campaign behavior according to their expectations of how the news-reporting process occurs.

Second, as a presidential campaign gathers political strength, it becomes better able to manipulate the phenomena that reporters are trying to cover. Thus, the political relationship between campaigners and newsmen alters according to the campaign's strength in the electoral arena. In 1975, Carter, for example, could only hope for national news coverage. By the close of the primaries, however, he was able to use his political leverage to enlist Mayor Daley in his effort to focus reporters' attention on the Ohio primary and away from other primaries on the same day. The Carter-Daley cooperation was a political maneuver designed to affect the nomination race through the attitudes and behavior of journalists.

Third, successful campaigns acquire a large retinue of reporters and correspondents that provides upper-echelon management with the means for influencing coverage. Competition between numerous journalists for access to the candidate and campaign staff allows the latter to deal with journalists as a group rather than as individuals. Tactics as simple as blocking follow-up questions—presumably to give everyone an opportunity to ask his or her questions—can add up to a pattern of influence. Moreover, reporters permanently assigned to cover a presidential campaign surrender their own physical location to the campaign scheduling office. Their job is to go where the candidate goes. Campaigners may exercise this leverage to focus newsmen onto a desired topic or away from others.

Finally, rapid travel curtails the flow of outside information and perspectives into the press corps, thereby increasing the reliance of reporters and correspondents upon information sources under the campaign's control. Campaigners cannot completely determine the internal information pool, but they can heavily influence it.

The relationship between news reporting and the campaign of an incumbent president is even more complex. The incumbent possesses at the outset considerable control over the flow of newsworthy items. Presidents have no problem receiving abundant news coverage of their actions or thoughts. Their interactions with journalists throughout a reelection campaign resemble the relationship attained by others only in the latter stages of campaigning.

As the campaign proceeds, politicians are better able to orchestrate horserace statements about their progress and prospects and less able to influence their image and issue stands. The horserace aspects of reports on a presidential campaign change constantly, while images are, by their nature, assertions about the enduring characteristics of the candidates. New events and new measurements of political support mean a continuous flow of predictions about the final outcome. By contrast, images and labels that summarize the candidate's appeal to voters develop more slowly. As the campaign unfolds, a particular characterization becomes linked to numerous events and other beliefs about the candidate in question. Once formed, these images are much harder to erase; they are less amenable to influence by campaigners. Regardless of whether or not image reporting is anchored in reality (was Ted Kennedy inarticulate?), these labels take on a weight of their own, especially as they are transmitted to the public and become linked to voting choices.[1] Images become the filter through which evidence is selected and judgments are rendered.

One should not conclude, however, that politicians lose control over their campaign themes to the journalists. In fact, both groups become increasingly less able to alter the imagery surrounding an election campaign. In terms of ability to orchestrate news coverage, therefore, once one moves beyond the simple chronicling of events staged by campaigns, politicians are more successful in the domain of horserace statements about the support-building process.

Reciprocal Influence

While journalists worry about manipulation, campaigners view their interactions with news-reporting organizations as greater than their efforts to orchestrate desired news coverage. Their activities throughout the campaign—let alone their direct exchanges with journalists in, for example, news conferences—are heavily conditioned by media considerations. Campaigners spend a good deal of their time reacting to actual news coverage or attempting to anticipate the news coverage that will flow from their actions. In other words, they allow themselves to be influenced by the work of journalists. Media politics embrace influence in both directions—orchestration and accommodation. The relationship is reciprocal.

During 1976 and 1980, campaigners often designed their politicial strategies around anticipated news reporting. For example, anticipating that New Hampshire would receive abundant coverage as the nation's first primary, most campaign staffs decided to enter that race. Believing, furthermore, that interpretations of primary showings depend more heavily on what is expected rather than concrete results, campaigners maneuvered to minimize press expectations of their probable performance. Anticipated news coverage, moreover, can affect major areas of campaign decisionmaking, such as which primaries to enter, how to describe one's political strategy, when to announce one's vice presidential choice, or how to present oneself to the electorate.

Our analysis also brought to the surface numerous instances in which campaigners reacted to the news coverage they were already receiving. Mo Udall altered the theme of his campaign to emphasize issues when early news reporting indicated his positions were vague. Terry Sanford learned that his fundraising plans were at odds with what journalists considered appropriate for a serious presidential bid. To obtain news coverage, he had to restructure his campaign organization to qualify for federal matching funds. After victories in New York and Connecticut, the Kennedy campaign decided not to campaign exclusively in the upcoming Wisconsin primary. His planners believed if they did, reporters would then comment that Kennedy could continue in the race only if he won in Wisconsin.

This research indicates that campaigns are most vulnerable to influence by news reporting when they are politically weakest. At the outset of the race, many of the nascent campaigns were unable to pursue their own political, thematic, or fundraising strategies in the face of journalistic consensus to the contrary. Unable to obtain news coverage at all or suffering from criticism from major political journalists, campaigners based fundamental decisions on the judgments of journalists. Even in later stages of the campaign, news reporting had its most profound impact on campaigns when they were in political trouble. In contrast, in gaining political support, campaigners validate their assumptions about the major determinant of success, and are able to gain acceptance, however grudgingly, for them by reporters and correspondents.

In summary, presidential campaigns are initiated in a position of reliance and subservience to news reporting. As they succeed in the nomination race, however, they become better able to influence the news coverage they receive. From the campaigners' perspective, this shift is both expected and assumed to be perfectly natural, because politicians conceive of their interactions with journalists as one of a number of politicial relationships.

They naturally exploit opportunities for improving their position in the reciprocal influence relationship, such as dispensing news collectively to an expanding press corps rather than responding to individual requests or rationing the candidate's time among competing news organizations with very different audiences. Campaigners are not, therefore, simply interested in orchestrating the content of each day's news; they are also attentive to ways in which they can increase their influence on news reporting in the future.

The Consequences of Media Politics

Certainly, media politics do not comprise the whole of modern campaigns for the presidency. The relationships described here exist simultaneously with the campaigner's attempts to influence segments of the politically active community. Parallel to their contacts with journalists, politicians respond to the behvaior and values of both voters and party activists on the one hand, while trying to influence their behavior on the other.

In some respects, the press corps functions as an intermediary and surrogate for the electorate and politically active communities. Reporters have unique opportunities to observe and question the candidates. They pass along the understandings they glean from such exposure in their stories. The fact that the news media offer a convenient channel to the electorate provides a major incentive for campaigners to develop news strategies. This is as it should be.

The problems arise because campaigners respond to the journalistic corps as more than simply a surrogate for the electorate. Indeed, many examples cited in this book indicate that interactions with journalists comprise an alternative sphere of campaigning. Politicians conform directly to the desires of reporters while trying to affect their behavior. At the point at which relations with the press corps begin to supplant or alter significantly dealings with the electorate, media politics come to have implications for the functioning of the electoral system.

Research by political scientists has not yet established whether information and evaluations transmitted by the mass media actually affect citizens' cognitions, attitudes, and behavior. However, politicians firmly believe in these effects—that is, that what journalists say about them will have a massive influence on their ability to mobilize political support. This assumption, in fact, forms the basis of their carefully calculated attempts to influence, predict, and respond to news coverage. However, because media effects on their audiences remain unproved, the conclusions discussed here are presented from both sides of the argument—that the content of news reporting can or cannot shape public support.

Assuming Media Effects Do Exist

The available literature on public opinion frequently distinguishes between politically active citizens—those attentive to and interested in politics and public affairs—and the rest of the electorate.[2] Particularly during the preprimary period, campaign news strategies target party activists who pay close attention to the news media for information about the candidates. From this active strata, campaigns seek to mobilize electoral resources that can be utilized in subsequent efforts to attract the support of voters. Volunteers and financial contributions are essential to underwriting the appeal for votes. Campaigners count on news coverage to aid these mobilization efforts. Campaigners mention the comparative ease of building a campaign organization when the news is favorable or the increased flow of money into campaigns that are receiving exposure in the news media.

Politics are less visible and important to the average voter under most conditions. Such insulation from politics must certainly be partially responsible for the inability of social research to demonstrate media effects. Qualitatively and quantitatively, different relationships may well exist among the attentive strata. These certainly deserve greater attention, for they form a major and possibly decisive link in the support-building dynamics of presidential campaigns. No systematic interviews were conducted with party activists for this research. However, the persistent finding that individuals making decisions for campaign organizations themselves respond to news coverage may be taken as partial evidence that news content affects the electoral process at the elite level. Unfortunately the transmission mechanisms for opinion and information from elites to the attentive public and ultimately to citizen voters are still poorly understood.[3]

The argument that news coverage, particularly of the horserace aspects, sharply affects campaigners' ability to mobilize political resources appears plausible. Scholars of electoral politics generally posit three reasons why individuals become active in politics. Some activists are motivated by friendly contact with other individuals; some are energized by policy concerns; and others are impelled by the material incentives that may accompany winning elections.[4] Joining the winning candidate early enough to secure access to that candidate and his upper level staff constitutes one of the most successful strategies for reaping material benefits or influence in policy matters. News content that describes one candidate as a likely possibility for the nomination can thus generate a flow of support to that campaign of attentive activists. The outpouring of such support may itself validate the prediction. Certainly, campaigners labor under this supposition. For example, campaigners often photocopy favorable speculations by prominent national journalists for mass mailings to party activists.

If we assume that media effects do exist on the level of the electorate, this cyclical process is repeated in magnified dimensions once the primaries begin. The rapid rise in Carter's or Bush's name recognition and preference polls after New Hampshire, for example, may have been transferred through nonmedia sources. However, in the face of cover stories by the newsweeklies, extensive network coverage, and nationwide newspaper headlines, news coverage is the more likely transmission mechanism.

Finally, at least a plausible argument can be advanced that in 1976 news coverage produced an outsider effect that benefitted Jimmy Carter. Because McGovern moved from an extreme long-shot position to become the party's nominee in 1972, the argument goes, journalists were highly aware of the possibility of that scenario repeating itself in 1976. When Carter showed some early signs of strength, reporters rushed to Atlanta to build sources within the campaign, to gain an understanding of Carter before he became isolated by the demands for access to his time, and to inform their audiences about his chances for nomination. The net result was news coverage for Carter far beyond that achieved by his competitors. In turn, this coverage generated greater political support. In effect, the argument proposes that by looking for a darkhorse victor, the media contributed to its happening.

This proposition, however, was not confirmed in 1980. George Bush benefited enormously in news coverage by his success in the Iowa caucuses. Polls at the time showed a marked shift toward Bush away from Reagan. Reagan strategists responded by actively and aggressively campaigning in New Hampshire, something they had intentionally minimized before Iowa. Although it is impossible to dissect how Reagan regained his support and won the New Hampshire primary, it is certainly clear that abundant and favorable horserace reporting was not sufficient to produce victory for Bush.

What can be said is that national news exposure transformed Bush from a little-known candidate to a formidable challenger to the frontrunner. As frontrunner, Reagan may have been more readily able to reestablish his political support in the face of all that news coverage for Bush than Carter's competitors, who had to attract support, not reclaim it. In addition, Reagan was covered by a large corps of journalists, which considerably eased his problem of effectively countering Bush's dominance in news space after Iowa. To be sure, news coverage alone did not make Jimmy Carter in 1976, just as it did not deliver the nomination to Bush in 1980. But saying this is not the same thing as arguing that it had no effect upon the political competition in those two years.

Without Assuming Media Effects

The consequences of the relationship between media politics and campaign politics do not end if news content has no effect on the attitudes and behavior of citizens or party activists. News reporting still has a direct effect upon the conduct of presidential campaigns, primarily because campaigners act under the assumption that media effects do exist. Many of the major campaign decisions in 1976 and 1980 were based wholly or in part upon calculations of news coverage. Collectively, these decisions certainly affected the outcome of the presidential race.

Counterfactual speculation would be required to argue that this process affects the election outcome. Consider, for example, the fact that Udall lost the 1976 New Hampshire primary by 4,663 votes. Would he have received more votes if he had not spent ten days campaiging in Iowa instead of New Hampshire? We cannot know. Udall's campaigners, however, are convinced they would have done better and might even have won. We do know, however, that if he had won in New Hampshire, Udall would have been on the covers of *Time* and *Newsweek* (both were prepared in case he won) and received far more network news coverage. Rewriting history cannot provide a decisive answer to the question of whether news reporting shapes the election or nomination outcome.

Relations with journalists, however, do shape what campaigners actually do in their attempts to mobilize electoral support. On a superficial level, large amounts of campaign activity go into the effort to generate news coverage. Scarce resources are thus diverted from direct attempts to influence voters and party activists. But it is doubtful that candidates and their upper-level operatives could directly contact more than a tiny fraction of the electorate even if they did nothing else. Nevertheless, media politics makes a deep imprint on the way in which campaigners approach their task. The quest for news coverage establishes the nature of the campaign's daily schedule. In pursuing local media to complement national exposure guaranteed by the traveling press corps, for example, recent campaigners try to schedule their candidate into three media markets each day. Contemporary presidential candidates are constantly on the move. Because the marginal returns in news coverage derived from remaining longer in one area decrease sharply after the first "reportable" event, campaigns try to cover as much ground—literally as many markets—as possible.

A century ago, presidential campaigns were conducted quite differently. During the 1860 campaign, Lincoln stayed at home in Springfield and refused to make political speeches, preferring to meet with supporters in small groups.[5] In 1876, Tilden cloistered himself in his New York mansion which he turned into a campaign headquarters, drawing political supporters to him.[6] Even as late as 1896, when Mark Hanna was organizing McKinley's campaign, he arranged for the Ohio governor to spend long social vacations in Georgia, where his operatives arranged meetings with southern politicians. In contrast to modern campaigning, these meetings were arranged as quietly as possible in order to minimize news coverage.[7]

Modern techniques are very different. Contemporary presidential campaigning does not provide frequent opportunities for lengthy, private meetings between the candidate and local political leaders. To be certain, politicians jointly appear on numerous platforms during the hectic campaign and attempt to stay in contact with each other. But there is no time for elaborate negotiations to arrange reciprocal political support.[8] Carter once described himself as the president to arrive in the White House least encumbered by political deals. Whether that was true, his statement ignored the benefits of negotiating a coalition of political support that would make it easier to govern once he achieved office. In part, this absence resulted from Carter's predilections; he was running against a political establishment. But it is also attributable to the demands of campaigning through the news media.

The depth of this change goes well beyond the surface relationship between campaigns and media organizations. Since the turn of the century, many of the communication links in electoral politics have been depersonalized. Appeals for support through lasting party structures once involved person-to-person contact. The ward boss dealt directly with his precinct leaders. In the process, at least he had to listen to their wants, grievances, and petitions to secure their support in delivering the vote. At each point in the communication structure, reciprocal influence was exchanged as human beings dealt directly with each other.

While contemporary electoral politics still involves a large measure of direct personal contact, the major change in campaigning over the last two decades has been the development of communication in depersonalized forms. Computer-assisted, direct-mail operations dispatch millions of letters to purchased lists of citizens. Volunteers staff telephone banks, calling as many voters as possible with a standardized appeal for support. Leaflets are dropped on computer-targeted geographical areas. And candidates reach out for voters through the mass media both in advertising and through their news strategies. There are, furthermore, methods for reverse communication, for receiving information about voters' concerns. Polling provides an opportunity for upward communication that is initiated by the campaign. These links, however, are detached from the downward-directed appeals for support. The information is structured by the priorities of the campaign and arrives as aggregated data.

The depersonalization of the major means of building electoral support at the mass level has removed the quid pro quo from large areas of campaigns' persuasive activities. If the nomination and office can be seized without making deals, there is little incentive for politicians to go through the laborious and constraining process of coalition-building. The promises that cement mutual support by their nature limit the flexibility of office-seekers who would prefer to keep their options open. As an alternative means of securing elective office, campaigning through the news-reporting process holds out this obvious benefit—candidates do not have to bargain away appointments or policies before taking office.

Perhaps this makes no difference. Perhaps coalitions are built once politicians are in office, through the process of governing. There are reasons, however, for suspecting that media politics may spill over into the actions of politicians once they control public institutions. In developing this argument, we take as a starting point a central assumption of democratic theory. A democratic political system should force those who seek or hold elective office to respond to the needs and desires of the citizenry. Are the preferences of the majority of voters reflected in the public policies pursued by elected officials?[9] What politicians in office do in the way of blocking or promoting certain public policies should, in theory, have an effect upon their electoral prospects.[10]

I do not intend to explore how effectively this process of representation now functions given the pivotal role of the news-reporting industry in the staging of contemporary election campaigns. Rather, I raise the linkage to suggest that the reverse relationship works equally well: How a politician secures elective office will affect his or her beliefs of what must be done once in office. The practicing politician does not know what the interests of the voters are in any concrete sense. Although politicians frequently speak publicly and forcefully about what the people want, the will of the governed is determined by partially informed hypothesis and conjecture. Far beyond deciding on narrow question of policy—whether the voters prefer guns to butter—the need to project assumptions onto the citizenry extends to the politicians' beliefs about the electoral mechanism as a whole and, indeed, to conceptions of governing. Thus, the technology of how one secures elective office shapes the behavior of the political system, transmitted through the assumptions which politicians bring to their work.[11] Media politics at the campaign stage, therefore, have profound implications for the process of governing.

As politicians gradually shift toward communication with voters through public relations rather than political organization, they also change their conceptualization about the electorate. A strong party system—meaning both effective mobilization of resources at the elite level through party rather than candidate organizations and definitive attachments for voters—would promote a conception of the electorate divided into competing camps.[12] Two groups of voters confront each other over the determination of public policy. Because these groups are more or less fixed over time, the basic parameters of electoral strength are known. The strategy of gaining elective office in these circumstances is to maximize the number of one's own adherents who turn out on election day, while seeking to split the opposition camp to minimize their vote. The enduring party organizations are geared to identify and communicate with supporters to stimulate turnout.

Politicians operating in this system think in terms of "us" versus "them"; their actions while governing will be conceived within this framework. This model of the electorate, therefore, provides an underpinning for coalitional politics and political patronage. In office, politicians reward their supporters so as to solidify their position, while seeking opportunities to win away members of opposing groups. Elaborate negotiations establish the mutual exchanges that are necessary to forge a coalition of support, a process that generates a working definition of who "our people" are. Finally, this model implies that there are opponents, those to whom it is legitimate to deny effective political power. Both sides understand that loss at the polls will mean political banishment. For practicing politicians, therefore, the "us-them" model implies that, for the sake of keeping their own coalition intact, they cannot negotiate for political support with certain political factions. Rather, politics and governance are accomplished primarily by maximizing power, cooperation, and mutual support within one's own camp and being willing to write off potential support from the opposing camp.

Current campaign technologies, at least on the presidential level, propel politicians toward a radically different conception of the electoral and governing processes. Instead of divided into two or more competing camps, the electorate is seen as a broad, relatively undifferentiated mass of voters. To be sure, there are some individual preferences, particularly in different perceptions of the personal attributes of a president, the intensity of specific governmental actions, or preferred public policies on widespread problems. But, these differences are minor compared to the divisions found in the strong party model. They allow contemporary politicians to think in terms of winning away voters from the opposition by emphasizing some themes while downplaying other aspects.

Because there exist neither enduring nor decisive cleaveages among voters, the politician's task becomes one of appealing to as wide a range of citizens as possible in order to maximize one's vote. Even while recognizing that opponents have supporters who cannot be courted away, the campaigners' goal is conceived of as drawing support from the whole electorate rather than from a finite segment of voters. The technology of media politics with its mass audiences facilitates reaching this broad cross-section. As politics becomes broad, however, it loses its depth.

For the sake of argument, this discussion has overdrawn the degree to which practicing politicians thoroughly embrace one model versus the other. Nevertheless, these exaggerations illuminate two notable consequences for the functioning of the electoral system. First, the political dialogue suffers; politicians seeking widespread support cannot be highly specific about their intended policies. Instead, their appeals are more likely based on their personal characteristics, on criticisms of present policies that are not linked to suggested improvements, or simply on suggestions that electoral victory is inevitable. In each case, the persuasive messsage is designed to attract supporters without alienating others. The calculation that some votes are expendable, much less undesirable, is emphatically rejected.

Second, for the sake of efficiency, politicians direct their resources toward citizens who will probably vote of their own accord rather than stimulating the maximum number of citizens to become involved in the political process by registering and voting. Most political pollsters, for example, narrow the range of individuals whose opinions they poll to those who are probable voters, based on their frequency of voting in the past. The advice they give to campaigners is geared toward securing electoral victory within the group of likely voters, not toward expanding dramatically the set of voters. The current low levels of turnout evident in U.S. elections may well be related to the fact that campaigns make broad appeals to habitual voters, rather than stimulate maximum participation.[13]

The consequences of adopting this marketing model of the electorate spill over to the governing process. Public officials with this view of politics conceive of governing as an effort to develop support levels among the population as a whole. Presidential popularity, as measured by the Gallup or Harris polls, becomes a conceptual substitute for building cohesive political coalitions based on a distinction of "us" from "them." Such polititicians also avoid the temptation of dealing with issues that pit one group against another. Rather, they engage in highly symbolic activities that have the perceived benefit of evoking widespread support without alienating specific groups. For example, foreign policy successes that may unite the nation loom as an attractive alternative to domestic problems that divide us. Politicians who live by this conception of electoral politics tend to avoid too strong an identification with particular organized groups. In the process, they deny themselves effective alliances that could promote their own agenda. When stymied in their efforts to enact desired legislation, these public servants are tempted to appeal for mass voter support to pressure other officials to do their bidding.

Many of these symptoms characterize our national governmental machinery, prompting a growing number of scholars to voice concern over stagnation.[14] Certainly all of the blame should not be laid to campaigning through the news media. But there is a disjunction between the requirements of promoting of public policies in Washington and what politicians who practice media politics believe they must do to be elected. In the short run, politicians may recognize the necessities of developing a concensus among elites such as representatives of key interest groups, appointed officials, career civil servants, congressional staff, and other officeholders. The dilemma for politicians is that what Mayhew refers to as position-taking and credit-claiming for the sake of broad popularity are likely to cripple effectiveness in coalition-building.[15] In this manner, the mind set brought to politics by media politics may contribute to the inability of our governmental institutions to deal responsively with major social, economic, and technological problems.

The contradiction between a fundamental concept of electioneering and the practical actions of governing may be related to the noted rise of cynicism.[16] Politicians are supposed to represent and advance the broad public interest, the welfare of the nation as a whole. They repeatedly appeal for electoral support on this basis. Specific policy questions and the institutions of government that must be engaged to resolve them, however, force public officials to balance much narrower questions of competing interests. In practice, politics become the corruption of ideals expressed during election campaigns and, therefore, can be a source of considerable antagonism.

Finally, no examination of contemporary campaign politics would be complete without consideration of the transmission of policy preferences. After the 1972 campaign, a number of media critics pointed out the low percentage of campaign news coverage devoted to public policy issues.[17] This problem is central to notions about the electoral process in a democratic polity. Assuming perfect information is a frequent caveat of formal democratic theories. Although no one actually expects perfect information to exist, the ideal of creating an informed electorate ought to be a goal of those concerned about the workings of our democratic system. News reporting should—and can—provide citizens with the information required to make vote choices.

Journalists themselves are aware of this shortcoming. They have a strong defense for their lack of issue reporting. The candidates themselves were unwilling to talk extensively about the policies they would pursue once in office.[18] This reluctance, according to our interviews, derived from three specific beliefs. First, many campaigners argued that complicated issue positions simply could not be communicated to the electorate through the news process. News reporting, according to this view, necessarily simplifies most questions. Tactically, if the campaigns themselves simplify the ideas they wish to communicate through the news, they have a higher probability of transmitting that message without filtering by reporters.

Second, many campaigners believed reporters would leap to point out weaknesses in their positions if they offered any specifics. Going into detail on policy positions, therefore, was seen as an invitation for a press crisis. The campaign would then lose control over the flow of news coverage.

Third, some campaigners simply believed that issues were to be avoided because voters would not respond to policy issues:

Voters are simply not, in my judgment, either interested enough or well enough educated to perceive the complexities. Our job as campaign professionals is to try to reach voters with messages that are appealing to them, not to try to communicate more than they are willing or able to absorb.[19]

Coverage of the 1980 general election campaign proved to contain a much higher level of issue reporting.[20] Analyzing stories on the CBS Evening News, Robinson and Sheehan found that issue coverage more than tripled after Labor Day. While they quoted one CBS official as saying that issue coverage had increased because the candidates had begun discussing public policy questions, they noted that many of the stories were initiated by the network without a hard news—that is, what happened today—peg. They conclude that, in part, the criticism of news reporting as failing to cover issues was itself responsible for network executives deciding to devote more space to the policy views of the candidates.

As argued in chapter 5, the issues that were given prominent news coverage were related to a candidate's electoral prospects. Reagan's hardline stands on many foreign policy questions, for example, could be directly related to a perceived electoral problem among women—that is, reporters were able to establish a link between the stated policy and negative consequences for the candidate's electoral support. Issues of this type receive sustained news coverage.

Given their assumptions about the low levels of citizens' interest in politics, politicians feel that only repetitive news coverage is likely to make a large difference among substantial segments of the electorate. Yet news coverage is more likely to focus on electoral prospects than to elucidate the major choices facing the nation.

During the 1980 primary campaign, Robinson and Sheehan found quite low levels of issue coverage, as in 1976. With near unanimity, those campaigners who were attempting to communicate issue stands complained about their inability to project these themes through the news-reporting process. They perceived journalists as unwilling to produce news coverage of their position papers or policy speeches in any detail. Given the low volume of issue coverage, their criticism seems plausible.

Here again, however, the argument is circular. Newsmen blame campaigners for the lack of issue content in electoral politics; campaigners point the finger at the news media. That both are probably correct does not raise hopes that the situation will be easily rectified. We are, thus, led to a somewhat dismal conclusion—the prospects for creating an informed electorate through the news reporting process are not great.

However, there have been major improvements in campaign journalism since 1972. In most cases these improvements, such as the profile reports carried by many news, outlets at the beginning of the election year, the stock speeches printed by the *New York Times,* the late night coverage of ABC News, and the special reports run in 1980, were the result of explicit decisions by news editors and producers. In the process, the media did make available much more information about the different candidacies than they had in prior years. But this one-time coverage does not satisfy the campaigner's need for repetition nor override the barriers to citizen attention. These improvements did not, furthermore, carry over into daily reports filed from the campaign trail by individual journalists trying to do a better job. Nor were they the result of some change in the behavior of candidates.

These improvements were initiated by journalists reacting to past criticism. This responsiveness by journalists may provide the only conceivable means of improvements in the future. Explicit attention to how coverage patterns affect campaigning might lead editors and producers to reevaluate how they report the presidential race. For example, the decision to move the entire network news team to New Hampshire or Florida lends a significance to those primaries that may not be warranted. Permanently assigned reporters traveling with one candidate narrows their perspective on the race as a whole. Campaign coverage that mostly follows the words and actions of candidates denies journalists the opportunity to initiate many stories.

Most attention in this study has been lavished on the strategic maneuvering of politicians in their efforts to use the news-reporting process. Even though they purport to operate in the public good, politicians will not voluntarily limit their flexibility or jeopardize their electoral prospects. Ironically, though journalists have not sought the influence on electoral politics discussed here—indeed many find it abhorent—if change is to come in the conduct of media politics, it will occur only when initiated by journalists.

Notes

1. According to the investment theory of voting behavior, individuals search for the means of reducing the time and effort expended in gathering information necessary to reach a voting decision. By this principle, once a decision had been reached, both the vote choice and the information which determined it should become enormously resistant to change. See Samuel Popkin and others, "Comment: What Have You Done for Me Lately? Toward an Investment Theory of Voting," *American Political Science Review* 70:3 (September 1976), pp. 779–805.

2. Studies that suggest this division include Gabriel Almond, *The American People and Foreign Policy* (New York: Praeger, 1960), V.O. Key, Jr., *Public Opinion and American Democracy* (New York: Knopf, 1964);

Donald Devine, *The Attentive Public* (Chicago: Rand-McNally, 1970); and James Rosenau, *Citizenship between Elections* (New York: Free Press, 1974).

3. The two-step flow theory provides one account for this translation. See Paul Lazarsfeld and others, *The People's Choice* (New York: Duell, Sloan and Pearce, 1944); and Daniel Katz and Paul Lazarsfeld, *Personal Influence* (Glencoe, Ill.: Free Press, 1955).

4. James Q. Wilson's exchange theory in *Political Organizations* (New York: Basic Books, 1973), chap. 3; or Robert Salisbury, "An Exchange Theory of Interest Groups," *Midwest Journal of Political Science,* 13:1 (February 1969), pp. 1–32.

5. Osborn H. Oldroyd, *Lincoln's Campaign* (Chicago: Laird and Lee, 1896), pp. 110–113.

6. Lloyd Robinson, *The Stolen Election: Hayes versus Tilden—1876* (Garden City, N.Y.: Doubleday, 1968), pp. 101–106.

7. Stanley L. Jones, *The Election of 1896* (Madison: University of Wisconsin Press, 1964), pp. 112–113.

8. National nominating conventions still provide a context within which some negotiation can take place at the convention site. For a case study of a convention in which the nomination question had been resolved, see Denis G. Sullivan and others, "Candidates, Caucuses and Issues: The Democratic Convention, 1976," in *The Impact of the Electoral Process,* ed. Louis Maisel and Joseph Cooper (Beverly Hills, Calif.: Sage, 1977), pp. 81–132.

9. For a thorough discussion of this question, see Hannah Pitkin, *The Concept of Representation* (Berkeley: University of California Press, 1967).

10. Related arguments that consider the interaction between politician's acts while in office and the electoral performance include David Mayhew, *Congress: The Electoral Connection* (New Haven: Yale University Press, 1974) and Benjamin I. Page, *Choices and Echoes in Presidential Elections* (Chicago: University of Chicago Press, 1978).

11. A similar argument is employed by Richard I. Fenno, *Home Styles: House Members in Their Districts* (Boston: Little Brown, 1978).

12. Richard J. Jensen, *Winnning of the Mid-West: Social and Political Conflict* (Chicago: University of Chicago Press, 1970), chap. 6.

13. Peter Lange with Christine Ridout and James Cooney, *Voter Turnout in Advanced Industrial Democracy: A Bibliographic Essay* (Washington, D.C.: Committee for the Study of the American Electorate, 1978).

14. See, for example, James McGregor Burns, *The Deadlock of Democracy* (Englewood Cliffs, N.J.: Prentice-Hall, 1963); Grant McConnell, *Private Power and American Democracy* (New York: Knopf, 1966); Theodore Lowi, *The End of Liberalism,* 2d ed. (New York: Norton, 1979);

or Nelson Polsby, *The Consequences of Party Reform* (New York: Oxford, 1983).

15. These terms are borrowed from Mayhew, *Congress: The Electoral Connection.*

16. On the increase in cynicism over the past two decades, see Jack Citrin and others, "Personal and Political Sources of Political Alienation," *British Journal of Political Science* 5:1 (January 1975), pp. 1–31.

17. Thomas E. Patterson and Robert D. McClure, *The Unseeing Eye* (New York: Putnam, 1976), p. 41; Doris Graber, "Press and TV as Opinion Resources in Political Campaigns," *Public Opinion Quarterly* 40 (1976), pp. 285–303.

18. This point was made by Thomas Wicker of the *New York Times* in the NBC forum on the 1976 presidential elections and by Martin Plisner in "Campaign Journalism: Professors Grade the Press," *Columbia Journalism Review* (November–December 1978), pp. 57–63.

19. John Deardourff, advertising manager for Ford in Jonathan Moore and Janet Fraser, *The Campaign for President* (Cambridge, Mass.: Ballinger, 1978), p. 155.

20. Michael Robinson and Margaret Sheehan, "How the Networks Learned to Love the Issues," *Washington Journalism Review* 2:9 (December 1980), pp. 15–17; and *Over the Wire and On TV* (New York: Russell Sage, 1983).

Appendix

Over 100 interviews with presidential campaigners in 1976 and 1980 form the principal data base on which this book rests. The interviews were tape-recorded, transcribed, and analyzed for commentary on the organizational, thematic, and strategic effects of interactions with journalists. Although the course of each interview was not determined by a precise inventory of questions, each interview did follow an informal agenda, so that each campaigner was questioned about the same matters. The interviews were conducted *on the record* with the understanding that they would not be used until after the election. In a few cases, campaigners asked to have parts of their remarks off the record. In these instances, which for the most part contained personal observations about other individuals, the tape recorder was shut off and the comments were ignored. The following is a list of interviews.

Anderson, 1980
> Mark Bisnow, Press Secretary, 7/9/81.
> Michael, MacLeod, Campaign Manager, 12/6/80.

Baker, 1980
> Douglas Bailey, Media Advisor, 12/7/80.

Bayh, 1976
> Gail Alexander, Deputy Press Secretary, 4/15/76.
> Jay Berman, Campaign Political Director, 7/10/75, 8/8/75.
> Ann Lewis, National Political Coordinator, 1/22/76.
> William Wise, Campaign Press Secretary, 7/10/75, 8/8/75, 1/14/76, 4/15/76.

Bentsen, 1976
> Jack DeVore, Press Secretary, 7/8/75, 1/21/76.
> Robert Healy, Campaign Director, 1/22/76, 2/18/76.
> Rochelle Jones, Deputy Press Secretary, 6/13/75.
> Ben Palumbo, Campaign Director, 7/8/75.

Brown, 1976
> Edmund Brown, Candidate, 5/31/76.
> Michael Kantor, Campaign Manager, 6/4/76.

Brown, 1980
> Byron Georgiou, Director of Delegate Selection, 2/3/80.
> Thomas Quinn, Campaign Manager, 12/6/80.

Bush, 1980
    David Keene, National Political Director, 2/2/80, 2/14/80,* 12/5/80.
    Robert Teeter, Pollster, 2/2/80, 12/6/80.

Carter, 1976
    Patrick Caddell, Pollster, 6/24/77.
    Barry Jagoda, Assistant Press Secretary, 3/22/76, 1/7/77.
    Hamilton Jordan, Campaign Manager, 7/22/75, 3/22/76, 12/12/76.
    Jody Powell, Press Secretary, 7/22/76, 4/22/76.
    Charlotte Scott, Press Secretary-N.C. & Pa., 6/9/75.
    Tick Sigerbloom, Coordinator-Pa., 4/23/76.
    Gerald Rafshoon, Media Director, 7/22/75, 3/21/76, 12/13/76.

Carter, 1980
    Tim Kraft, Campaign Manager, 2/2/80.

Church, 1976
    William Hall, Press Secretary, 8/25/75, 1/21/76.
    Deborah Herbst, Press Aide, 10/7/76.
    Robert Koholos, Deputy Press Secretary, 10/7/76.
    Mike Novelli, Campaign Director-Cal., 6/5/76.

Connolly, 1980
    Charles Keating, Campaign Manager, 12/20/79.*
    Eddie Mahe, National Political Director, 12/6/80.

Crane, 1980
    Laura Broderick, Press Secretary, 9/7/81.

Ford, 1976
    James Baker, Campaign Director, 12/12/76.
    Bo Calloway, Campaign Manager, 8/7/75.
    Bradford Hayes, Southern Political Coordinator, 3/22/76.
    Peter Kaye, Campaign Press Secretary, 7/13/76.
    Thomas Moran, Comptroller, 7/14/77.
    Larry Peck, Press Secretary-Cal., 6/8/76.
    Larry Speakes, Deputy Press Secretary, 1/22/76.

Harris, 1976
    Ralph Collins, Campaign Director, 1/15/76.
    Frank Greer, Press Secretary, 7/8/75, 1/13/76.
    James Hightower, Campaign Manager, 7/8/75.

Jackson, 1976
    Brian Corcoran, Press Secretary, 5/20/75, 6/12/75, 3/12/76, 5/20/76.
    Robert Keefe, Campaign Director, 6/12/75, 6/12/75, 1/7/77.**
    Sterling Monroe, Administrative Assistant, 2/8/77.**
    Ben Wattenberg, Issues Advisor, 8/6/76.

Kennedy, 1980
  Peter Hart, Pollster, 2/2/80.
  Paul Kirk, National Political Director, 2/2/80.
  Gary Orren, Campaign Pollster, 5/29/81.
  Carl Wagner, Director of Field Operations, 2/3/80.

Reagan, 1976
  Mike Deever, P.R. Advisor, 9/5/75.
  Lyn Nofziger, Press Secretary, 6/5/79, 1/22/75, 8/6/75.
  John Sears, Campaign Director, 1/14/75, 8/7/75.
  Carter Wren, Coordinator–N.C., 3/22/76.

Reagan, 1980
  Lyn Nofziger, Director of Communications, 2/3/80, 12/6/80.

Sanford, 1976
  Paul Clancey, Press Secretary, 7/7/75.
  Dorothy Lyons, Treasurer, 1/17/76.
  Terry Sanford, Candidate, 2/19/76.
  Jean Westwood, Campaign Director, 7/9/75.

Shapp, 1976
  Norvall Reese, Campaign Director, 8/28/76.

Shriver, 1976
  Linda Cook, Press Aide, 1/16/76.
  Richard Murphy, Campaign Manager, 1/14/76.
  Don Pride, Press Secretary, 8/6/75.

Udall, 1976
  John Gabusi, Campaign Director, 8/8/75, 12/10/76.
  John Marttila, Campaign Director, 2/20/76.
  Robert Neuman, Press Secretary, 7/6/76, 1/21/76, 6/12/75.
  Richard Stout, Campaign Press Secretary, 1/21/76, 4/23/76.
  Stewart Udall, Campaign Manager, 7/8/75.

Wallace, 1976
  Joseph Azbell, P.R. Director, 7/25/75.
  Billy Joe Camp, Press Secretary, 7/24/75.
  Charles Snider, Campaign Director, 7/24/75.

*Interview conducted by John Carroll, Jeffrey Kampelman, and Robert
Moorman
**Interview conducted by Scott Moeller

Index

About the Authors

F. Christopher Arterton is an associate professor of political science and management at Yale University. His research and writing focus on American electoral institutions and the behavior of political elites in those institutions. In addition to this work on the importance of newsmaking to presidential campaigns, Mr. Arterton has written on political parties, national conventions, the management of candidate organizations, and campaign finance. He is a coauthor of *Explorations in Convention Decision-Making* (H.W. Freeman, 1976). He also serves as an advisor and consultant to the *Newsweek Poll.* His most recent research concerns the relationship between communication technologies and the political process, especially citizen participation in policymaking.

Robert A. Fein is an attorney with the Boston law firm of Testa, Hurwitz & Thibeault. He received his J.D. from Harvard Law School and his B.A. in political science from Yale University.